Imaginal Reality

Volume Two
Voidcraft

First published 2011
by Aeon Books
London NW3

www.aeonbooks.co.uk

© Aaron B. Daniels

British Library Cataloguing in Publication Data

A C.I.P. is available for this book from the British Library

ISBN: 978-190465-856-6

Imaginal Reality

Volume Two
Voidcraft

Aaron B. Daniels, Ph.D.
with Laura M. Daniels, M.Ac.

Aeon Books

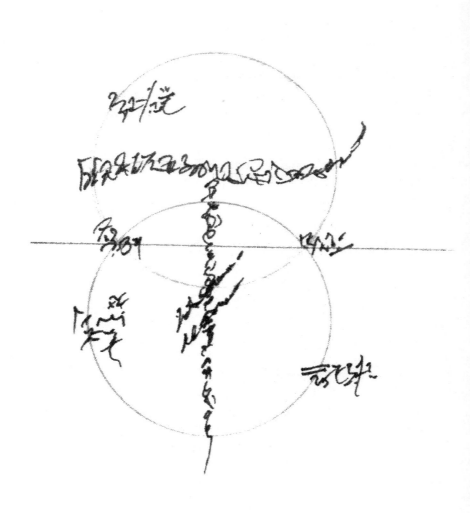

Contents

Acknowledgements

As this second volume is an extension of the first, all the gratitude from the first holds doubly true here. I would like to further thank Aeon Books' Alex Thornton for her superlative (cross-cultural) editorial skills, graphic layout, and cover design for both volumes. I would also like to express again my undying gratitude to my wife, Laura, for her able graphic manipulations, patient editing, insightful guidance, and unflagging support and love.

Introduction to Volume Two

Aliens, The Alien, and Alienation

How will we know when we make first contact with aliens? Surely our three pedestrian dimensions, together with our rigid temporality, rather limits our capacity to recognize entities for whom our spatiality may be merely a flickering, visible only in their periphery. Will we recognize the difference between their armor, spacesuits, and clothes, and their 'bodies'—should such a term even prove appropriate? What of their means of transport? Putting aside space-warping engines and eldritch gateways, what alterations of even our most fundamental means-of-knowing will be necessary in order for us to simply recognize their emergence into our world? And then, of course, there's language. Or not! So fundamental is our inveiglement with the bald-faced lies of signs, references, and symbols, that we cannot conceive of any interaction with another sentience that does not fundamentally convey meaning. We are made of such misdirections, after all.

Hiding behind all these speculations is the far more pressing, but oddly difficult to answer, question: How do we recognize the alien here and now? Because, of course, the vast majority of the time we don't. To whatever extent I am an 'I', I am a structured defense against the other, the alien. Volume One attempted to bring us closer to this consistently uncanny nature of the means by which our lives unfold. It promised a *Journey to the Voids*—both intimate and distant. Through becoming more familiar with the no-one in which our various 'I-s' emerge and dissipate, the text offered the reader the possibility of becoming less certain, but more free.

With that first arc, the reader encountered the overall approach and purpose of this work. Taking a hard gaze at the 'imagination of magic,' these texts endeavor to bring us more fully face to face with the existential voids that define the true limits of our lives, but also create the stage upon which our lives unfold. Moreover, with an eye for the various fictions with which we create our lives, we have tried to show that most of the 'givens' of life are far more mutable and abstract than our various storylines seem to concede. We have, to our detriment, become so alienated from the fundamental structure of experience that we cannot see the marvelously fictive nature of our lives. In order to offer some means of access to the imaginal reality of our lives, Volume One enumerated eight voids. Grounded equally in existential phenomenology, imaginal psychology, and a type of mystical nihilism, these voids provide invitations to live more fully, deeply, and in accord with the structural truth of life-as-lived. They are also the terrifying vistas against which we create our abiding and life-strangling defenses.

The first volume laid out in more explicit detail four of the voids:

* **Immediacy:** All time extends imaginally from a perpetually unfolding 'now.'
* **Undifferentiation:** All identities and alterities are configurations of the segregation of experience.
* **Madness:** All rationalities are simultaneously revealing and concealing stances, grounded in shifting images.
* **Chaos:** What we see as various structures of cause-and-effect are perspectives, derived from a vast sea of intersecting systems.

Along the way, Volume One also offered exercises, stories, and amplifications from the metaphors of magic to illustrate the ways in which we may defend against, or open ourselves to, these structural realities. Ultimately, the imagination of magic came to reveal the physics of the Imaginal.

This current volume moves more explicitly into the practice of magic—that is, the ongoing journey of claiming our lives more fully and deeply. This cultivation of intentionality and vision, though never a one-time decisive victory, can become a more habitual attitude. To gird these hard-fought realizations, this volume presents the other four voids in detail.

The Remaining Four Voids

* **Nothingness:** Individual things and the thing-sets with which we populate our worlds are the set-dressings that illustrate the scripts guiding our life plays.
* **Meaninglessness:** The world will never, to us, yield either fundamental meaning, or some ultimate 'point.' The process of meaning-making *is* the meaning of life.
* **Freedom and Responsibility:** Only through claiming life in its structural truth, through a responsiveness to the imaginal reality of life, can we truly live out the freedom that is always, already, our birthright.
* **Change and Finitude:** Nothing abides and any clinging to concepts rooted in 'permanence' will yield a bitter and morbid shadow.

To catch us up more fully to this point in the story, I refer the reader to Chapter 20, 'Midword,' in which the fuller evolving theses of this work find voice.

Why 'Voidcraft'?

Let's move back to the genre of high science fiction. When initially adopting 'Voidcraft' as the subtitle for this current volume, I researched the term to see if others had used it. Reading China Miéville's stunning *Embassytown* (2011), just a few days after deciding to go with this speculative compound word, I saw that he adopts the term in an intriguing reference to the spacecraft that ply the 'Immer'—a fascinating interstitial space that connects places and planets in weird but navigable ways. (Miéville's work presents toothsome meditations on the questions briefly raised at the beginning of this introduction.) 'Voidcrafts' show up in other speculative fiction and science fiction cosmologies as deep space exploration vessels and, perhaps distantly, as metaphors for abjectly alienated individuals and collectives, adrift in the blackest of expanses.

I deeply resonate with these images and, thus, felt all the more sure of this subtitle. Building on these resonances, I intend my use of this term to have (at least) two distinct meanings. First, the term refers to a type of imaginal praxis. Against the backdrop of the existential voids, we live out our stories, and as this overall work asserts, much of the real magic of life is claiming the authorship of our many meaning-ensorcelments. Thus, 'voidcraft' is a word like 'witchcraft.' We are weaving our narratives with the audacity of one who seeks to live his or her ownmost life.

The other sense of the word is the construction of those vessels that take us on these various journeys. A vessel is, after all, necessary to ply these strange imaginal tides. Thus, 'voidcraft' is also a term for the identity structures that allow us to escape the gravity wells of various image-planets, and move to new psychocartographic realities.

Just such a journey informed the creation of these volumes. As mentioned in Volume One, through the cultivation and exaggeration of one particular vector of me, I sought to achieve escape velocity from the limits of perspectives that may or may not have been serving my most liberating interests.

Seeds and Magical Personas

The ideas that form the grist for this overall work—the *prima materia* for this odd alchemical opus—emerged from an exercise I began in mid 2006. Having made it well into my fourth decade surprisingly intact, I set out to discover: how did I get here? To begin to address this question, I asked Michel de Montaigne's fundamental question, *'Que sais-je?'* 'What do I know?' That is: what are the comments, aphorisms, approaches, old saws, bromides, realizations, rules of thumb, and abiding wisdoms that have endured, and sometimes sustained me through my peregrinations as a student, psychotherapist, clinical supervisor, academic, ritualist, and religious traveler? That exercise led to a lengthy laundry list that read something like Polonius' rambling parting advice to his son Laertes in Shakespeare's *Hamlet* (Act 1, Scene 3).

Snippets from favorite theorists and ironies dominated my first collation, such as C. G. Jung's observation that no real problem is solvable by its own terms, or my realization that 'magic always works' (just not in the ways we expect it to). Meaty, perhaps, pithy, even, but the product was mostly a cipher of ideas that interconnected in only the most loosely intuitive of ways. Yet, underlying them, I hoped that I had a greater picture and not just a series of 'good ideas.' This greater picture, I suspected, might help me address not so much *what* I had accumulated along the way, but how I have *made* my way.

My questioning was not an effort at self-congratulation. Although far more settled with the person I had become than, say, the 21 year old I had been, I was also seeking to make more effective and deliberate changes in my life. It seemed to me that I was still working against myself in too many ways. Thus, I hoped that my gathering together of these ideas might help me find some sort of way forward.

Staring at this partial collection of my thoughts, I concluded that to encourage that greater picture to emerge I should undertake a long-term magical working—a course of initiation. I find most of life's initiations are not deliberate, conscious efforts. Car accidents, disastrously failed relationships, and being fired from a job are just some of these 'growth experiences' which call us to change or die. After these often life-threatening transitions, we are usually simply grateful to have our limbs still attached, and walk away to later reflect on whatever transformation may have occurred. An explicitly magical perspective, however, demands that we enter the underworld more purposefully. So, I took on the name of a character who had been bouncing around in various short stories I had written: Niel V. Estes. Niel's name came from a play on words based on a Latin motto: *nihil veritas est*—'nothing(ness) is truth.' He became an embodiment of a sort of hard-edged postmodern mystical nihilism. Concentrating on his attitudes, imagining his reactions, and eventually having active imaginal conversations with him, he became an increasing reality to me. The Jungian term might be that his image was 'individuating'—emerging from the unconscious to constitute its own reality. His voice dominated the next draft of the manuscript. He provided the vehicle (the 'voidcraft'?) for the vivification of the bare bones laid forth in my previous laundry list.

Having a collection of fractured separate personalities foisted upon you, by, for example, severe and repeated trauma, is pathological. Choosing an alter ego, a magical name and persona, can be equally, but differently, pathological. Brother Mehrwein, introduced in the first story in Volume One, once asked me if I thought it was sick that he had divided his life up into discrete personas—a magical one here, a familial one there, a professional one elsewhere. The bigger answer is, of course, 'no.' We all shift personas continuously. This ability is often a sign of vigorous health, so long as a certain flexibility and fluidity prevails. Nevertheless, when attempting to deliberately bring up and integrate material from the unconscious, what at first may seem to be merely a persona, or the product of a creative exercise, can very soon become wholesale possession of the ego by an archetype.

As noted in the first volume, those who undertake the formal work of magicians are well aware of this style of possession and create elaborate rituals of 'invocation' or 'evocation' to try to partition such experiences into ritual spaces by the use of magical circles, talismans, and banishings. (The rest of us use the commute home, getting dressed up, or a stiff drink to make transitions between various parts of ourselves.) These partitioning rituals are undoubtedly effective for the sort of small magic that occurs in temples or during a work project; but the greater magical work of our unfolding lives plays out these possessions on a far more vast scale. No magical circle or banishing can contain, in one fell swoop, the forces that ultimately create the substrate for our personality itself.

Thus, Niel V. Estes took on quite a life of his own. He simultaneously encapsulated and amplified aspects of my personality—some I liked, others not so much. Niel was a fierce anti-theist, a brutally efficient thinker, intolerant of lazy logic and complacency. He was not satisfied until he had reached a postmodern, nihilistic, self-devouring conclusion. He was, at best, an abrasive conversationalist unless you were ready for a sort of scalpel-juggling. Although classical Jungian thought won't quite allow for a man to have one, Niel was my *animus*—an inner, unintegrated masculine ideal that was cruelly efficient and unsatisfied with anything short of dark brilliance.

Niel's manuscript, the second draft of this work, was consistent with his personality. It read like the works of Martin Heidegger but without the benefit of footnotes, recapitulations, or commentaries. It was a dense prose poem at best, a self-indulgent series of cryptic aphorisms at worst. When I would edit passages, I would finish with a smug sense of satisfaction: *Haha! Yes, that says it rather concisely.* My first warning that something was terribly wrong was when Mehrwein read a draft while running a fever and happily declared that it read like one of his rants but could provide no substantive edits. Indeed, it was a rant: an unmediated irruption of a part of me—one upon whom I had relied for many years, assuming it my only unique talent. Seeing my gift for brutal deconstruction as my sole redeeming feature had its drawbacks, the worst being how it eclipsed those traits my friends and colleagues actually liked about me: my sense of humor, warmth, and candor.

In the end, Niel had to die. Both Niel—not quite 'me'—and the 'me' that was not Niel had to be transcended in order to yield a new configuration. In what is popularly known as a Hegelian dialectic (i.e., thesis + antithesis = synthesis), Niel was the emergent antithesis to my personality's initial thesis. The two volumes of this work are the ultimate synthesis. Finding a new voice that integrated my experiences, my failures, my realizations, and my growth proved to be the work of the third and final draft of this work. No longer heady speculations *about* experiences, the work became devoted to experience itself. By adding stories and exercises, this work came to life — *my* life.

Territorial Tales

The interconnecting timelines I weave into the stories in these two volumes are not offered as autobiography. (I personally feel like I should be paid the usual psychotherapist's fee of $120 per hour when reading many people's autobiographical material.) The stories rather exist to give voice to important convergences of images and to bring the messages of this work into the realm of real experience, without which this work would topple under its top-heavy preposterousness. The stories, though sometimes weak on specific facts, are true to the territory I seek to describe.

This volume does indeed go deeper into my youth and the often overly-earnest struggles of my young adulthood. I hope many readers find them humorous, I certainly can now at least chuckle at the strange configurations I twisted myself into when attempting to make one unified sense of my life. Other readers will undoubtedly shake their heads, bewildered that anyone could put so much effort and sincerity into what was undoubtedly a defensively misdirected waste of time in the face of far more pressing issues. However, a third, but not necessarily mutually exclusive, category of readers may discover parallels to their own private journeys. It is for them that I have written these tangled snapshot memoirs.

As noted in Volume One, many people come to the esoteric, the New Age, spiritualism, or Wisdom Traditions as young adults, if not young teenagers. These meta-narratives often hit the seeker like a lightning bolt, jarring them from angst-ridden slumbers with revelatory Truths. Regardless of their existential veracity, these traditions are vehicles with such a profound sense of provenance and uncanny insight that they can make the spiritual traveler feel engaged and spoken to, perhaps even *seen*, at a heretofore unimagined depth.

For me, my youth and teen years were so soaked in these narratives that they were the very territory from which I unwittingly sought escape. Beginning with my mentor's General Semantics, but rapidly expanding into Existential Phenomenology, Taoism, Zen Buddhism, Postmodern Philosophy, Apopathic Mysticism, and other language-bending undertakings, I found life-engaging foils for my early spiritual morasses.

As odd as my experiences may have been, I do not believe I am alone. Thus, I offer these stories as a call to those who have not really found one concise label with which they can summarize their Crooked Path. Such is the case with this first story, in which I found myself firmly face to face with that which defies expression, but demands engagement.

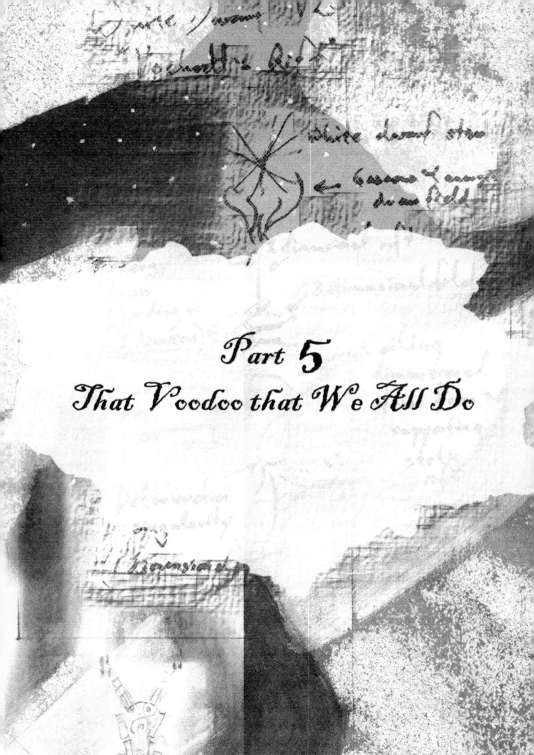

Part 5
That Voodoo that We All Do

My former work has been misunderstood, and its scope limited by my use of technical terms. It has attracted only too many dilettanti and eccentrics, weaklings seeking in "Magic" an escape from reality. I myself was first consciously drawn to the subject in this way. And it has repelled only too many scientific and practical minds, such as I most designed to influence. But
MAGICK
Is for
ALL

Aleister Crowley, Magick Book IV: Liber ABA, Part III,
Magick in Theory and Practice (1929)

19
Mentoring
Images of Resistance and Realization

I type away furiously on the keyboard. The ideas come flooding up and I am glad to be able to finally express them in this journal entry that is taking shape on the computer monitor glowing in front of me. The bluster of New England's late autumn rattles the windows and gives the work a peculiarly Romantic gravitas. This is a liminal sort of moment for me. I find myself once more in-between, an apprentice, a novice — after all these years and experiences.

Serves me right. My travels (hopefully not tourism) through the worlds of religion, philosophy, mysticism, the occult, and magic left me always on the move. I was so bitterly disappointed by so many would-be gurus, teachers, and sages that I stayed in motion — *propelled* actually. A year in this practice, six months in that one. I gave them a chance, but soon I found that the nonsense outweighed the benefits for me. Money-grubbers, narcissists, and fakes abounded. Of those that seemed to have some value, they fell into three disillusioning camps: either they had no psychological insight but an overly earnest devotion to some school of magic or mysticism; or they were rooted in psychology but had merely a winking 'magical realism'; or, basically, they showed themselves to be just plain nuts and without a redeeming sense of humor, although they were often admirably tenacious in their convictions.

And so now, at enough past 30 to find it awkward, I have a 'mentor' to whom I am writing a journal entry. The role of mentor here is really more that of a companion and witness. He was clear from the start that he was not going to be some sort of Yoda to my Skywalker. Instead, he speaks as one who has himself gone through this same yearlong process of self-examination and inventory — of expanding boundaries and gaining a grounding in how we actually practice. This process is about refining what *I* do and not what the system or tradition prescribes for me to do. This mentor-witness is someone with whom I can speak frankly and openly about *everything* I do, not just about 'spells,' 'gnosis,' and other partitioning nonsense. Though we have not yet physically met, we have had frequent phone conversations and email exchanges. We get along famously, having similar tastes in literature, music, and aesthetics.

Although I am old enough to find this novitiate a bit off-putting, I am also just mature enough to make the best use of the opportunity for it. This is, after all, not my first experience with mentorship.

My first real mentor was named Richard Kelly. He came into my life when I was a teen and remained an important part of it until his death, in his late 80's, when I was in my mid-20's. A long line of pastors, elders, and family friends had given me support and guidance throughout my childhood and teens, but Mr. Kelly was truly my Mentor—someone who took on my struggles as his own, developing a bond unlike any other. Our relationship had various configurations. After the death of his wife, I was, for a time, his household assistant. Eventually, he came to live with my family as he put his estate in order. Throughout it all, with calmness, love, and endless packs of unfiltered Pall Malls, he transformed me from a blustering idealist into an exacting philosopher, planting seeds that are still coming to flower.

Alfred North Whitehead, Alfred Korzybski, and S. I. Hayakawa were my curriculum. We spent most of our time with me on a couch and Mr. Kelly sitting in his easy chair. (Perhaps this was the model that my psychotherapy practice sought to replicate.) He could fiddle with the tip of a cigarette for nearly an hour before lighting it. As I hurled out onto some half-considered idea, he would draw in a loud, sharp, snort through his nose. He would then purse his lips, tilt back his head, and peer through his silver browline glasses. Finally, if I still hadn't taken the hint to stop my ill-conceived onslaught, he would make a distinctive hum: a strange, quick, almost whale-like glissando into his gravelly basso. He taught me to consider the nature of 'ideas': their associations to each other, their functions, versus their intentions, and their relationship to different types of experiences. He taught me to think about levels of abstraction. These descriptions don't do justice to the personal transformation I underwent. Under his tutelage, I became aware of *having* ideas, not just the ideas themselves. He was, and will always be, my sensei, my sifu. His voice guides me today as I teach, struggle with life, and write.

Although not entirely typical of our interactions, one evening stands out in my memory, when my father and I shared a dinner at Mr. Kelly's house on the lake. To add an extra resonance to this mentorship, Mr. Kelly had also known my father well as a teen. After dinner, we sat in the living room drinking tea and munching on pastries, rambling through a series of topics and 'solving the world's problems.' In a way, it was an opportunity for my father to understand the process I was undergoing.

I can't remember what the exact topic at hand was, but I recall that I found myself championing my mentor's perspectives and also trying to connect, to integrate my father's New Age spiritualism into a larger summation of 'Life, the Universe, and Reality'—hey, I was a teenager, so the intellectual narcissism was age-appropriate.

I was making broad statements, but managing to avoid the 'sparkling ambiguities' of which my mentor warned. I remember seeing a warm and proud smile creep onto the faces of both my father and Mr. Kelly as I held forth on some topic. However, at the time, I was so truly hungry for, yet uncomfortable with, personal praise or even validation that I channeled my discomfort into redoubled philosophizing. As my diatribe reached a precipice of ideas, I was overcome by a strong sensation of interconnection for which I couldn't find any words. I stammered and tried to speak around the feeling, hoping to find the right framework to encapsulate, to crack open this pressing enigma. It felt important, vital in a way that I had never before experienced in the realm of thought. I realized that the 'shape' of this wordlessness lay within the same mode as that in which I perceived, and played, music—structures, forms, inter-relationships, contrasts. But I still couldn't find the words.

Finally, frustrated, I described seeing a chest locked shut that hummed with what was inside, but which I just couldn't figure out how to open. I dropped my efforts and the evening ended with warm hugs and a sense of the value of the mentorship I was undergoing.

Staring again at the computer monitor, rereading the email to my new mentor, I think back to my time with Mr. Kelly. I've come a long way since then. I've taken on the role of 'supporter-of-process' myself. I've assisted more than a few clients. I have also seen snapshots of the kind of development I underwent in students I have had for a class or two. Now I am trying to navigate the often-difficult relationship of being a full-time faculty member and mentor to college students over a span of years with sometimes daily contact, and I guess I'd better be able to see myself through a serious commitment like this novitiate before I ask it of my students. I know that my job with my current mentor is to raise *my own* issues, challenges, and insights. I volunteered for this process and I am finally ready to make of it the best use I can.

This current journal entry sits on a cusp—a tipping point. The process I undertook is to be one that is explicitly magical, but, up until this point, it has been mostly focused on meditative practice and shifting awarenesses. Now, I come squarely to the question of 'practical magic.' For a couple of weeks, my journal entries and phone chats with my mentor have danced around this issue but now I am squarely staring at it. In the world of people who call themselves 'magicians,' one ill-defined term tends to separate practitioners into two very distinct camps. That term is 'results-based magic.' The idea here is that some people are practicing rituals that are, unto themselves, supposed to lead to increased enlightenment—a 'Yoga of the West' as some have characterized it. The other camp pooh-poohs this approach and states that, with the application of some rigorous methods, a magician can alter seemingly concrete events in their lives, such as car repair, political events, weather patterns, and so on.

As these debates wage, I can hear Mr. Kelly smacking his lips and commenting that we seem to be 'separating with language what cannot be separated in fact.' Indeed, the idea of 'results-based magic' creates a false dichotomy. Being wrapped up in either side of the equation seems like a losing battle to me. On the one hand, I've become somewhat reluctant to practice any form of ritual designed to effect a 'measurable concrete change' for fear of falling into a blind pursuit of 'things and stuff' — not to mention delusionality. The other side of the equation, the 'enlightenment' side, scares me just as much with its irrelevance — how easy it is to settle into self-examination and never act.

I continue to type, laying out a series of objections to 'practical magic' as I see it portrayed. I present the concerns not so much as a form of defiance but in the hope of catalyzing some sort of shift. I write in a sort of short-hand that my mentor and I have built up over our series of conversations and notes:

From: flummoxed mentee
To: long-suffering mentor
Subject: Impractical magic?

What *really* are my struggles with 'Practical Magic'? (I suspect that to address these, I might come up with some kind of 'statement of purpose' for my magical work or at least a sort of 'ground for rhizomes' into which the work can grow.) Here's a partial list of my objections:

- *What is it that I would want in such a way that I can't/don't pursue it with the most powerful magic (i.e., action)?* Aren't some people drawn to magic because of an overall impotence and ineffectuality in their lives? Whether through a lack of simple philosophy or a complete ignorance of psychology, these people would rather spend money on vapid pap than read a book that might demand having a dictionary open beside them. Change is hard and no spell will take care of fundamental personality flaws. In fact, I suspect it will only amplify them!

- *What version of 'me' wants this change?* How do I engage in an adequate discernment to determine what configuration of 'me' has this desire (or is 'had' by it)? Desire for specific things is so often a form of becoming stuck in a particular identity which, ironically, leads to no change at all.

- *Doesn't the leprechaun phenomena kick in, i.e. be careful what you wish for?* How do I know the consequences of sating this small desire? Even if I don't care and state that I am willing to accept whatever consequences may come, am I not in actuality doing spell-work for effects that are mostly beyond my kenning? And I suspect that this is indeed where the role of preparation comes into play. The very act of contemplating change is a grave prospect.

- Why should I want anything other than annihilation in the Divine Void? (Or some other far more abiding and ultimate goal, rather than whatever specific desire I concoct.) In other words, why worry about smaller concerns in the face of the Great Work? To varying degrees, all spellwork is going to be in service to some version of the Great Work, if only because it participates in some magical paradigm that has an implicit or explicit Ultimate Purpose. Does one not need to be quite careful when ferreting out the underlying implications of the magical technology in which one participates? Is there such a thing as magical work that is not part of some sort of Great Work?

- We are so surrounded by spells, sentient patterns, programs, etc. shouldn't I spend more time trying to undo those spells, rather than in doing my own?

- Moreover, I am personally pulling spells on myself all the time. Wouldn't these tend to color all my other spellcraft?

- Doesn't temple ritual work remove the most powerful aspect of most of our magical work? Isn't that the shifting in our subtle day-to-day patterns? Should we not move more directly to control those quotidian technologies? (I suspect I can answer this one more easily since temple work actually *should,* more often than not, manifest as a series of 'shifts' in day-to-day work.)

- Don't I usually simply need to change myself, rather than the world? In a way, this refers back to the first objection. And, again, I think magical work *does* change me.

- Is it not amongst the highest callings in magic, to live life itself as ritual? But am I there yet? Although life may not have a purpose unto itself, the very unfolding and expanding of Kia automatically speaks to a path which we each tread in our individual Great Work. Does not magical technology for its own sake beg the question of complete meaninglessness? That is, doesn't the simple actuality of continually working to discern and pursue greater liberation, *différance,* possibility, rhizomes, and en-Kia-ment automatically cast endless ripples/spells about us?

I look forward to your response,

ABD

I finish the email and fire it off after a quick edit. I am pleased when I receive a call two days later and find that my cryptic shorthand resonated with my mentor. I can hear him lighting up a cigarette as he settles in for a long discussion with me. We talk about my objections. He genuinely seems to know where I'm coming from.

He pauses. I hear him blow out a long exhale. (For some reason the cigarette-smoking mentor has become nearly archetypal for me.)

'Aaron, I guess, well... We both know life is pretty much without purpose, you know?'

I quibble with semantics a bit regarding whether 'life' or 'the world' is meaningless; but we come to an agreement on terms and he continues.

'So, you're asking this basic question, "why?", and given where you're at,' he pauses again, 'I guess I would say, "why not?"!'

His answer is a play on an oft-repeated tale of a philosophy final in which the professor writes a one-word question for his students: 'Why?' The student who gets highest marks responds with a two-word answer, 'Why not?'

After a somewhat nervous chuckle, I get past the glibness of his answer and start chewing on it. I look around me. I am in the home temple and library my wife and I share. Candlelight plays off the spines of the impressively diverse volumes: fiction, religion, history, magic and the occult, a handful of rare books, Chinese medicine, Asian topics... The threads of thick incense smoke play with the candle light and for a second, it seems like I can read characters in the wafts. I am enveloped in swirling text — ensigilized by every breath.

Why not, indeed? What am I really fighting against here?

I realize that I have been silent for longer than a phone conversation usually allows.

'Huh,' I eloquently begin. 'I guess that's really it, isn't it? We're at it already. If I really believe magic is everything, I'm already doing it — but I'm not claiming it — not taking hold.'

My mentor responds and sounds relieved. 'Yeah, exactly!'

I think I've passed some sort of test here. Taking on older novices like me is often a bit of a risk for a mentor. When we're younger, we're full of desires that are untempered by moderation or restraint. We *want* everything and usually *have* precious little. Getting a younger person to whip up a ritual for some desire is easy: more sex, more money, revenge, health, success, and on and on. As we age, even if wisdom doesn't really mellow our ambition, we tend simply to have more stuff — we want for a bit less.

My mentor had mentioned this early on in our relationship. He noted that some people tend to drop explicitly magical work once they hit their 30's because they really don't have any more unbridled ambitions. For me, that's not so much what has drawn me back to magic again and again. Of course, I want things, but I know, as my email notes, that action is the best magic. In fact, as we continue our telephone conversation, I'm slowly starting to understand that all action *is* magic — magical — en-magic-ed?

A bridge starts to build up in me — or perhaps a bridge finds reinforcement and allows for a bit more traffic. I feel a shift in gravity — as though something large is creeping up from below. My more mystical, sometimes ascetic side has never had great relations with my more playful, intuitive, and imaginative side. A strange—and, I now realize, 'false'—divide has made it difficult for me to integrate these two camps.

The place my mentor helps bring me to feels warm and real, not heady. We live. We go on doing it, until we don't. Propositions about ideals and 'shoulds' are all well and nice, but if they aren't livable, they are of little use. Moreover, if they aren't about *how* we live, they run the real danger of removing us from engagement with the process of living itself.

Suddenly, I sit up. I feel a strange weight upon me—not unpleasant but odd. I feel simultaneously larger and stronger, but also heavier. I try to explain these interconnections and insights to my mentor while puzzling out the sensation. We finish the conversation on a good note but I still can't quite peg the experience that emerged during our talk.

The next evening, I sit in quiet meditation. The temple space is cool and comfortable. My body feels natural and at ease, maintaining a solid upright posture that seems to support itself. My eyes are nearly closed and the candlelight creates a golden glow through which I let my thoughts pass.

I've just hit a nice 'hum' when the sensation from the previous night comes back. There seems to be no use in ignoring it. I think at first that it might simply be the after-effects of having years of objections and divisions removed; but even as I try that idea on for size, I realize that the relief of that liberation feels quite different. No, this current sensation isn't quite 'relief.'

What is it then? I let the feeling take residence. A firmness. A solidity. I try to clear my head enough to listen for the words that might emerge from this state. Three words strike me and echo through my head: 'THAT WE LIVE.' With them comes a series of wildfire associations. With the way the words resonate for me, I realize that I suddenly have an embodied sense of the integration of ideals, pleasures, desires, and an odd sort of peace. Of course, we desire. Of course, we hold ideals. Yes, we find varying degrees of pleasure and pain in different activities and states. These are all, I realize, states, stories, the marvelous swirling narratives through which our lives flow. Realizing this fictionality doesn't change that we still live the stories, it simply makes our tale a bit more postmodern in its meta-narratives. The ultimate reality, *that we live,* always confronts us. This doesn't mean 'material biological' life, but rather life *as experienced.*

The words begin tripping over themselves and I return to the experience. I try to let it simply permeate me.

This is it, I tell myself, *this is as important as any realization you've ever had.*

'And I can't even put words to it!' I say aloud. In that second, I remember the locked and sealed chest from that evening all those years ago with my father and

Mr. Kelly. This is why I couldn't find words for it, because it was about something ineffable—not ineffable because it is too abstract, nor because I haven't reached some level of enlightenment. The ineffability is because *it is the sum of all life*, all words, all living. To say it all, in its entirety, is to live a life fully and deeply. The sealed secret is *that we live*, and that changes everything, while simultaneously changing nothing.

And with that, my meditation ends. I stand and bow toward the altar—left hand wrapped around my right fist, Chinese style.

'I give thanks to the mentors who have brought me Here.'

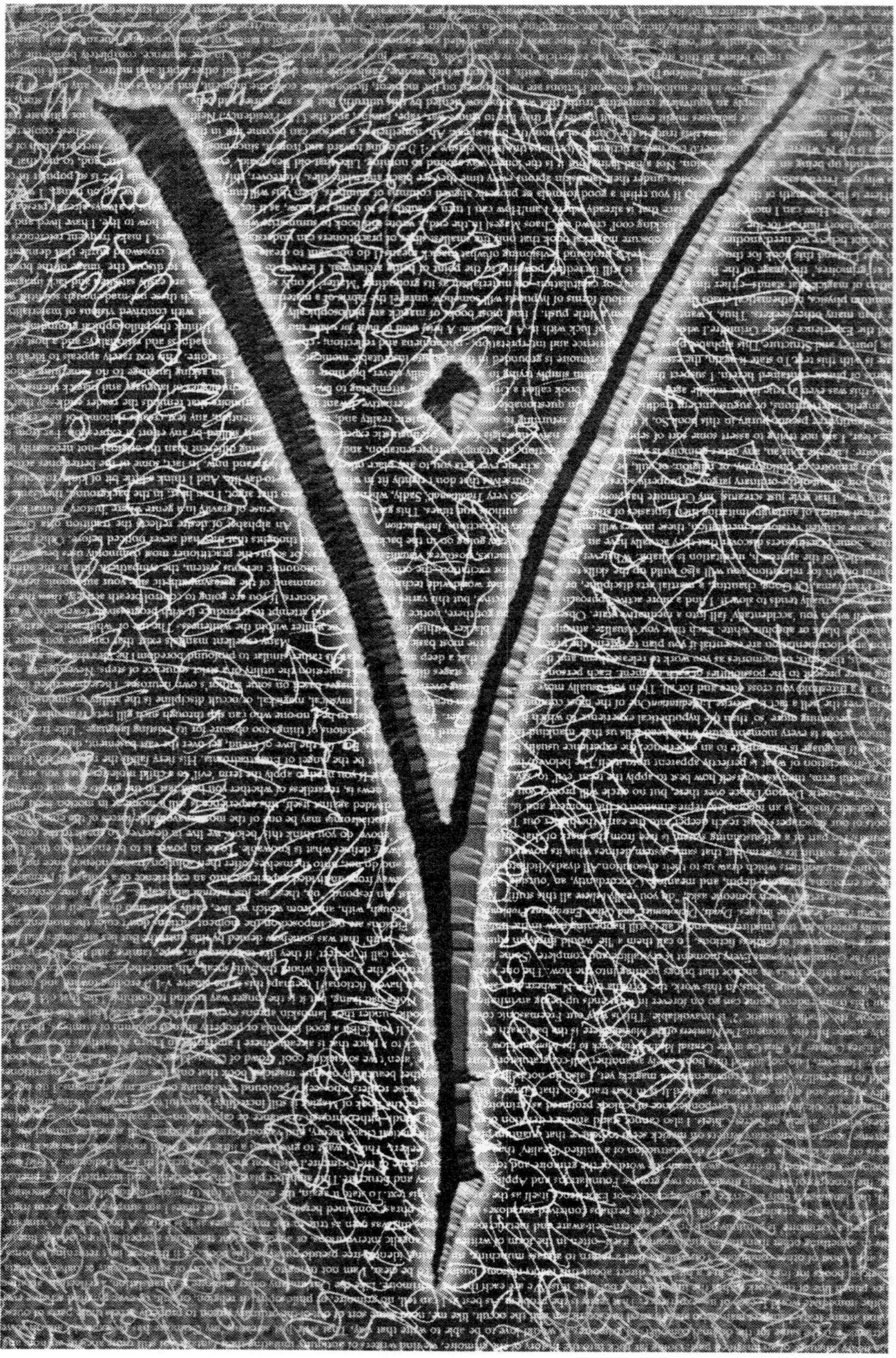

20
Midword
A Summing-up-so-far

If a work can have a foreword and an afterword, then it can also have a 'midword.' Volume One brought us halfway through the voids. With the preceding story's hints at interweaving life and lived magic in mind, our journey through these aethyrs will start to accelerate from hereon out. Now that we have a sense of some of the core principles underlying this work, we have made a shift to looking at how our lives themselves unfold—that is, magic. These interconnections, nets of meaning, defenses, and longings propel us through lives that are mostly out of our control, regardless of the illusions of agency into which we may buy. Deliberate, intentional magic, as opposed to the unwitting worship of our quotidian ziggurats of images, is an audacious act, a Promethean act, and, for some, even a Luciferian act. We must defy the popular trances of 'how things work' in order to gain awareness of what has always been hiding in plain sight—actually in the very act of seeing itself. Nevertheless, this liberation is neither a permanent switch nor an isolated choice.

As should be clear by this point, most people who take charge of the imagery by and through which they live do not think of their choices as sorcerous. They may cherish the fullness and depth their lives carry and they may have perhaps a sense of the 'magical' in their lives because of these choices. Magic that only exists when we are in temple spaces, wearing robes, in church, at psychotherapy sessions, or attending self-help retreats usually helps us to stay stuck in the pre-existing lives we live outside these spaces—even and especially when it is these very lives we seek to change. This is because with these isolated acts we ensigilize spells of segregation: 'Here, in this incense filled room, I can imagine anything I want. Here I am safe and sequestered from the banal influences of day-to-day life. I must commit strange and unusual acts within this space so that I can continue to live like everyone else outside of this space; but, hopefully, somehow, because of this ritual in here, I will covertly achieve my goals out there.' (The same segregating devil's bargain can be seen when parents or administrators commit some unconscionable act against their child or employee with the excuse that it is 'for their own good' or the 'good' of the family/corporation.)

Good luck with that. Is it okay with you if I stand a safe distance away from the inevitable shock waves of dissonance this segregation will engender in your life? To be clear, I am not necessarily advocating for you to roam the halls of your Fortune 500 employer in robe and cape, wand waving merrily about in an effort to live an authentic, integrated life of magic. What I *am* advocating is the recognition that the supposedly 'banal' day-to-day world of 'normies' is actually soaked in spells, ensigilizations, and seemingly supernatural forces. I am advocating for a certain 'ritual awareness'—a figurative and mythopoetic imagination that sees not beyond everydayness but *before*. That is, I want to help people to see how the most common of acts, the most menial of tasks, and the simplest of events in our lives are only possible in a vast sea of images.

Beyond Figurative Magic

I suppose that you could read this book and think that I am merely trying to co-opt the language and imagery of 'magic' for a more poetic view of life. I have a broad swath of colleagues in the broader world of Depth Psychology as well as the more specific niche of Imaginal Psychology who are quite content with this perspective. Too many altars and robes make them either a bit giggly or a tad nervous. You could, moreover, assume that I actually don't think magical rituals themselves are of any value and that those people who practice them are misled at best and delusional at worst. Most of the rest of my psychology colleagues really hope that this is what I actually intend with this book. To be clear, this is *not* my intention, but you could read this work in that way and still get some value out of the perspectives I'm pushing.

With this work, I have definitely sought to expand the definition of the Mage beyond the realm of self-avowed 'magicians' to include dreamers, innovators, creators, 'highly effective people,' artists, and others of intense imagination. I have also wanted to express what I think is a common yearning for a sense of the magical in our lives. This longing is neither whimsical, escapist, nor delusional. Quite the opposite. I believe that this fundamental call for the magical is actually existential. I believe that we are drawn to, or perhaps repulsed by, the magical because it can serve as a gateway to the Imaginal—the very ground of our being. Yet beyond a figurative and mythopoetic attitude, I am also strongly of the mind that humans are inherently creatures of ritual.

From the undifferentiation of our infancy, through the as-if play of our childhood pretending, to the intensity of our teen dramas, we subtly misdirect ourselves with ideas of 'reality' to ignore the deadly serious play of our lived rites. Our minds are metaphorical, symbolic, and never literal. The 'literal' is an idea, not a privileged 'fact.' We learn to produce answers for our teachers that betray our own experience in favor of a socially acceptable consensual, but flimsy, reality. Transcendent 'Reality' or 'Truth' are powerful images, but they are as fictional as any other aspect of our lives. They are often successful, effective, and useful, to be sure, but, like every other perspective, they are still fictional. However, this does not mean that we each get to simply construct our lives whole-sheet based on our whims. This is not a book about subjectivism and the solipsistic nihilism to which that leads. Far from it. For most of our lives, we are made by images, not the other way round. Creativity is actually the ability to navigate between imagery, not simply the ability to create images.

Thus, in order to cultivate this ability to navigate the Imaginal, we must encourage other ways of knowing, new ways of seeing. Practicing overt rituals—engaging with the imagination of magic—encourages a type of awareness, which, so long as we are not merely substituting spiritual fundamentalism for material fundamentalism, will offer us new eyes by which to see our many worlds of possibility, instead of one disanimated world of inevitability. Temple rituals, fiery circle ceremonies, regalia, rites of passage, and sacraments are the stuff of life as lived. By developing the sort of ritual awareness these events engender, we can reclaim our lives from the unconsidered imagery that has calcified our lives into rigid networks of brittle defenses. Rather than accepting that life of desperate segregation, by claiming the magic of our lives we instead navigate through the whirling spheres of multiplication.

Magical Curricula

Entering the world of explicit magical practice is rarely a deliberate, systematic, or well-monitored process. From my experiences with clients, students, friends, and myself, it seems that high emotions, intense privacy and shame, (fed by questionable literature and websites) and fits and starts of experimentation typically mark these—usually unwitting—forays. Spurred on by the lure of the imagination of magic, young people glom together idiosyncratic practices and perspectives that are diverse enough to make even the most eclectic chaos mage's head spin. Often the teenager, stretching from childhood's complete-immersion-in-fantasy toward fantasies-of-adulthood's-power-and-confidence, is the first to dabble in the application of rituals in order to effect changes in his or her life. Ouija boards, urban legends, intense petitioning prayer, lucid dreaming, and many other diverse practices are cobbled together, fueled by naïveté, sincerity, angst, garbled sexuality, and passion, in order to produce highly charged syncretic practices. More often than not, the dramatic results scare the teen out of his or her mind. In response, neophytes quickly retreat into bland 'normalcy' leaving their dalliance with sorcerous power a distant but haunting memory. For a few people, later in life, these early frights may become justifications for the pursuit of purely 'High' or 'Ritual' forms of magic (e.g., orthodox religion), yet may also simultaneously provide a seductive narcissistic shadow.

(Childhood itself is, of course, inherently magical—which is not synonymous with 'lovely.' However, children are so immersed in the Imaginal, with scarcely a single functioning identity, let alone the polycentric multitudes of 'I-s' they will use as adults, that it might be best to say childhood itself is more magical than are the individual children themselves. The ability to carry forth this childhood wonder into adulthood finds its best hope in a mythopoetic attitude toward life.)

In order to channel these early impulses, the idea of a 'magical curriculum' has become common in many modern magical texts, beginning in the late 1800's but becoming more robust from the 1960's. (And I think many of us secretly long for Hagrid to show up and sweep us off to Rowling's *Hogwarts School of Witchcraft and Wizardry.*) Typically, New Age magical texts give the reader a psychotheocosmology, including some rehash of the cardinal directions, and then offer a series of visualizations, a catalog of magical tools, a scrying technique or two, and finally some spells. Perhaps the text even includes holiday and/or Sabbat rituals. Charming though these ideas may be, these texts rarely stretch even a few feet outside of the circle of warmed-over Gardnerian Wicca—which is itself a pastiche of late-Victorian peri-Masonic Romantic eclecticism. Moreover, even when the texts are clearly creative endeavors on the parts of authors, most of them still try to lay claim to a literal historical, rather than an experiential, provenance. These pseudo-arcane New Age curricula are rarely existentially-grounded and, as such, are forms of indoctrination that impose the systems' assumptions, styles, needs, and limitations onto a calling that, to be truly magical, ought to be giving you the tools with which to liberate yourself from such programming.

Although many contemporary magical texts may leave themselves open to criticisms regarding their lack of philosophical depth, these authors are hardly alone in their desire to cover over life's uncomfortable uncertainties. This propensity for imposition is as true of many life coaches' self-help curricula as it is of various cults' brainwashing systems. Countless approaches to psychology also pedantically reduce humans to wonderless automata. Whether through trite and dismissive terms such as 'positive thinking' and 'self-fulfilling prophecies' or the mechanistic bleakness of 'learned helplessness' and 'repetition compulsions,' psychology seems bent on ignoring life-as-lived in favor of an exclusive focus on aspects-of-life-that-lend-themselves-to-quantification. The desire to give into these reductionistic perspectives is easy to understand. Faced with a world, and lives, that retreat from easy explanation, we hunger for systemizations, whether psychosociological, magical, or cultic, that promise to explain away the uncertainties and ignorance inherent in life. Nonetheless, any explanation that does not respect—and perhaps even begin with—the fundamental role of the unknown, the mystery, and the ineffable frontiers of life is condemned to fail in its addressing of the human condition.

Many texts on chaos magic would seem to allow for this essential indeterminacy. Letting efficacy be their guide, the best of these authors eschew highflown cosmologies in favor of rough-and-ready existential schematics. However, afraid to admit that they might not *always* be bloodletting, goat-humping, and Cthulhu-worshipping, too many texts on chaos magic balk at pursuing the idea of the ubiquity of magic to its logical end—that is, that *all of life is magic*, even when that life is pathetic, uncool, immature, and banal. Not that chaos magicians don't live and understand this truth, they just don't like to write books that emphasize its possibility. In truth, the chaotes I know who have reached any level of maturity and accomplishment have bookshelves far more stacked with philosophy, linguistics, religion, psychology, biology, folk-lore, and imaginative fiction than black and hoary tomes on making unspeakable eldritch entities do your housework. Trying to make broad statements about chaos mages is, however, a fool's errand. The fevered individualism that marks these explorers is notorious. Nevertheless, success in any magical pursuit, but most especially a chaos approach, always entails a powerful and sometimes downright goofy sense of humor, as well as the ability to play very seriously. In this sense, these volumes fall firmly within the chaos tradition.

An Existential Magic

I say all of this by way of summing up much of what I've tried to convey in Volume One. For most of us, most of the time, life unfolds in the unconsidered assumptions. My major criticism of most books of magic, let alone how most people pursue religion, philosophy, and their lives, is that they don't dig deep enough to consider these fundamental lived assumptions. In addition to an unimaginative concession to a belief in 'matter,' most people live out philosophies that only address exceptional, ideal, or hypothetical situations. These 'speculative philosophies' scarcely account for the mechanics of our work-lives, relationships, or fears. (A brief note to anyone hoping to establish a successful cult: Unless you lock your members away in carefully controlled 'retreats,' your brainwashing system will only prove successful if it accounts for everything your subjects experience in the course of a normal day. This is, of course, why most cults put most of their energy into isolating and insulating their members from as many types of real-life situations as possible.)

In response to these lifeless approaches, I have tried, thus far, to account for life as everyone experiences it. This existential focus is painfully absent from most approaches to anything like 'magic' because most perspectives on magic are efforts to *escape* the existential facts of life. Through ill-conceived ideas about spirituality, vague supernatural agents, and an insupportably rigid sense of a core self, most contemporary magical systems are simply wish fulfilling, philosophical porn. By not confronting the limits of knowing, current systems of spiritual-ity, esotericism, and magic simultaneously lay claim to, and betray, the wisdom traditions from around the world.

The unavoidable existential frontiers to human experience are not heady phil-osophical constructs. They are painfully obvious, however there is little doubt that we construct much of our life in order to misdirect ourselves subtly away from the realization that:

* we all die;
* we cannot know ourselves or other in the same way we know 'things';
* the past and future are projections from the present;
* we are all making meaning in the moment;
* which makes us both completely free and responsible for this ever-present moment;
* and all the rules, certainties, logics, categories of things, causalities, and identities by which we would hope to capture this ever-unfolding life, are as ephemeral and insubstantial as a diamond's sparkle.

Paired with a sense of wonder rather than dread, I contend that the stuff of magic need not be contrary to a thoroughly considered existential philosophy. Because to be human is to be a creature of imagination, we are all already always doing magic—magic is how we make and live out meaning. To be a mage is to take hold of the technology of imagination, to enter the Imaginal. In the Imagi-nal, the assumptions of life come into stark contrast. We come to see the images through which we live, the images that underpin our lives. Identity, alterity, interpretive systems, goals, memory—so much of what we take as 'given' in life shifts uncannily beneath our feet as soon as we move to a different constitutive image.

Nevertheless, because the same 'I' with which we would hope to awake to these powerful images is itself contextually defined by these same underpinning images, we need to make a shift away from a rigid sense of 'Facts,' 'Truth,' and other thing-like concepts if we hold the hope to ever gain any emancipation. Because this shift cannot be absolute and because every moment presents us with new and ensnaring certainties from which we must extricate ourselves if we want real liberation, I have chosen to call the presence-to-the-Imaginal, 'no-one.' No-one is similar to a Jungian sense of psyche, a Buddhist sense of our original nature, and a chaote's sense of Kia.

Engagement with no-one may give us a sense of 'soulfulness' but it isn't a soul. Learning to see from the perspective of no-one may offer us ways of living more deeply and fully; but it will leave us more certain that we will die. This perspec-tive values multiplicity over unity, diversity over homogeneity, polycentrism over an integrated Self. I am, in a way, advocating for the 'Balkanization' of the personality, because, until we see diversity in our many selves, we will never truly make a place for diversity in the world. The limitations of the ego and its obsession with the 'reality principle' constantly drives us to assert our permanence through a worldview of unity. Thus, our dreams of peace are too often the fascist nightmares of an obsessed monomaniacal ego desperate to assert its dominance. Only by letting go of our universe will we see the cosmos—the appearances in and through which we live—as an invitation to join the multiverse.

Conclusion

Although the ideas and exercises in these volumes may bring many assumptions with them, these perspectives are, hopefully, far more obvious and malleable, for both the budding and the experienced practitioner, than the derivative 'certainties' of far too many magical systems. My aim is to honor, through a system of inventories, the magic that is already present in our lives—the magic that creates our lives. Through increased attentiveness, a sort of meta-magical and life-as-lived outlook can evolve uniquely for each person.

Even if we are not addressing explicitly magical practices, this text draws no hard distinction between overt self-styled magic and far more ubiquitous undertakings such as prayer, wishing, visualization, superstitions, creativity, piety, daily rituals, self-help, and, overall, lifestyle. Regardless of your approach, the key is, as ever, awareness, beginning with the simplest of questions, 'What am I actually doing?' as in Volume One's Application 2.

With Chapter 22's sixth application, we bring the life inventories to their conclusion. Further exercises will deal with specific magical practices, but this final set of ethical perspectives offers heuristic questions, which aim to speed the process of claiming your own magical style.

But before we get there, we must journey to the eternal midnight of the Crossroads in order to consider the bargains we've already struck, and make some fundamental choices about what sort of magical life we want to live.

21
Magic

Now we come to it: the crux of the matter; actually, the Crossroads—with all the attendant gods and goddesses from around the world who oversee this liminal space of in-between. The Crossroads always mean a choice, whether or not we call upon the Old Stranger to strike a pact. This chapter is no different, it poses us with the fundamental questions about how we will henceforth choose to live our lives.

We have the ideas. We see the cosmology. We understand how images constitute us, how they constitute our world, and how *we* see things in return. Now, what do we do about it? How do we go about the business of leading a life—of actually *living*? Not so much living-with-really-cool-ideas-floating-about-our-heads, which is a grand way to stay stuck in a life you don't really want. But living in accord with how we realize life actually works.

Given the radically contingent and contextual nature of the imaginal reality we've described so far, simple 'action' is, actually, not so simple. The unconsidered images of life can so easily fool, mislead, program, or entrance us, to such an extent that we have no idea of what we are doing. We can be doing something quite different from what we think or say we are up to. Ideas such as 'intention,' 'action,' and 'consequence' are often epiphenomena—a surface froth above leviathan constitutive images.

Should we conceive of a need or desire, what in fact is it that decides whether or not we achieve it? Surely, no single factor can receive credit for that. Hosts of dynamics collaborate, coordinate, and constitute the journey from desire to accomplishment. Even the most hard-minded of us still indulge superstitions to 'hedge our bets,' dimly intuiting that our efforts are, unto themselves, drowned in a sea of variables such as are laid forth in Volume One's presentation of the void of Chaos. To reach our goals we ritually research, hermeneutically hope, and enthusiastically engage epistemologies. Do our 'informed choices' lead to better paths? Typically, it seems to be so. But was it the quality of the information or the nature of the ritual of deliberation that led to the clearer discernment? Most of our intellectualized ritualizing is unwitting, but we do it with the same sort of earnestness as the seven-year-old wearing the same pair of 'victory socks' for his next t-ball game.

We are inherently ritual creatures, creatures of imagination (i.e., *homo imaginalis*, since our shifting 'sapience' stands within the far more fundamental mundus imaginalis). And we are magical. Our imaginations express themselves in the language of magic. The life-engineering that is accomplished through engaging the imaginal level of existence is indistinguishable from 'magic.'

Thus, if we plan to navigate the waters of the Ocean of Images, we must have a sense of humor about, and perhaps a little bit of derision for, the limited ways in which most people think things get done in this world. Perhaps we need to make use of that deadly predator of these waters, the snark, in order to liberate ourselves from infantile ideas about magic and claim our creative birthright. The snark can be brutal, of course; but worse than its cruelty is our more common practice of depriving the snark of proper nutrition. Well-fed snarkiness lives on irony and parody. It is a means of critique. Without satire, the snark becomes a bitter and baseless creature. And so, although this chapter may get a little snarky, it is with a purpose. My intention is to address the hosts of unexamined assumptions that we carry with us — ideas about the mechanics of the universe, vague divinities, and symbolic actions. As we integrate our ideas thus far toward a vision of magic as the means by which we claim our lives, we may need to cast a few sneers, a jaundiced eye or two, and perhaps even reclaim a sense of skepticism from those superstitious scientists. Magic has for too long been the purview of the painfully credulous and the intellectually flabby. Let us now reclaim it from the fakes, the deluded, and the fearful. Perhaps the best way to begin is with a few basic questions.

First, do you like your life?

Do you like, nay, *love* everything about your life and the world in which it unfolds? Good. Put down this asinine book and report its perverted author to the nearest Authority who has graciously fabricated your marvelous existence for you. In truth, I don't mean this sarcastically. I believe that some people find that their story has unfolded to a marvelous place in which they have rich experiences, fulfilling relationships, and a surprisingly limited number of dust-bunnies. If you are in this position, I would not recommend mucking about in the worlds of magic. The magic in your life is giving you what you want or at least telling you that what you have *is* what you want. Fairy tales clearly show us that journeying into magical realms tends to throw everything into flux, leaving us suddenly adrift and uncertain.

Regardless, no matter how pleasant your life is, it *will* change. Hence, the best-constructed lives have powerful rituals, simply built into them, to mark and catalyze these moments of transition, often in the form of rites of passage. As such, magic is a liminal companion in many lives that are otherwise carried by those cultures that have not drifted too far from life-as-lived. (Hermes is, amongst his other duties, a god of these crossroad rituals of transformation, as well as one of magic.) Thus, most people within these functional cultures will find that they need not travel too far in order to allow the reinvigorating waters of the Imaginal to wash over them. Rituals of birthing, naming, bonding families, coming of age, marriage, career transitions, and a host of other critical moments-of-growth abide in some of the world's more tenacious communities.

On the other hand, many of us find ourselves in cultures that deny that they even *are* a culture. In our postmodern à la carte world, we select appetizers of religions, soups of philosophies, and salads of cultures. We confuse the over-full bloat after this meal with actual satiation. We believe that the prefabricated, warmed-over menu from which we choose offers us real freedom. But in this Cheesecake Factory version of life, a giant menu doesn't actually mean real choice. We cannibalize religions, exercise and diet systems, philosophies, aesthetics, and self-improvement strategies and yet somehow don't feel the richer for it. We tell ourselves that we are at least 'doing something about it,' whatever 'it' is. Yet our efforts may merely be the preprogrammed, impotent 'alternatives' that keep our stagnation firmly in place. Still, on this first level of being 'happy with our lives,' many people are pleased enough with their unhappiness and their various, often ineffectual means of addressing it. Leaving aside the question of whether or not this is another form of 'happiness,' any move away from this stagnation and toward truly recognizing and working with imaginal reality—that is, genuine magic—will only screw up that tenuously (mal)contented configuration. This leads us to a second question.

Do you dislike much of your existence but think you deserve it?

Pray harder, you schmuck. And for G-d's sake, confess to someone for polluting your eternal soul by reading filth like this. Many people do live within a religious framework that tells them that what happens is the product of a single omniscient and omnipotent Divinity (always Capitalized) who controls all aspects of Reality. This is the theological stance of 'strong theism.' That sort of Divinity, of course, has a whole lot of explaining to do, but those who believe in such abhorrent abominations deserve the Divinity they get.

(These sorts of prepackaged certainties are wildly popular, except within the Halls of Academia where they receive at best a wink and at worst a dismissive sneer. Although I have met a small minority of academics who have respect for religion in the West, most equate *all* Western religion with superstition and see it as the source of most, if not all, of the ills of the world. The soft humanism that passes for faith in the world of scholars has evils all its own, not the least of which is a tacit materialism. Oddly enough, this secular materialism can quickly deteriorate into the same sort of orthodox, literalist fundamentalism as that of its hyper-religious rivals.)

The big problem with 'faith' is that this word has become synonymous with 'blind obedience,' when it need not. Unfortunately, those who attempt to use the language of various faith-traditions without this sort of foreclosing inscrutability find themselves in a lonely place, drifting rapidly toward 'heresy.' High emotions come along with discussions of faith. Through all of life's most awful and painful moments, literal believers have staked their sanity and their well-being on a Divinity who not only heard their prayers, but who also knew best, and dispensed both Justice and Succor.

Even without this sort of Kung-fu-Grip 'strong theism' Deity, people use 'karma,' 'Justice' (poetic and otherwise), the 'Rule of Threes' (i.e., 'what you sow you shall reap threefold'), together with a host of other Universal Principles to make themselves feel better about what goes on in the world, and in their lives. In the worst cases, this attitude turns into a resignation from engagement with life, a disavowal of our freedom and responsibility. Nevertheless, the concept of believing that what occurs in the world is ultimately out of our control, and that what befalls us is probably what we deserve, has a huge swath of fans, many of whom are not 'religious' at all.

(I have wrestled with this particular concept for many years, growing up in a family that was firmly Monotheistic, although in some unusual ways. In particular, the concept of propitiatory and petitioning prayer in the Face of an omnipotent Divinity has been a point of contention for me. This issue receives treatment in 'Chapter 24: A Young Lutheran Struggles with Prayer.')

Finally, do you want to make changes but have found your previous efforts ineffectual?

Maybe you don't resonate with any of the previous caricaturizations and want to make a few adjustments. Good for you! Waggling about a lovely wand and reciting some butchered Hebrew may do this for you. At least it will distract you from what a cesspit this world is. As an alternative, go out into the woods, strip naked, and rub up against the nearest warm body (or tree). At least your distraction will be a bit more fun than the wand schtick.

Regardless, if any of the above 'magical' approaches tickle your fancy, you should also put down this awful book and thank your nearest divinity and/or cult leader for fabricating such a marvelous delusional system that can keep you distracted from—and yet still *in*—the immediate moment that has proven so unsatisfactory for you. The vast majority of 'magical systems,' 'New Age' vagaries, and pseudo-Oriental Western glosses are, after all, simply hobbies, wardrobe repertoires, and niche magazine and blog demographics. No matter the aesthetics, source scriptures, wardrobe choices, names for divinities, ultimate concepts, or principles, most religions, philosophies, and magical systems fail to truly, radically revision reality itself. Thus, the postmodern world offers a host of 'alternatives' but few genuinely novel choices.

But, if you have persisted so far with this book, then you really are a sorry sort of an ilk. Something like me.

(I apologize in advance.)

If this latter proposition is the case, then we must sort out some bizarre inconsistencies that the aforementioned 'happy,' 'guilty,' and 'deluded' have left for us. A few basic observations should prove a good start. These perspectives sum up many of the viewpoints presented in these volumes so far, but now with the emphasis on claiming the magic in which we always already participate. Although rooted in the imagination of magic (the imagery, trappings, and ideas that are the argot of people who call themselves 'magicians'), these ideas are much more about the magic of the imaginal—the magic of imagination.

Let's have at them.

Everything is Magic

Cars, cell phones, hypnosis, celebrity, power, healing, email, governments, toilets (oh, especially toilets!), money, clothes, sickness, pharmaceuticals, weaponry, comedy, and on and on… All of it is magic. Hell, occasionally even pentacles and wands are magical.

Magic is the physics of an imaginal universe. Any experience is the product of the convergence of various magical currents. Magic is not the exception to the rule. *Magic creates the rules.* Even 'the thing unto itself'—that amazingly empty nihilistic notion underpinning materialism—depends on an informing, underlying image for its seeming self-evidence, its meaning and purpose. Materiality and its schools of magic, the 'natural' sciences, merely form an incredibly pervasive and successful system of magic.

I am not saying that various schools of magic don't have *qualitative* differences—the types of resulting experiences *do* vary. What I am saying is that most self-declared 'mages' are too busy trying to assert how cool, traditional, or different they are to notice how much other people are not only more successful at making car payments and getting laid, but also at making changes with sorcerous technology.

All Acts are Magical

Worshipping ATMs (or toilets), driving, praying, signing a contract, lying, researching, painting, working, dancing, voting, singing, mugging, reading, lighting a cigarette, using a remote control, paying bills, showing your passport, and everything else we do floats through a dreamland of impossibilities that we blithely accept. Because so many of us have given up on asking 'why?' we believe that the answers must either be irrelevant, known only to experts, or so subjectively individualistic as to be imponderable. And yet our millions of contingent and half-considered 'whys' are *how* we wake up in the morning, relate to ourselves and others, eat, sleep, dream, and either do or don't blow our heads off. We drift between complexes of images that provide fabulous justifications, scripts, identities, distractions, purposes, reasons, and accessories.

Doing magic—as opposed to being done by magic—is the process of claiming some of the technology of meaning, desire, choice, intent, language, representation, identity, and so forth, for your own ends. This is far from an all-or-nothing equation. Our relative agency exists along a continuum and may vary greatly from one part of our lives to another. That is to say that life spans the gamut from those times when we are most aware of and able to consciously exercise these technologies, to those other times when these technologies work for or against us, with little or no intervention or awareness on our part.

All Sex Acts are Sex Magic

Let's be clear, however. If you've gotten this far, then you understand that 'magic' is not automatically synonymous with 'wonderful', right? As best as I can tell, sex takes a little bit of work to do well. Most people don't actually have sex anymore. They have elaborate fantasies—usually driven by the aforementioned unconscious 'phantasies'—in which another body may be obliging enough to play a representative role.

Whether you are creating a little homunculus, trying to forget a lousy work-week, celebrating having an erection, praying for the disinhibiting effects of alcohol to outpace the dampening effects, hoping that the pleasure and beer goggles will blind you to the less attractive attributes of your partner(s), reciting Tibetan phrases backwards while breathing through only one nostril and maintaining positions named after amorous primates, rutting like angry wombats, or jacking off to blurry clips of celebrities—all of these actions deeply reinforce the patterns of behavior leading up to, and at that moment of, orgasm. This is the essence of sex-magic, but most writers on sex magic feel compelled to couch this 'secret' in their fantasies of tantra, (dis)inhibited Edwardian gentry, or various other marvelously creative fictions.

Nevertheless, these 'sex magic' writers too often ignore that the couple having sex in the dark, in the missionary position, and later praying to be forgiven for their sinful ways are also practicing sex magic and getting exactly what they ensigilized in their work. So too are those practicing sex with bonking buddies for whom they have no love.

Sex transfixes us, especially when we don't admit that it does. The vast majority of religions cannot even conceive of a reality that transcends the ubiquitous mechanics of this marvelous act. Sadly, these same religions simultaneously conceal their libidinal well-spring in contrived symbolism that induces sniggers in smart-ass occultists, who like their version of sublimated sex-acts better. The Magical Revival, its Romantic roots a response to the dehumanizations of the Industrial Revolution, unfolded over the same time-span as various sexual revolutions. Thus, the imagination of magic in modern occultism is rife with quaint, convention-defying sexual imagery and ritual. (So common are the various substitute sexual acts in neo-pagan ritual that a Wiccan High Priest friend of mine once opined, 'Well, it's all about the pole-in-the-hole, isn't it?')

I am not trying to question the power of sublimating libidinal energy or so-called kundalini into symbolic acts. What I do have difficulty swallowing is the monomaniacal focus on the sex act as the founding and sole metaphor. In Volume One we discussed 'puzzles and secrets,' the first type of mystery. Finding out that the drapes to your tradition's Holy of Holies are actually labia is precisely this first kind of mystery. What, exactly do you *do* with this insight? Perhaps this realization could help undermine false divisions in your life. Maybe you can even get to that alchemical epiphany of having both spirit matter and inspiring matter. But, unto itself, 'deciphering' the sex codes behind every cave, mandorla, standing stone, and shaft is a tired pseudo-Freudian trick that, unto itself, leads to an empty nihilism. Sadly, countless magicians remain stuck on 'sex' as some sort of universal secret. These occultists somehow contend that overt sex magic gets you far more in touch with the 'real-you.' (With apologies to Thelemites, 'hriliu' is what Crowley described as the 'shrill scream of orgasm' to be uttered at the transubstantiative peak of his Gnostic Mass, *Liber XV*. This likely tells the reader much more about Crowley's overly-erudite approach to love-making than it does about the secrets of 'sex magick.')

Sure, looking into a partner's eyes, breathing deeply, and delaying orgasm may enhance your skills as a lover, and may prove good for both your health and your relationship. But don't delude yourself, getting good at those tricks doesn't mean every *other* orgasm you have doesn't somehow ensigilize its own reality as well. Psychological and neurological research continues to confirm that an orgasm is one of the most reinforcing rewards a human can experience. Thus, both adulterous dalliances and porn can adhere to the addictive cycle. Moreover, as some of us know, 'those other playmates don't mean anything to me, baby' is a sorry excuse to a partner who thinks they mean quite a lot.

Whatever You Do, You are Ensigilizing that Reality

Don't like your life? Change something. Hell, *change anything*. Practice changing again and again and again until you get it: that you *can* change. Keep changing things until you realize how much can be changed—until you realize that the things you thought were simply the 'givens' of life are as mutable as fashion trends. Otherwise, you will continue to perpetuate the great rut of all existence — so-called 'inevitability.'

Why are we so fond of writing diaries, books of shadows, blogs, and a host of other self-referential texts? Why are cities covered with graffiti 'tags'? We need to ensigilize the tenuous fictions of our lives and identities. Imagine what would happen if we spent as much time writing *new* fictions as we do onanistically writing and rewriting the tired old ones? (Then again, sometimes our fantasies are just thinly veiled versions of the same tired conflicts we haven't figured out how to overcome.)

Practicing magic is an audacious, mendacious arte. It defies the dominant narrative of what and how things are. Magic will always, to some extent, deceive — just as all image complexes do; but magic is a self-employed deception. This arrogance and oppositionalism touches all magic with Darkness. This inherent Shadow Nature is the reason occultists so often associate the Adversary with all things magical, and rightly so. Real, intentional magic emerges both to liberate, and to undo, convention.

As such, True Magic can never be a tradition. The Mage is the one who, with a light touch, surrenders to no-one. No text can tell you how to be magical; it can only offer you possibilities, which you must claim for yourself. Of course, we all hunger for a tradition and a community, a sense of belonging. These are fundamental human needs. But ultimately, this journey is a Crooked Path — an individual, tangled and twisted unfolding story. In a way, we are all mages, but most of us deny and never claim the technology by which our stories progress.

(As an aside: when practiced well, several forms of solution-focused psychotherapy, notably Neuro-linguistic Programming, Narrative Therapy, Cognitive Behavioral Therapy, and even Ellis' Rational-Emotive Behavior Therapy, operate under these same change-centered premises, simply using different vocabulary. These forms of treatment simply help clients to identify what they want to change, and then walk them through an assessment of their attendant thoughts, actions, imagery, and stories in order to discern what supports, and what inhibits that desired change.)

Your Life is Magic

Whether you realize it or not, your life is an unfolding, mystical journey that follows the imaginal physics of magic. In most cases, no matter what the supposed 'intent' is of whatever ritual or initiation you are attempting, you will most likely be *doing* the magic for which your life is screaming. This is because our strongest ensigilizations are rarely considered 'magical'; yet they easily undercut any shallow pretending we may occasionally do while wearing a robe and magical ring.

Thus, when we open the various ritual spaces of our lives with the aim of claiming greater potential, will our desire to commune with some contrived god-form outweigh our fundamental struggles with a co-worker? Doubtful.

With that in mind, making oaths and statements inconsistent with your life-as-lived-outside-the-ritual-circle is an odd practice. It conditions a fundamental disconnect that is the exact opposite of will-working but is sadly what most people hope for when they do 'magic.' It is far worse than hypocrisy, since the hypocrite may at least know that he is being false. Some magical practitioners make use of a separate magical persona in an effort to disconnect their temple work from their day-to-day work. In these situations, I have always been curious what exactly these practitioners are doing their temple work *for* and where they hope to observe the results of their work. This disconnect is just as true for formal religions, corporate retreats, and the sort of commitments to changing our lives we make when in a stupor of melancholy inebriation.

Humans, whether possessed of a mythopoetic sensibility or not, are storied creatures. We live out our narratives with every act, every intention, and every value judgment. We hunger to claim our authority, our authorship, but we scarcely know how. Look to the ghost story genre to understand this dynamic. Ghosts are playing out their stories but remain imprisoned within the limitations that encompassed their deaths. Ghosts impotently seek for their story to reach a real resolution. We live like ghosts, in denial of our deaths, desperately unhappy with our lives, demanding revenge for our wrongs, and mostly ineffectual in our efforts. Our attraction to ghost stories is a hunger to give voice to our longing for catharsis, for resolution, but also, more fundamentally, it is a hunger for the language of our larger narrative, to go into that Light rather than to merely be forever played by Fate. The frightening tone, the eerie, uncanny, and the eldritch horror is the ambience of a life lived bleakly in opposition to itself.

People who claim real encounters with ghosts, faeries, or past-life remembrances often spend their entire existences trying to validate their claims within the limited confines of a scientistic epistemology. What a strange story these seekers choose to live out! What resolution could they possibly hope for? The very methods of today's Scientific Method preclude the necessarily individual nature of these supernatural encounters. Far more important is to question what sort of story you are living. These paranormal irruptions are genre-defining. Rather than looking for material proof of these experiences, we should ask ourselves the more literary question of how these stories unfold within the popular fiction of psi phenomena and ghost stories. This tack of questioning will at least provide answers grounded in the Real, rather than some particular 'reality.'

Any 'reality'—that is, your take on 'what is' and how things work—is merely one part of your story. It forms the background cosmology from which your story unfolds. As any reader of great science fiction knows, spending too much time on your cosmology and not enough on character development may get you devoted fans but will preclude you from the annals of real literature. Becoming fixated on 'proving' aspects of your story to be cross-fictional (i.e., true for everyone) is a pointless pursuit guaranteed to endlessly distract you from your own life. Look what happened to poor Fox Mulder of the *X-Files*. Until he learned that the truth was 'in here' and not 'out there,' he couldn't get on with his life.

Psi research, both the profession of parapsychology and its portrayals in popular fiction, is a parody—a shadow spoof mocking the methods of materialist science. Sadly, these wannabe-sciences are just as shabby as the psychics, charlatans, and disembodied knocking they seek to investigate. By definition, when we set out to investigate 'exceptional occurrences,' we will miss what is not an exception. We will miss life itself.

Claim Authorship of All of Your Magical Acts

Claiming our authority is the secret of a Magical Life, rather than simply an isolated practice. We are absolutely free and, thus, absolutely responsible for our lives. Sadly, the instruction booklet (i.e., the True Grimoire) is written in the very fabric of our life, our storied flesh. Thus, it takes a little practice to get the necessary perspective to read it.

In Volume One I made it clear that *The True Grimoire is made of your flesh written in the alphabet of your desires*. Not in someone else's incredibly complex writings, not in another ancient language, and not in obscure angelic/demonic formulae. Your life is the only text you need to read to learn the most hidden of magical secrets. Most of the metaphors of lost Golden Age civilizations, spiritual prequels to our lives, and hidden archaic wisdoms are merely metaphors for the wide-eyed mystical potential we possessed in our youth—and may still uncover in the moment. In current psychological research on happiness, 'meaningfulness' comes out as the highest and most abiding level of satisfaction—above getting cool stuff or even having memorable experiences. This is the sense of the 'magical' in our quotidian lives—an engagement with the meaning-making, the imaginal level of our existence.

Lovecraft teaches us a powerful lesson with his stories about the madness-inducing Grimoire-of-grimoires, the *Necronomicon*. His terrified characters provide testament to the awful cost of becoming so alienated from life itself, the True Grimoire, that every turn confronts them with the unspeakable, rather than the ineffable, with horror rather than wonder, with disillusionment rather than transformation. In a life that isn't about life-as-lived, the life-affirming power of the True Grimoire mutates into the maddening alienation of the *Necronomicon*.

Even setting aside the metaphors of the imagination of magic, committing to accomplish the simplest of tasks in our day-to-day lives creates incredible layers of complexity. How do we plan it? How do we remember what we set out to do? How do we assess progress? How do we imagine our goal? How do we reconfigure our sense of self to be the one-who-gets and not simply the one-who-wants? The vast majority of the time these factors coordinate seamlessly and what we want falls firmly within the parameters of the paradigm we occupy. When, however, we seek to do what is far less likely, or even 'impossible' within our current context, we must learn to navigate strange landscapes in order to find new means of achieving—new ways of being.

In spite of all of this ennobling rhetoric, we want all kinds of things and it should be painfully clear that 'wanting' is not the adequate pretext to 'getting.' Not even wanting, jacking off over a whole lot of cryptically ensigilized portrayals of what you want, censoring all your thoughts of any other desires, praying very, very hard, or giving more money to the nearest church, tantrika, or con artist will get it. In part, this is because of the so-called 'lust for results.'

Intentions and Wishes May Keep their Opposite in Power

We are some seriously perverse creatures, no? This disastrous disconnection between intentions and results has plagued those people who attempt to live out the imagination of magic. To their credit, many people who call themselves 'magicians' honestly note, and are vexed by, this problem. This is why so many 'rather impressive magicians,' usually falling firmly within the 'results based magic' camp, will tell you to cast your spell and then fuggetaboutit—fire and forget. (This has a similar feel to making a wish on your birthday candles but not sharing the wish with anyone.) The idea of letting the desire fly forth and forgetting the ritual—often ceremonially destroying the components that went into it—is meant to undo the complexities of wanting, worrying, hoping, trying, failing, and so on that get in the way of us actually 'getting' what we want. Perhaps, in a sense, this is an effort to sneak past the reality-principle-obsessed Demiurge of our egos and let the ritual simply reconfigure the imagery of our unconscious. Thus, with this magical virus implanted beneath its awareness, our egos can blithely go about their self-deluding way, but the overall dynamics of our psyches will lead us inexorably to our ritual desire. (Begging the pardon of its advocates, but, sadly, this sort of overblown psychological explanation pleases many of the ritualists of whom I speak, but it also operates more as an 'intellectual' talismanic bluff *against* further innovation and investigation, rather than *for* it. Essentially this approach states that any further investigation will lead to undoing the efficacy of the spell.)

However, these same fire-and-forget proponents often also tell you to keep working toward your goals. How, exactly, we are supposed to move toward the goals, but forget that we did a rather unusual ritual in order to try and hedge our bets, remains unclear. And all of this 'doing and not doing' all rides on the assumption that we actually have, in the rest of our lives, been doing everything we possibly could and in the most fruitful ways possible (big assumption!). So, maybe the reality is a little more nuanced than some impressive sounding bromides.

The so-called 'lust for results' that many a mage will warn you against is only one of many constellations of desire that can stand between a wish and the achievement of one's desire. The idea of 'lust for results' reminds us that 'wanting' too often casts the 'wanter' as the one who doesn't (and may never) 'have.' Images are almost always dyadic by nature. Hence, simply tapping into a god-current of 'prosperity' can equally get one 'poverty'—its shadow and constant companion. Most of the capitalist West sits firmly within that particular vicious dyad. To gain a better grasp on this mercurial issue, let us ground ourselves once more in some good, old-fashioned existentialism.

Rollo May is a startlingly readable philosopher and psychologist who has made existential thought accessible and palatable to America—no small feat. He gives us a formula rather more utile than some you may read of in popular 'Books of Magic':

$$Wish + Choice = Will.$$

Many of us can wish quite easily, although some people fear truly letting themselves give in to its seduction. On the other hand, choosing is a bit more difficult than it seems. This is in large part because each one of us is not a single conscious entity. There's more than one of you in there. This should be fairly clear to anyone who has attempted will-working, except that will-workers keep calling the other centers of themselves things like 'demons,' 'Holy Guardian Angels,' 'god-forms,' and other terms from the imagination of magic, while simultaneously not creating a cosmology in which they can meaningfully claim these 'things' as also themselves. (Although it remains possible that the secrets of the 'upper levels' of initiation within magical societies do actually reform epistemologies in such a way as to account for these experiences.)

As we shall see, ferreting out all of the spells we constantly cast that conflict with our newest overt, articulated 'will' is a lifelong task. Most magic seems to 'fail' because all the other magic you are doing is concurrently working as well. The new spell works, but in cryptic, perverse, and unexpected ways. Nevertheless, magic always works.

Magic Always Works

To a greater extent, whatever we wish for, let alone choose, we experience. These procedures—wishing or choosing—are only the smallest sliver of what can be called 'magic.' Our perception of 'failed magic' is when our wishes, choices, or ensigilizations don't come how, when, or where we want them. Nevertheless, the forces we invoke, evoke, cast, or ensorcel *always* manifest. Most of the time, it is we, not the universe, who must bend and move to be in the right place at the right time. It is usually not the world but us that needs to change. Consider the implications of the entirety of reality being imaginal. Hence, if magic is indeed a means of accessing the imaginal structure of experience, where do we expect to see the results of our work?

Portrayals of magic, both 'fictional' and 'non-fictional,' have much to teach us. I contend, however, that we must take a simultaneously less serious, and more serious, gaze at this topic. 'Less serious' in that we must stop trying to turn magic into some sort of paranormal, scientisitc 'phenomena'; and 'more serious' because we must finally at long last address how we make meaning, how we grow—in short, how we *live*.

Stories about magic, and our imaginings of magic, are ultimately not about levitating, shooting lightning bolts from our fingertips, or transforming Pb (82) into Au (79). The romances, tragedies, and fantasies of magic describe hubris, fear, transformation, discovery, perilous journeys, and unimaginable forces—in short, they are the stuff of life. Only when we engage in these stories, only when we wake up to the dream logics with which we cobble together our own stories, will we awaken to the magic that permeates every moment of our existences.

Thus, to make this most subtle and monumental of shifts away from a derivative, freeze-dried life, (no matter what the packaging) toward a life uniquely our own, we must take stock of the occult forces we bring to bear every day.

Application 6
Magical Inventory

If you have done any of the kind of magical journaling I described in the story about my mentors, then you are familiar with the idea of assessing the efficacy of your efforts — magical and otherwise. In some traditions, the term *Book of Shadows* applies to this personal diary, marking milestones in awareness and efficacy. This discipline is a vitally important habit since overt magical practice represents a level of audacity to which most people do not dare aspire. Thus, learning to look beyond your temple space, your church, or your management retreat, and into your life itself with a magical and ethical eye is essential. (Day-timer systems such as those proffered by the *Franklin Covey Company* adhere to the same principles.)

As should be apparent from this text, many formal magical practices are usually quite petty and ineffectual compared to the much greater spells in which we participate every second of our lives. Some of these spells are obvious: telecommunications, cartography, transportation, medicine, and so on. Other spells we cast upon ourselves are more subtle and arguably more pervasive, such as hope, ambition, and success, but also low self-worth, hostility, longing, despair, and so forth. Although we are apt to hold 'individuals' accountable for having such emotional stances, they do not occur in a vacuum. We live in a world soaked in overwhelming emotional solicitation. (Ever see a commercial that says you're a good person, who needs nothing additional to make you happy, and, oh, have a nice day?)

When we have the experience that an effort at working our will — a spell, sigilization, prayer, positive thought, business plan, or other magical procedure — 'doesn't work,' it may be because all the other incantations, invocations, and conjurations of our daily life eclipse its effects. That is, we often work against ourselves. Magical practice is, for too many of us, an excuse to sequester our desires into our temples or strategy meetings, and concede the rest of our lives to the vagaries of the world's currents. Beyond the language of magic, we use expressions like 'shooting ourselves in the foot,' 'working against our best interests,' and the various popular paraphrases of Voltaire's sentiment, 'the better is the enemy of the good' in order to describe a host of configurations of acting against ourselves. Most of us, most of the time, are mired in overwhelming tangles of crossed agendas.

Thus, as a means to discover what sort of Mage you actually are, try performing an assessment of your various life domains. If some of these questions seem to be more in the realm of ethics and lifestyle, then you are catching on. Remember that we said 'ethics is the highest form of magic.' Thus, this exercise is an extension of Volume One's ethics inventories in Applications 2 and 4.

To begin, ask yourself:

* Where do I spend my money?
* Where do I spend my time?
* Where do I get my money?
* What (usually-not-called-) rituals do I perform daily?
* How and to what do I allocate the square footage of my living space?
* What do I eat?
* What do I desire?
* How often do I find it necessary to distract myself with television, drugs, videogames, porn, and alcohol (as opposed to the intentional application of these technologies)?

Time and Money

Almost every magical system has some sort of subtle 'energy,' which is supposed to shift, flow, extend, and thus accomplish the practitioner's will. Whether some form of qi, or libido, or lifeblood, or an extension of the aura, the central metaphor is a sort of New Age electricity, which powers the system's vision of 'magic.' According to the endless shelves of books on such topics, once aspiring wizards, healers, martial artists, or yogis learn to feel and manipulate this energy, they can use it to create defenses, cast their will, and cure diseases. I like the idea of having some sort of imagined force that can be both visualized and felt—honestly, I realized a few years ago that I am still trying to become a Jedi Knight through my mastery of the Force. Nevertheless, I think most Westerners would do well to get over these 'energy' metaphors and understand the incredibly diverse and systemic implications of terms such as 'qi' in their native usage. Moreover, I think these specialized terms, which supposedly reveal our astral mechanics, can simultaneously serve to conceal what are the far more common currencies of a lived magical economy: *time, money*, and *space*.

Some ethnically based folk-magical systems understand this behavior-based value and place money—actual or proxy—and artifacts of life-investments on the altars to the gods. Liquor, family photos, sex paraphernalia, food, timepieces, holiday cards, shells, and a host of other symbols of what we value in our day-to-day life occupy devotional spaces the world around. Frankly, this practice seems close to archetypal since children unexposed to these folk practices will naturally place items they value in animist altar-like arrangements. (Whether we explicitly create altars or not, we clearly live out our values through the ways in which we make use of space and decorate our homes, as well as the things we keep 'private.')

Therefore, instead of worrying about the hyper-attenuated subtleties of your aura, open up your eyes to how you spend your day and your paycheck. Even when you know exactly what you have to do for the next week, lay it all out on a schedule. Look at how much time you dedicate to shopping, eating, talking on the phone and texting, watching TV, sleeping, commuting, reading, and in actual contact with humans of your choosing. No amount of magical ritual or prayer will overcome 'voting with your butt.' Where you spend your time says much more about you than what you *say* you value.

The same is true of money. Actually *look* at your bank statements. Many online banking sites allow you to sort your expenditures by type and a fair number of credit cards send you these categorized lists at the end of the calendar or fiscal year. Money is pure magic. It is abstract enough to be nonexistent and yet the investment of purpose is so unconscious that we cannot conceive of the 'meaning' of money—we can only speak of what it *does*. It just is valuable. In an ironically concrete and tautological sense, money has become value itself. Questioning the value of money and our unbridled pursuit of it is undoubtedly wise, but most of even the wisest of us still use it. Therefore, trying to deny its value in our life while simultaneously participating in its world-trance will likely blind us to how our use of it portrays our lived values—our magical investment.

Once we are able to answer the surface question of which types of businesses our money goes to, we can then look deeper. Where do those businesses spend their money? From where do our goods actually come? What are the labor practices in those countries? From where does our food come? Who produced it? How? What resources went into the production of the food? What is necessary for them to grow? What are the consequences of those approaches to agriculture? Increasingly, 'natural' and 'organic' are becoming moot terms that ignore the effects, implications, means of production, and business practices of producers. The key term for agriculture in the 21st century is *sustainability*.

Keep in mind, that, although this book may seem to have a stereotypically 'liberal' viewpoint, I am, in no way, advocating for any particular political agenda—unless 'thoughtful consideration and intentional living' are political. By all means, shop at your multinational-corporation-run stores in suburban America that drive local stores out of business. Buy chemically-laden, out-of-season produce from distant countries that exploit their laborers. Support the torture of animals through feedlots, animal testing, and the unbridled use of antibiotics. Invest your retirement money through and in corporations that undermine the basic principles of common sense and decency. And do all of this in a petroleum-based, environment destroying, climate-altering, war-encouraging big-ass SUV! I genuinely admire you if you have looked deeply enough into your life choices to understand the ramifications of your standard of living. Just, don't do all that and *then* think you can overcome all those gods-eclipsingly massive investments of Power with a little plaque by your door that says 'Dream' and a yearly donation to those same child laborers on whom your standard of living depends.

Intentional Living

From the perspectives in this work, the True Mage is the one who *lives intentionally*, who strives to calibrate desire, perception, ideals, and action into a seamless whole. Overt deliberate rituals are one time-tested way of trying to bring these four vectors into accord—of *orienting* yourself. (Many magical rituals begin with reference to the cardinal points, often beginning in the East, the 'orient.' The East is where the sun rises, from where hope comes. As much as this text may scrutinize the heroic, triumphant, and too-often egoic associations of the sun, it is, at its purest, a symbol of rebirth and new beginnings. How often do we check in with ideals and compare them to our actions? Such an opportunity for deliberation will inevitably re-orient us and offer us new opportunities, new beginnings.)

Every one of us struggles to match our way-of-living to our ideals in the light of our many wants and needs. Often, these tensions prove irresolvable, since our ways of seeing and knowing—our perceptions and epistemologies—enslave us to prepackaged values and desires. These freeze-dried ethics direct our eyes elsewhere, away from the lived values, and toward conveniently compartmentalized charities, causes, and indignation-eliciting injustices. We feel bad about other countries' famines, genocides, and natural disasters. We donate money to our favorite aid organizations. We may even picket outside businesses or government offices, but do we scrutinize how we speak, where we spend our money, who our friends are, and how we eat? Although there are no easy answers, only the relentless asking of these questions yields true ethical awareness. Sadly, many people give up on these deliberations and shuffle through the rest of their existences conceding control of their destiny to the powers-that-be.

Although my various identities will always be tied to some particular agenda and perception set, I must interrogate the lived values of those ways-of-being if I intend to be any more than a contingent 'I.' No-one lives and expands through this path of awakening. That is, our own sea of possibilities opens up to us when we reclaim the authorship of our lives from the innumerable soul-consuming patterns of this world.

As our world hurtles through yet another time of cultural flux, multicultural contexts emerge all around us. The laughably irrelevant term 'white' is finally in its waning days and many of the populations of the world are shifting toward a beautifully rich shade of 'brown'—even if their skin is pale. However, we are also seeing new intersections of disparate cultures yield heretofore unknown conflicts. Much as when waves of immigrants came to America at the dawn of the 20th century, today, many ethnic groups find they must codify and pursue ethical systems that help members to heighten both their sense of investment in the group and an awareness of their lived magic, their life choices. Diet is certainly one of the central points of intervention. Systems such as the I-tal of the Rastafarians, the Halal of Islam, or the eco-Kashrut of Reconstructionist Judaism create a culturally-grounded practice that reaches beyond simple considerations of health, tradition, or animal cruelty. These practices go further than the narrow 'we are what we eat' to the more global 'we are *how* we eat.' This approach is a shift away from the narrow-band viewpoints of materialist causality and into the magical fields of a chaos-based systems-living perspective.

Intentional living, intentional communities, and some forms of social anarchism are further examples of individuals seeking to claim their ethics away from conventional 'goodness.' Whether sharing resources, channeling investments, consuming sustainably, or creating goods, intentional communities remind us that we all live out intentions, but few of us know what those intentions are. We must deliberate, we must see in new ways, we must endlessly question if we want to craft a life that grows and transforms—a life that serves no-one.

In the Western world, we have made important progress advocating for individual rights. America has gone from being beholden to a Constitution designed to empower mostly wealthy, white, male landowners to a multicultural landscape of near-universal suffrage in which intellectuals and politicians have the luxury of wrestling with how best to encourage people to claim their rights. But, in this process, America has also witnessed the precipitous decay of community and culture. Globally, we have become so fixated on the construct of the 'individual' that the threads that link us to the environment, our families, our generations, and our society have broken, leaving us isolated islands in urban sprawl, suburbia, or blighted rural wastes. In our supposedly post-colonial world, the colonization of psyche, together with the infection of individualism, seems to have escaped the attention of most revolutionaries.

Although many people who define themselves as religious may see our current age as one in which 'belief' has become a rare commodity, I would contend that we have come to believe in both the individual as well as an individualistic definition of belief. In this self-trance, we are blind to the corporate beliefs in which we participate with far more zealous tenacity than our supposedly more faithful ancestors did.

Too often, books on magic are far too busy begging the question of an individual identity to truly understand the far reach of magic. The sorts of identities with which we wrestle in the West—and, increasingly, in much of the rest of the world—are products of the isolating forces that fueled the Industrial Revolution. As the inexorable tide of Renaissance Humanism blossomed in the smoke plumes of smog-choked factory-states, villages, communities, and even genuine families dissolved into the toxic sludge of 'industrialization.' Soon, the 'nuclear family' emerged, just in time for the nascent science of psychology to observe its world and, like the demiurge, blissfully ignorant of its history, declare the incestuous mommy-daddy-baby to be the healthy and normal model. Thus, bereft of centuries-old rituals and generations of support and tradition, and cluelessly thrust into a bewildering world gutted of purpose, the 'individual,' like all newborns, blinked its eyes and let out a horrendous cry, the echoes of which we can still hear today.

The so-called 'magical revival' came from a Romantic revulsion at this hideous condition. At the dawn of the 19th century, fantasies of Greek gods, Druidic rituals, and Ægyptian cosmologies served as preferable distractions to a world going rapidly and inexorably mad. In the absence of viable and relevant religions, the dominating influence of a generic Protestant Bourgeois Individualism created a fantasy of the guilt-ridden individual, divested of any overt symbolism and ritual, attempting to work out a relationship to a single, personal, and omnipotent Divinity who, through the machinations of war, colonialism, environmental matricide, and free-market capitalism, became increasingly irrelevant.

Thus, the individual 'human' is rarely the most meaningful unit of analysis in any system. Too often, 'humanism'—whether in its Renaissance or 20th century versions—is a watered-down philosophy that serves to support the status quo. In the hands of this bland 'humanism,' gods are rendered anthropomorphic allegories, psychologizing explains away all abnormality, and a vague normalcy rules the day. At best, humanism sees ethics as perhaps a natural human expression of our unique cultures, or a desire for functional community. But humanism can reach neither the transpersonal, nor the ecopsychological, nor the magical.

In order to free ourselves from these leveling 'humanistic' trances we need to ask questions about our sense of 'the normal.'

The Tyranny of Normalcy

Now, ask yourself:

* What do I consider 'normal'?
* When I appeal to these sorts of ideas, what do I feel like physically?

* When do I find myself speaking of what 'most people' want or do?
* When and how do I make use of ideas such as 'middle of the road' even when I speak of it with derision?
* When I speak of 'Americans'—or 'Canadians' or 'the British' or 'Mexicans'—what do I imagine? What do I mean?
* In what ways *am* I 'normal'? How do I define these commonalities? How do I feel about them?
* Where am I accepted? Do I notice when and where I can walk unmolested? Are these places where someone else of another class, gender, or ethnicity would be detained, abused, objectified, denied entry, or offered 'redirection'? On the other hand, where do I face those discriminations? Is it a 'privilege' to enjoy treatments that are unavailable to others? (Regardless of your self-identification within a 'majority' or 'minority,' or the historical and current inequality relative to your group, answer this last question as fully as you can, based on your own experiences.)

On a fundamental level, humans appear to always be checking in on their normalcy. This is, clearly, not a conscious act—most of the time. Largely, this conformity-status-check is positive and necessary. It allows us to move in crowds, drive automobiles, carry on conversations in the midst of other chatter, sit in audiences, and perform a host of other group activities. Nevertheless, the 'tyranny of normalcy' shows its ugly face when these unconsciously conforming attitudes color our conscious declarations of value. As discussed in Volume One's Chaos chapter, from a 'normal' perspective, outliers are troubling, irrelevant, or a threat. Thus, we need to become aware of our gut-level judgments about what is 'okay' and what isn't. This heightened awareness doesn't mean we should eschew all apprehension, fear, or prejudging ('prejudice')—far from it. We need these reactions. We *must* listen to them, but only as one source of information.

The Life We Live is Our Only Life

My focus on these concerns of daily life grows out of my observation of too many self-declared neo-pagans who spend hours playing Massively Multi-player Online Role-Playing Games, memorize whole passages of Tolkien, possess intimate knowledge of half-baked pseudo-histories, know exactly what planet is ascendant, what's in retrograde, and when the next transit is, and yet don't know where their food came from. The life-sapping influence of 'spiritualism' is a blight upon paganism—upon any religion, frankly—and it renders disengaged, bloated 'individuals' floating in irrelevant aethyrs of self-importance. When we focus on what our 'spirits' do, we easily lose sight of that with which our now-vestigial flesh occupies itself.

As we isolate our various selves and sequester our magical practices into our temple spaces, our churches, our psychotherapy sessions, or our 'magical retreats,' we cut off the lifeblood of our practice. Elaborate psychotheocosmologies full of angels, spirit guides, totems, and assorted other tutelary and defensive entities can be a marvelous means to garner the help we cannot give ourselves; but they can just as easily progressively remove us from the challenges of our lives. A tutelary spirit is only as good as its ability to help guide you through difficult life decisions, it must not insolate and isolate you from the consequences of a life unlived. I have often thought of creating a bumper sticker that says, 'Your Holy Guardian Angel may think you're a Rock Star, but the rest of us think you're an ass-hole—so hang up and drive.'

In the face of the Void of Undifferentiation, our tenuous grasp on identity quavers in mind-numbing panic. We have all suspected at some point that our habits, typical behaviors, and preferences don't cobble together adequately to create a cohesive and consistent 'I.' At these angst-ridden moments, we usually go buy something or have a conversation with an old friend in order to revisit—and recreate—'old memories.' Responding to these challenges to a singular self, we not only bolster our well-defended egos, but we also re-entrench our hidden away 'true selves.' Unfortunately, this 'core self'—this fantasy of a carefully protected 'real me' deep inside—condemns us to a half-life of perpetual inauthenticity. Any cherished *private* self runs the risk of blinding us to our complicity in countless *public* activities. *I am as I live, not as I imagine or hope I am.* From a Jungian perspective, the Self is not some sort of 'treasure' to be hidden away and protected. The Self is a glorious story unfolding through our lives!

With apologies to all those introverts, poets, songwriters, and artists who feel that nobody understands them, and who take comfort in their own special internal life: GET OVER IT! Introverts can at least have close friends. Poets must produce works that reach *someone*. Songwriters must perform. Of course, we often grind away in obscurity, we retreat to create, and frequently we feel that our work is irrelevant or ignored. Nevertheless, we must also bounce up against our audiences and our critics—shaping and refining our works. 'Artistic integrity,' remaining 'true to your vision,' and not letting anyone deter you can be brilliant signs of real moral fiber; but they can also be excuses that cover up laziness and fear. We must perform, publish, create—in short, we must live!

The fantasy of a hidden 'true self' often exists in counterpoint to a history of abuse. Children learn to protect themselves by fracturing their experiences. Teddy bears, fantasy lives, and a host of other shards of experience hold onto a part of the child, which he or she hopes will remain unmarred by the brutality of parents incapable of raising children. Even when the parents prove adequate, our schools, religions, and cultures often prove equally violating to children, especially during their indoctrination into the fictions of gender, socio-economics, and 'race.'

Therefore, when we appeal, as adults, to ideas of a hidden away 'true self,' we re-fracture and re-traumatize ourselves—we reinvest in our inauthenticity, our ineffectuality, and our suffering. *We are as we live,* not as we want to live, not as we think we should live. Not even our self-consolations in regard to all the bad things we aren't doing will make this experience-fracturing any less real. The myth of the dragon protecting the giant pile of treasure, usually with some sort of pale virgin in tow, speaks to this all-too-common configuration of personality. The hero or heroine defined in opposition, yet chained to this dragon is struggling against personal, familial, and cultural programming; yet stays mutely miserable. The true protagonist must overcome these false divisions, at great peril to self and reputation. The hero or heroine must reclaim that power that was always his or hers, but which lays unclaimed. Otherwise, the treasure lies fallow, distant, and life-damning.

Taking inventory of our lives takes bravery, tenacity, and a strong stomach. 'Necessity,' 'mere-ness,' 'inevitability,' and 'facts' pin us in on every side so that we convince ourselves that we have no choice in the matter. We are all, in one way or the other, simply 'following orders.' As futile as it may seem, if we are to make any real changes in our lives, we must make it an ongoing practice to look into what we actually *do*, which sits in too-often sharp contrast to what we imagine or hope we are doing.

Literalism creates endless blinds behind which agendas, consequences, implications, and values hide. To exist in a world of things, we abdicate responsibility for our meaning-making—unsuccessfully, but we still try. Until we return to the most serious of play—ritual and magic—we will remain victims of our own design, prisoners of our assumptions and our limited imaginations.

23
Some Ideas about the Rituals of Life
The Wheel of the Year

A fine line separates compulsion and ritual. Even so, I think we can venture a litmus test. A compulsion is something we feel that we *must* do, and which renders us 'less' for having done it. A ritual should enhance, inspire, orient, organize, and carry us to a deeper and fuller living for having done it. By this definition, of course, any given act could be either a compulsion *or* a ritual, depending on how the practitioner takes it up.

Our lives are—hopefully—ripe with meaningful routines, which heighten the pleasure and meaning of various experiences. Consider: the often elaborate rituals for mixing drinks or pouring a glass of wine; the physically intensive alchemy of baking bread (when not using a bread machine); or snuggling down to watch a film at home with just the right pillows, accompanying munchies, and beverages.

What if we were to approach traditionally less-pleasurable tasks with the same ritual glee? What if balancing the checkbook and paying bills involved a favorite pen, appropriate incense, and the occasional check-in with long-term financial goals and their accompanying patron deities? (…as well as spreadsheets and calculators—or maybe an abacus.) In today's technology-intensive world, uploading new software or defragmenting and virus checking a hard-drive may well have far deeper resonances than any traditional ritual for renewal or cleansing. Our dreams make use of such symbols, why shouldn't our rituals?

Each day we go through our routines of waking and going to bed. Why not recognize these routines as the rituals they are? Shaving, putting on rings, locking our home as we leave, starting our cars—we animate these acts already; thus, acknowledging their inherent power can raise our awareness of the barrage of spells we ensigilize with the power of these routines.

The Witch's Sabbath and the Neo-Pagan Sabbat

Today, the roughly secular holidays that punctuate the year are a mash-up of political, religious, and pre-Christian festivals. However, rather than the Bishops, Priestesses, and community leaders to whom our ancestors may have turned, our current tradition-defining elders are Martha Stewart, Rachel Ray, and the rest of cable television's panaceas for the sense of isolation, meaninglessness, and anomie we regularly experience in our suburban sprawl.

The emergence of Wicca in the mid 20th century offered the fantasy of a Romantic return to an imagined past that was more animated, integrated, and soulful than the industrialized world that surrounded its 'revivalists.' Beyond this Romantic neo-pagan esthetic, Wicca also 'reclaimed' the language and imagery of the Witch's Sabbath. From this rich font of imagination, Wiccans crafted their eight holidays marking the solstices, equinoxes, and cross-quarter days—their Sabbats. The imagery of the Witch's Sabbath before this New Age co-option was rooted in a thousand years of the fevered imagination of Christian Europe's formidable shadow. Whether from monks imagining the forbidden activities of mythic witches, authors creating satanic orgies, or painters seeking an excuse for another flesh-scape, the Witch's Sabbath carried a scandalizing and titillating power of darkness and sexuality.

Wicca's founder, Gerald Gardner, with his sky-clad companions, may have hearkened distantly to these dark resonances in the founding of their tradition, but their aim was not so much to confront Christianity with its shadow, as to trump modern Europe with a more archaic provenance—fantastical, to be sure, but one whose time had come. Thus, in the hands of these pagan revivalists, Sabbats and Esbats—lunar celebrations—lost a bit of their outlandish Satanic fuel in order to gain a certain green orthodoxy.

Actually, to be fair, the Wiccan Sabbat shied away from blood-soaked orgies only in the actual practice—the public's fevered imagination is still pricked by its scandalous possibilities. Thus, the imagery of the Witch's Sabbath did not disappear. Leaving aside for now the theatrics of various Satanists, Andrew Chumbley's Sabbatic Craft was an effort to bring back some of the dread power to this gateway of the Imaginal.

I present all of this by way of a differentiation between the Witch's Sabbath and the Sabbats of contemporary neo-paganism—two images that have become, in their wider application, quite distant. You are more likely to encounter the Witch's Sabbath in the Industrial and Metal Music 'scene' than in most neo-paganism. Likewise, the holiday traditions once relished by many Christians of European extraction are far more likely to appear in the homes of neo-pagans in the form of, and around, the Sabbats.

Moreover, most of this imagery has little to do with how adherents of alternative and new religions go about their daily business. In fact, both these categories of images exist by and large to present a sharp *contrast* to day to day life. Both the Witch's Sabbath and the neo-pagan Sabbat exist in an altered time and space—the kairotic time introduced in Volume One. The Witch's Sabbath takes place at the eternal midnight. The neo-pagan Sabbat exists in a transcendent and perpetual space of cycles—the Wheel of the Year turning on and on.

I am a big fan of both classes of imagery. I love the bawdy, randy antinomian-ism of the Witch's Sabbath that shows up in dance-clubs and certain festivals. Similarly, I have a profound soft spot in my heart for the tender hearth and home power that the best of Wiccan Sabbats can invoke. Nevertheless, I still wonder how we can bring this power to our lives rather than redirecting it into our fantasies that either Elvira or Gandalf will come to whisk us away?

The Cycle of the Year

What can we now, in a world driven by 'progress,' gain from a rapprochement with the cycles of the year? Have we not 'secularized' the year into arbitrariness with our artificial holidays and our industrialized nightmare of constant labor? Perhaps, but we have not yet overcome the sun, the seasons, and our own growth and development, as well as the strange clockwork of our own wants and needs. Although our psyches may well be colonized quite completely by the imagery of our defensive structures against the voids, the unsatisfying sterility of these defenses leaves us hungry for something 'progress' will never address.

The constant cycles of the year, in whatever argot they speak, defy the 'onward and upward' fantasies of modernity. Here, the fickle cycles of the Wheel of Fortuna of which we spoke in Volume One, become the certainty of the Wheel of the Year. These Sabbatic moments call us to seize Kairos in a different way. In this case, Kairos is not merely opportunity, but a piercing through into the great (un)certainties of life. Progress, after all, will always bring with it a shadow of decay. A cyclic year reminds us that modernity's promises to eventually tran-scend all of life's cycles and limitations are empty propaganda. Sadly, as religions changed to keep pace with modernity, they created a liturgical year that became a thing unto itself, devoid of relevancy to life as it was lived. Modernizing religions offered, at best, a sentimental pretending.

Sadly, in a perverse rebellion against, yet capitulation to, traditional religions, neo-pagans created supernatural fixations and experience-distant historical re-enactments. So many of the tools, garments, festivals, and traditions of overt magical traditions are merely today's fantasies of the everyday items of yesteryear. To be clear, this serves an important purpose. It pulls us out of our everydayness so that we might experience something entirely *other* to our day-to-dayness. In this way, the alterity of these trappings help wake us up out of our chrono-logical stupor and into the searing reality of Kairos. And yet, in the end, I must repeat one of the fundamental theses of this work: does this same alterity not run the risk of further impoverishing our daily lives? Worse yet, it may drive us to travel constantly from fantasy literature and comic book conventions, to neo-pagan gatherings, to BurningMan-esque events in an endless junkie-like quest to escape the very banality it simultaneously helps to define.

What of our lives? Is the quotidian truly the enemy? If so, then you will not have been able to endure this far into this text. If we are not to abandon our lives as lived in favor of dissociative fantasies, then we must seek to reclaim the animating forces of the immediate world around us. As celebrated today, the Sabbats, as well as other folk and neo-pagan holidays, seek to claim *the natural cycles that our ancestors could not help but observe.* Thus, many of today's holidays find their roots in necessities that we no longer encounter. In order to revitalize or reconstruct a firmer engagement with our own life cycles, perhaps we should pierce a bit deeper into the agrarian cycles that form the underpinning of many of the festivals synthesized into the Sabbats. (While examining the seasonal shifts, we may do well to keep in mind that most of Europe exists at latitudes north of the contiguous United States. Thus, the extremes of light and darkness as well as weather are much greater in the lands from which the traditional festivals originate.)

I resolutely doubt that our ancestors riotously celebrated while toiling in the fields. They did not gorge themselves on slaughtered beasts simply to mark some random calendrical happenstance. Moreover, with gifts coming from one's own larder and handicraft, our earliest ancestors did not produce gifts to adhere to Hallmark's schedule of holidays. The symbols, gifts, traditions, and music of our cultural pasts are expressions of a drive for survival. As religion becomes a thing-unto-itself, it easily leads us to disembody our festivities, to forget their bloody and desperate origins. Today, most of us do not think of our survival in terms of our winter supplies. If meat goes bad in our refrigerator, we throw it out and buy more from the nearest store. But are we any further from our basic survival needs?

Instead, have we not exported, extended, and spread out the networks on which we depend? More than even our most animistic ancestors, our lives depend on anonymous, mysterious, and only dimly understood powers (e.g., 'electricity,' 'computer networks,' 'government oversight,' 'infrastructure'). More than ever, we need the vivifying, life-and-death perspectives that the festivals of our forbearers contained. Not necessarily through an artificial pretending, historical re-enactments, nor separatist fantasies; but through a frank assessment of the world in which we live and the cycles in which we participate. Only the bourgeois agenda of leisure and distance from toil can create a religion and ethos that glorifies life-alien forces that we must accept 'on faith.' Thus, let us examine some ideas about the origins of various festivals, and then consider what necessities we face today that may parallel those of our ancestors.

Samhain-tide

Samhain, the neo-pagan overlay for Halloween is, at least in the northern hemisphere, right about the time when farmers assess their stored goods and livestock before hunkering down for the Winter. It is the so-called 'final harvest,' a euphemism for the slaughter of those animals that would not make it through the Winter due to the depletion of the silage. These same butchered animals will provide an important supplement to the laid in fruits, grains, and vegetables from the preceding five months. These stocks will provide sustenance for the humans who must endure the encroaching darkest portion of the year. Strong evidence suggests that the Celts celebrated this as their New Year. Their year began not with hope in the midst of darkness, as a midwinter New Year provides, but with a sanguineous culling—a dark in-turning in and preparation for hardship.

Growing up, my family would acquire a substantial selection of beef or lamb in the Fall from a local farmer. We would freeze the cuts and eat on this meat until Spring. It proved affordable and simultaneously disengaged us from the troubling and expensive complex of supermarkets, middlemen, and factory farming. Although vegan and vegetarian lifestyles are now certainly a viable choice when done with a strong eye for nutrition and sustainability, many of us continue to consume meat, often with a guilty but temporary cringe. In order to alleviate this guilt, the conscience-pricked consumer often prefers to purchase small portions, well packaged, and comfortably distant from the slaughterhouse. Is there a price for this scruples-ablating sterility? Gaining closeness to the source seems without drawback until we examine the level of discomfort so many of us have with where our food comes from. Thus, the Samhain Sabbat could become a time to reassess our food choices and perhaps make a commitment to a more intentional slaughter if not a cruelty-free diet.

Wiccans also use the Samhain Sabbat to meditate on, propitiate, and contact their departed ancestors since the veil between the worlds is thought to be thin on this night. This idea, of course, extends the All Saints and All Souls traditions which themselves adhered to long-standing pre-Christian rituals regarding the departed. Today, the pursuit of genealogy is easier than ever through websites, digitized public records, blogs, and widely used computer programs. With television programs devoted to genealogical research, religions for which a well-maintained family tree is central, and the new capacity to genetically research your mother- and father-lines thousands of years back in history, we are clearly hungry for a connection to our antecedents. Yet, oddly, encyclopedias tell us that ancestor worship is common only in 'primitive' and 'ancient' societies.

Guy Fawkes Night, now revived for audiences with anarchistic leanings by the film *V for Vendetta* (2006), is famously linked by Thomas Hardy in his *Return of the Native* (1878) to the pagan bonfires of the Samhain-tide. And what better reminder of our civic responsibilities can we ask for than the explosive aspirations of Guy Fawkes to prepare us for Election Day.

Election Day. In America, the Tuesday after the first Monday of November represents a recurrent and serious question mark in the stuttering history of the nation—at least every four years. Civic engagement is a strange thing in a nation so large and so diverse. Although many countries have much higher levels of voter turn-out, to make comparisons between countries the size of one American state and America as a whole is specious at best. Trying to make generalities about America, especially from a historical perspective, is even trickier. America reinvents itself every decade with new administrations, new waves of immigrants, new and different conflicts and wars, and demographic shifts with which it is almost impossible to keep pace. Americans are asked to identify with the mythology of their country, but the mass and breadth of the nation makes this allegiance vague and rife with subtext.

Our ancestors had a strong sense of their village, their neighborhood, or perhaps their county, but could scarcely conceive of a multi-million member group, let alone embrace it as 'us.' Festivities draw us together in common practice with those whom we call 'us.' We celebrate together. But as our holidays become more and more pre-programmed, the suburban mall tends to create far more antipathy than solidarity. We retreat into our homes and carefully control the flow of those whom we call brother and sister.

Little wonder then that politicians in communities facing the reality of multi-culturalism struggle to redefine civic pride—too often a term used by the dominant majority in order to cement their vision of the 'greater good.' Thus, national holidays become ephemeral and deeply subjective impositions. Nevertheless, where we see the real shifts and actions that help communities to grow and progress is through the *local* unity: the block, the borough, the neighborhood. You may have lovely friends across town with whom you profoundly identify, but they won't be the ones to call the fire department when your house is ablaze.

Events such as elections have a much greater imaginal charge, for many people around the world, than do archaic remnants of lost past civilizations. Yet, perhaps in a misapprehension of the separation of Church and State, we segregate our festivities from our civic duties. Or, maybe, we just don't want to be around our friends if our preferred candidate loses.

Thanksgiving. In Canada, this holiday precedes Halloween and is thus a classic harvest festival. In the United States, celebrated as it is on the fourth Thursday of November, this holiday is a somewhat more artificial enshrinement of middle-class excess. At its best, it stands atop the natural cycles of farmers who are no longer called to prepare for winter and thus gather friends and family together in order to consume the fruits of late Fall, together with one last batch of animals to be slaughtered.

Putting aside the saccharine imagery of Native Americans who somehow ignore the genocidal potential of the incoming colonists, Thanksgiving appears to have become a celebration that crosses cultural boundaries, within a nation that struggles with its breath of ethnicities. Ecumenical services, typically of Abrahamic faiths, tend to happen around this time of year. Efforts to reach out to the poor and homeless reach a peak. And families often come together and, at least temporarily, put aside the differences they have gathered over the year — and their lifetimes.

Thanksgiving has also become the day before the Christmas shopping season begins.

Krampus. In early December, Central Europe honors a fascinating shadow figure to the benevolence of St. Nick. Krampus is a devil who punishes bad little boys and girls. Sometimes, he is also Santa's chauffeur. The origin of Krampus, a tale to scare children into better behavior, finds its best explanation when we realize that families must live in much closer proximity throughout the winter. Moreover, the next three months would, historically, prove economically and culinarily difficult for all but the wealthiest families. Today, the developed world remains blissfully untouched by the sort of infant mortality that marks the history of most of the world. That newborns, toddlers, and young children could easily die from the challenges of winter is a dark reality not lost on our ancestors.

Many communities have some sort of parade or celebration to mark the beginning of December's festivities, as well as the frenzy of the shopping season. Krampus' day, typically on the 5th of December, is just one such expression. Nevertheless, every year, Christmas specials, ministers, and weary parents bemoan the crass commercialism befouling their cherished imaginings of a pristine midwinter's holiday. Although many of us can distantly relate to the idea of wanting farmers to have a good growing season, the success of a local shop owner has a much more immediate impact on our well-being. Yet multinational corporations channel away profits from communities around the world to their corporate lairs. This renders any pro-Capitalist sense of consumerism as 'community economic reinvestment' hazy at best.

Perhaps we have forgotten that midwinter contains a very real threat against the survival of the individual and the community.

Midwinter

Midwinter, the Winter Solstice, is that 'darkest night of the year' that brought Robert Frost to pause by woods on a snowy evening. Although a time of introspection, it is also a time to gather families of birth and choice together. Christmastide, regardless of religion, is a necessary affirmation of our shared condition. Although we are small compared to the wrath of Winter, our glow is fierce.

So strong is this need for hope that early Christian church fathers moved the birth of Jesus, which, although still a item of debate, seems most unlikely to have happened in late December, to this dark time of the year. (It was also a nicely timed distraction from the pagan excesses of the Roman Saturnalia, itself an effort to distract Romans from a crushing defeat in the third century BCE.) In Northern climes, the Winter is well and truly in force. This is the time for one last hurrah, a sharing of those supplies that won't keep much longer. A time to can, preserve, cure, and otherwise prepare what is left, in order to endure the rest of the winter.

The gifts associated with this time of year link to a home and hearth 'crafts time' that the end of the growing season afforded our agrarian predecessors. The wool shorn in late spring has become the sweaters of midwinter. From the cuts of wood stored up for the fire have come figurines, boxes, tools and toys. Hides have been worked, linen woven, spirits fermented and any remaining supplies from last year's larder used up lest they go bad.

Today, December is not a time of home and hearth for most people. It is shopping, school plays, church services, company parties, and a frenzy of other high priority 'special events.' Habituated to this hubbub, traditions have become dislodged. Many people find themselves longing for a 'traditional Yuletide,' yet they have only nostalgic books and DVDs to inform them of what these traditions might be.

This hunger, however, may not be purely a result of the discontinuity in culture that our postmodern world has wrought. The festivals of the dark half of the year are themselves times of story-telling and the passing on of customs. This is particularly true of Midwinter. Recipes, legends, family lore, the news of the preceding year, and a general reaffirmation of 'who we, as a people, are' come together in the light of the fire. The hope that 'the best parts of us' can come out at this time of year resonates with this renewal of our identities. Our identities are, after all, flimsy things, in desperate need of reaffirmation, if not wholesale transformation.

New Years. Truly an extension of the Yuletide, the traditions of this holiday are often secularizations of ancient folk and religious practices. Pushing aside the bad luck of a year gone by is also an expression of the hope of preserving our family, through the rest of the winter, in the face of disease, infection, and pillage. The sickle of the Old Year's Saturnine Father Time is the same sickle that can strike livestock and family. In a curious example of eternal return, this season now culls the human stock through drunk driving and other hazardous road conditions.

Epiphany. In Christian tradition, the arrival of the Wise Men ends the Midwinter celebrations. The 12th day of Christmas, January 6th, has come and the tree is out on the curb. The decorations are down, and now insulating strips, storm windows, snow tires, and safety kits have become the new accoutrements. Even the most secular of homes experiences a sense of austerity setting in as January unfolds. Snow or ice storms, frozen pipes, and long gazes out the window punctuate this expanse. Winter sports prove a welcome distraction from this season's indifference to our survival.

Most of us, however, consider austerity to be without virtue. New bourgeois values so thoroughly inform cultures around the world, that we view any restraint, whether financial or behavioral, as a sign of poverty or mental illness. We leave little time for reflection, introversion, and melancholy. Thus it is no surprise that the next Sabbat is among the most neglected in wider culture.

Imbolc

Imbolc or Candlemas. Around the beginning of February, we come to wonder if we'll make it—if it will ever be warm again. Groundhog Day is such a questioning of how the rest of the winter will play out. Will another animal need to be slaughtered?—a far different prospect to the late autumn cull.

Bludgeoned by lack of light and cabin fever, seasonal affective disorder (SAD) becomes solidly ensconced in those susceptible to it. However, evolutionary psychology scholars inform us that this may be less of a disease and more of an adaptation. Humans may have evolved to slow down and turn within during these introspective months. This sense of melancholy, therefore, may be a means of bonding couples and families, preserving resources, and conserving energy. In an odd parallel to historical rituals, one of the most effective treatments for SAD is light therapy. Indeed, Candlemas was a time to gather together the candles one had labored over since the rendering of fat and gathering of honeycombs in the fall and present them to be blessed in the community's sacred space. Paralleling this 'sacred light' archetype, the overlaid Christian holiday celebrates the Presentation of Jesus at the Temple.

Personally, I see this holiday as an excellent time to replace batteries, change light bulbs, and cook warming stews. Occasionally, I will go about the house and unplug every appliance and gadget I can reach—followed by harrowing combat with dust bunnies crankily roused from their hibernation. In the aftermath, I sit and realize how accustomed I have become to background hums and whines. I also think that this inward gaze provides the perfect opportunity to prepare your taxes. For many of us, this offers a far better opportunity to assess our previous year than the wine-induced recitations of the Yuletide. It also provides an opportunity to create a budget—appropriate as the winter-enforced austerity continues.

Mardis Gras. As with all the dark-half festivities, celebrations are rarely rooted in our ancestor's excesses. Instead, once again, our ancestors had to look into their pantries and discover what was close to rotting and needed to be used up in recipes designed to provide some welcome relief from the routine of a limited diet. This last winter's feast heralded an ongoing fast linked less to piety and more to the concerns of not reaching spring with adequate food. 'Lent' is a Christian overlay that introduced a world-denying purpose for a season deeply rooted in the earth's cycles.

Even as the earth threatens to radically shift her fecundity away from our needs, those in the first world still live in obscene abundance. The underfed in America still have access to resources in excess of more than half the world. The idea of restraint, self-imposed strictures, or prescribed dietary limits smacks, for many neo-pagans, of the sort of dogmatic religions against which they sought to rebel. However, given the inequity of the Western world's foodways as well as our general ignorance of our food's sources, might a season of fasting and/or food restrictions not prove informative in a far more visceral fashion than outrage-inducing books and films such as *Supersize Me* (2004) and *Food, Inc.* (2009)?

Valentine's Day. Although festivals of fertility, sexuality, and ribaldry abound throughout human history, the West has settled on this one in particular to channel its libido in a socially acceptable fashion. This holiday has scarce seasonal resonance as a randy spring-ing forth, except in the more Southern climes of the Northern Hemisphere where winter's hold may be loosening. However, for those still in the grip of Winter's grasp, this holiday is a welcome reminder of our need for warmth and love to carry us through our darker days.

Ostara

Spring arrives at different times throughout the Northern hemisphere. Thus it is that St. Patrick's Day has become far more of a pagan celebration than most of the revivalists' Sabbats. Drunkenness, (green-clad) sexuality, and a hazy sense of ancient tradition make this holiday a popular celebration of the Spring Equinox, albeit a few days early. Thus, the green may conveniently hearken to Irish cultural identity, but it is more deeply the green of Ostara or the Vernal Equinox.

With previously stored supplies dangerously low, March represented a first chance to move the livestock out of the barn, plant some first seeds, and air out a home sealed tight for four or more months. Spring cleaning, with its accompanying runs to donation boxes, recycling stations, and garbage bins is actually quite in tune with this season's message. We have survived, and it is time to strip away the wooly chrysalises of the winter and face the new challenges of a lightening year. Both Easter and Passover carry these liberating messages and are opportunities for families of all types to gather again, to share in the hope and relief the end of winter brings.

Town Meetings are also often held in the Spring. Although most famously observed in New England, we can trace the origin of these right back to early human subsistence in a fixed location. Spring is an excellent time to come together once again to survey fields, mend fences, plan for planting, settle disputes, and renew the covenant of the community.

As 'individualism' has become the contemporary ethos, we seem to forget that the custom of gathering to discuss those issues that are most relevant to our community has been the way of our species far back into prehistory. Life skills such as passionate but civil debate, conceding to the good of the many, sustainability, and a sense of belonging to a society rather than just a bloodline are only some of the virtues these gatherings can engender. As disenfranchised as many people feel today, we ironically tend to focus on national politics, or perhaps on the wranglings of a county board or city council—levels of organization that are typically beyond our influence. Many of us may not like our neighbors, or perhaps we like them just fine at the carefully controlled level of exposure we maintain. It seems well and good to discuss 'brotherhood' in the abstract, but actual neighborliness is all too rare today. We want a la carte associations and friendships.

Organizations such as Rotary, the Lions, and Kiwanis are gradually giving way to far more specific special interest groups. Today, we can be much more aware of the plight of children half a world away than the struggles of someone five doors down the street. However, as much as we cannot suddenly hearken to the wisdom of elders who were themselves not prepared to take on the role, we cannot suddenly turn to our neighbor and create a covenant overnight. Our laws and statutes engender pseudo-independence, an illusion of separateness that masks the fundamental interdependence of the members of a condominium, housing development, city block, or neighborhood. Spring may well be the time of year to assess what scant threads of this mutual reliance are still discernable, and to speak to them. Perhaps this is the time to renew the tradition of the stone soup—in which we come to realize that the small contributions of each community member can come together to benefit everyone.

Earthday now supplants Arbor Day, and the Christian Right justly casts this April 22nd holiday as a pagan festival. Indeed, Christianity has for too long given a faint lip service to our 'Stewardship' role over nature. Now, ecological and civic agendas once again coincide with this celebration of spring and our entwinement with unfolding nature. This holiday's message, and its ethical charge, make it a far better candidate for celebration than the ancient holiday that comes nine days later.

Beltane

Beltane or MayDay. Many people who write about neo-paganism and magic would appear to be very sex-positive people. It is difficult to reclaim the relics of our ancient past and not be confronted with prominent breasts, splayed labia, and erect phalli. Nevertheless, the idea of an unsegregated sex life is, for me, a terrifying thought. The bedroom door, the carefully constructed subtle innuendo, and a sense of sex as a forbidden pleasure are time-honored and healthy boundaries, I think. After all, is not lingerie meant to partially conceal?

Nevertheless, most people are severely alienated from their sexuality. Most of us are so far from the nudity–loving ethos of today's neo-hippie that we really don't need to worry that a little self-awareness and intimacy-cultivation will turn our homes into touchy-feely love-ins. Leaving aside the question of whether we should not be more comfortable with public displays of affection, let alone sexuality, most of us would do well to become more comfortable with pleasure and our own affections.

MayDay may now need to become the holiday to buy new sex toys, or at least put new batteries in them and acquire new lubricants. For those interested in seasonal resonances, it may also be the time to see various doctors, acquire new prescriptions, and stock up on prophylactics and birth-control.

(That MayDay became, for a time, a worker's celebration of the nobility of Labor and, eventually, a type of communist ideal, makes sense when we consider the summer as a time of labor in the fields, as discussed below.)

May is also the season of graduations. Commencement ceremonies, with their speeches of variable relevancy, are being reinvented with each successive generation of students. As a far broader swath of the world is completing high school and higher education, this rite of passage is fast becoming a cultural cornerstone. Rituals previously observed as children entered their teen years—the beginning of adulthood in earlier times—are now observed at 18 or 22 years old. Ritual robes, doddering elders, proud mentors, cryptic regalia, and a mass gathering of the community mark public rites of passage the world over. Commencement has simply become the substitute, or perhaps the surrogate for these previous traditions.

Memorial Day, in contrast to Beltane, is a far tamer herald of the end of spring and the beginning of summer in America. It falls on the final Monday in May. Grills, baseball, trips to the beach, and the unpacking of the summer wardrobe mark a clear line between winter's chill and summer's heat. The holiday originated to honor those fallen in war. However, after the tumult of the mid-20th century, America became far more divided in its opinions about warfare. Honoring soldiers seemed too close to celebrating war—and, frankly, in the past, there was little difference. Yet, refusing to address complex and painful issues because of a discomfort with controversy seems a slippery slope toward indifference. Too many people see jingoism or protest as the only two choices available to express their opinions. Education, debate, dialog, and the subtle nuance of a genuine memorial seem lost in a world capable of only absorbing the briefest of sound bites.

Midsummer

Midsummer or the Summer Solstice. Strangely enough, the shift from agrarian, to industrialized, to post-industrial cultures has flipped the work cycles of the year. Although we still celebrate the late summer harvest festivals of a farming ethos, most people vacation in the summer, rather than laboring through the growing season to prepare crops. The school year, after all, was founded when children were needed back on the farm to labor in the fields over the summer months. Our current system of labor throughout the winter and increased leisure in the summer—or any leisure at all for that matter—is a powerfully bourgeois perspective on the year.

In a few cultures, notably the Québécois and the Irish, St. John's Eve offers a celebration that retains midsummer resonances. Falling six months before Christmas, the parades, bonfires, and effusive festivities provide a chance for Christian Communities, broadly defined, to express and encourage their ethnic and cultural identities.

The Fourth of July. Since Memorial Day overshadows any celebration of a June 21st Midsummer in America, Independence Day has become a sort of American 'High Summer.' (Canada Day on the 1st fulfills nearly identical purposes but with a rather more singable anthem.) Historically, this holiday falls too early in the growing season to enjoy the fruits of a first harvest, but with today's transportation and agricultural machinations, this is now truly a first harvest festival. Evidence of this 'progress' can be seen in the addition of today's limitless, carbon-footprint-intensive cornucopia of previously not-yet-in season fruits and vegetables. At one time, not so long ago, the full range of July 4th foods was confined to potato and pasta salads and various meat delivery systems. As a new pagan holiday, July 4th concerts, fireworks, cook-outs, street-fairs, and parades burst forth with the season's life coursing through the earth itself.

Lammas

Lammas takes its name from 'loaf mass'—that is, the first harvest of grains. Corn and wheat dominate this holiday. Just as Christian traditions supplanted the original pagan Celtic festival, Lughnasadh, (Labor Day in America), now presents an industrialized image to supplant the agrarian beginning of this grain harvest.

In many parts of the world, this holiday heralds the hottest season of the year and leads many to leave the cities for cooler country or a last escape to seaside retreats. In the tropics and subtropics of the developed world, this season is the time for highest energy expenditure. Air conditioning, as pleasant as it can be, is a glaring symbol of our inability to live in harmony with our world. We do not design our homes to make use of natural passive heating and cooling; we are active during the hottest times of the day; we rely on energy distribution systems that are stretched beyond capacity; we recreate in giant artificial pools filled with toxic chemicals because our rivers, lakes, and oceans have become septic; and we measure the cost of this disharmony by the relative cost to our budgets rather than the environmental and cultural impact.

What would a Sabbat look like that spoke to the searing hostility of Sol Invictus? Instead of centering on the skin-cancer-inducing rituals of 'getting a good tan,' might we not find a holiday that comes into full swing after the sun abates? In desert and tropical climates, sunset signals the beginning of the real party. But these cultures also often embrace a nap during the hottest part of the day, as well as a work day that typically begins later in the morning. As with all of our seasonal celebrations, ethics and lifestyle hide just below the surface, but remain obscured only through the practiced application of seasonally-dissonant rituals.

Mabon

Mabon, or the Autumnal Equinox, is the second harvest of fruits, vegetables and the remaining grains. It is also the season of homecomings and county fairs. These communal gatherings are a hint of the gathering and turning-in that will come over the next few months. Over the past two decades, Farmer's markets, community-supported agriculture (CSA) associations, kitchen gardens, and farmers who sell direct to the public have been making a hard-fought comeback. This holiday, more than anything, is their celebration—a call to a direct relationship with what we eat and how it is produced. Through government subsidies, the practices of unscrupulous multinationals, bizarre taxation schemes, the invention of the supermarket, and a generally growing (and carefully cultivated) public ignorance regarding agriculture, the actual costs of our food have remained occulted. However, through films, lectures, books, and living room conversations, the message has finally spread widely enough to cross political boundaries.

In the Northern Hemisphere, the school year is underway by this time. Most people spend a minimum of 13 years in this system—too often a means of 'industrializing' students rather than actually educating them—yet unless we are parents, we have only the most distant of relationships to our regions' school. In fact, a non-parent at a PTA or school board meeting receives more than a few glares.

What our schools teach is too often the focus of discussion within the topic of education. Nevertheless, the real question should be *how* our teachers teach, and how our students learn. The lion's share of the information taught will be forgotten or outdated in less than a decade. But the means of learning, the hunger for insight, and the lust for growth can last a lifetime. Turned into babysitters, parole officers, and clerks, even educators with the best of intentions are worn down by school districts pursuing systems that are mere artifacts of long-extinct necessities. Disgusted with the crime in your town? Worried about the mental health of your community? Concerned about the welfare of children? Public health? The mentality of your fellow voters? If you want to change the world, educate your children. Efforts made to target adults for reform and innovation of various social issues may have their value, but these programs pale in comparison with the breath-taking social efficacy of simple initiatives for better funded education, engaged students, safer schools, and innovative classrooms. For example, to reduce drug addiction, you can pour money at specific anti-drug campaigns, or you could actually have your students read serious literature around the subject, study and debate social issues, and, perhaps most vitally, learn biology in order to understand the delicate chemical balance of the human body. The dollars spent on childhood education pay off as soon as those students become members of your community. Why is it that we don't enshrine the role of education in a Sacred Holiday? Surely a Sabbat is necessary for this function of the community!

What Cycles Do We Actually Live?

So, perhaps you try to eat seasonally. You may even have a garden. Maybe you work in a profession that is tightly allied to the agricultural cycles. But the vast majority of people do not. We may hang a different seasonal banner outside our homes, we may even celebrate the Sabbats and re-tell the legends of a mythic agrarian past—but it is ultimately a type of pretending.

However, we are still surrounded by the cycles of the world in which we find ourselves. Blinded by hazily Romantic notions of the past, we do not allow ourselves the eyes to see these cycles. There's no doubt that people living in farming and coastal cities have 'natural cycles' thrust upon them. Tides in port cities play a visceral role in the feel, function, not to mention the smell of your life. (We need not look to subtle and arcane zodiacal shifts when more obvious changes hide in plain sight. Who cares about astrology, the positions of Mercury or Uranus when an entire ocean changes elevation by several feet in the course of a normal day's tidal cycles?) But other patterns mark the succession of our years.

What are your local festivals? Chili cook offs? Rummage sales? Book fairs? When does the Carnival come to town? Communities that maintain traditions over the decades create a continuity for which we are desperate in a world in seemingly perpetual flux.

Moreover, do we enshrine our quotidian tasks with the reverence they deserve? Taking out the garbage, recycling, housecleaning, oil changes, and paying bills may not have a hoary resonance, but your life depends far more on these tasks than honoring John Barleycorn in an autumnal reel.

Birthdays and anniversaries, company retreats, and vacations punctuate our years with far more lived meaning than some widely recognized Bank Holiday. If we ever find ourselves settled enough in one place, we can actually set doctor, dentist, and optometrist appointments in a predictable yearly cycle. I rarely watch broadcast television, but view it with rapt attention every two years as the Olympics come on. This biennial treat alters my life course, my conversations, and my outlook on the world far more than most of the seasonal celebrations that may have survived until today.

What I mean to say is that the sanctification of the daily can raise us up enough from our disanimated stupor to make us recognize the values we actually live, rather than the distant resonances we may feel around 'patriotism,' 'community spirit,' 'family,' or even 'love.'

Magical Tools

For most religions, traditions, and magical systems, some sort of range of implements defines the person, and space, of the adherent. Crucifixes, prayer beads, ritual knives, icons, home altars, statues, talismans, candles, bracelets, incense, door charms, and a wide range of other symbols adorn the homes of the faithful. So too do posters, prints, family photos, calendars, action figures, mirrors, cooking implements, appliances, and a host of other symbols that typically tell you much more about the person than their avowed orientation.

Although I am no fan of the hypocrisy that seems to accompany many larger organized religions, I do not intend disrespect to the religious impulse. I do, however, ask that we examine the layers and textures of meaning soaking our every moment—the imagery with which we construct our lives. I do find it odd to see a neo-pagan lift a sword in a ritual when, essentially, she does not participate in any militaristic or warrior-oriented profession; the sword is, itself, completely impractical and if ever used would have been in the hands of a patriarchal oppressor; and she has far more psychic resonance with her favorite can-opener than any ritual blade. ('Guardians of the Watchtower of the West! Unseal for us the secrets of your Depths! Let us taste of your hidden Bounty and partake of your Savor!' *Whirr-rrr-rrr-rrr—kachunk!*)

What are the magical tools of our day-to-day lives? Car keys? Shredders? Staplers—especially that red Swingline stapler from *Office Space* (1999)? Both the Zippo and Bic lighters have hit the level of icon so widely that some magicians do actively use them in ritual, not as a concession to the convenience of modernity, but for their habitual resonance. In the film *Practical Magic* (1998), the state investigator discovers that his badge's five pointed star can banish a demon—not so much because of the star's magical shape, but because of the conviction and meaning he assigns to it. The same film also makes marvelous use of a substitute cauldron in the form of a blender full of margarita mix, as well as a dust buster in place of a besom broom.

In an early undergraduate class on mental health institutions, my professor explained that an in-patient client once revealed to her what the major difference between them was. 'You have more keys!' the client said. The metaphor perfectly aligned with the wad of keys every staff member carried for rooms, floors, alarms, supply closets, and prescription lockers.

I once sublet an office in which the owners had unexpectedly added a tissue box in which the tissues came out of the nose of an Easter Island head. A first client giggled and thanked me for the effort at brightening her day. The next client glowered and said with searing sincerity, 'That's not respectful.' The tissue box is a potent symbol in every psychotherapist's office. We know, even on an upbeat day, that this is a work of tears. Thus, whether keys or tissue boxes, the most banal of items are also magical tools, overflowing with potential meaning.

As impractical as fireplaces may be, they are a powerful symbol in many homes. The hearth, the mantel, and the tools all carry sentimental and atavistic associations even before a fire appears. Once lit, the flames exert a hypnotic power over us, pulling us to revelry as well as reverie. Bachelard dwells on this power in his *The Psychoanalysis of Fire* (1938) and his posthumous *Fragments of the Poetics of Fire* (1988).

Photo albums, as well, have served a ritual purpose for more than a century. However, the 'family portrait,' the 'only picture we have of him from that time,' and other visual gems seem to be threatened with an ignominious drowning in an overabundance of digital snaps. Nevertheless, the ritual function of the image is so fundamental to us that screensavers, PDAs with photo files, pictures on social networking sites, and digital frames are renewing and redefining it. ('Oh! Your granddaughter has grown so *much*!' 'Yes, she's 44 now…')

If we are to revitalize the practice of rituals in our times, we must look to what contemporary symbols carry the primal forces invoked by great rites. Thomas Moore once quipped that, in today's world, the gun is no longer a phallic symbol—rather, the phallus has become a gun symbol. Some initiatory organizations actually substitute firearms for swords. They realize, perhaps, that the immediate threat and terror that a firearm provokes is far greater than most swords can engender. The cocking of a revolver's hammer or the *click-clack* of a semiautomatic's slide evoke responses far more visceral than any blade sliding from a sheath.

As mentioned above, the toilet is itself a powerful magical symbol. From a time when most of us cannot make use of the first person, we learn with delight the magical power of the Flush. I have wondered if this discovery is also not the origin of our current environmental conundrum since we have come to believe that when we flush, our poop really and truly goes away. We need only consider our panicked responses when the water level instead begins rising precariously toward the rim—'oh sh-t!'—to recognize the incredible power this procedure still has over us. Many people remain transfixed and powerless before the rising fecal tide, such is its archaic power.

And to round out this selection of tools of lived ritualistic power, we can consider booze and cell phones. Liquors, such as tequila and absinthe, have elaborate rituals associated with them. People become passionate about the exact way of preparing their favorite drink. Our brand loyalties to various beers, preferences in wine, and ideal martini make statements about social class, self-restraint, and character. Many homes are far more likely to have an altar to alcohol than any other domestic deity. (Ah, Bacchus, you win again, you old goat.)

In practical terms, mobile phones and their growing number of mutations are scarcely 20 years old. Yet in this brief time, they have reshaped the world. Few technologies can penetrate so thoroughly through socio-economic and geographic barriers. The very nature of connection and aloneness are completely redefined. As I can attest from my classrooms, some students are physically incapable of not remaining connected to this digital umbilical. Texting has reinvented writing. Motor vehicle operation has returned to an era of ridiculous endangerment of driver and public. Cell towers have changed our skylines. And most people have unwittingly volunteered for being surveilled and tracked at levels previously reserved for SciFi films. With the speed of innovation increasing more than exponentially, it seems foolish to predict the future of telecommunications, even looking ahead a scant ten years from now.

This current work would bloat well beyond its mandate were we to look at the increasingly ill-defined realm of the 'computer'; but we need only look at the systems of automation that guarantee our minute-to-minute survival to realize that a mere 70 years of technological innovation has introduced a transformation of existence to such an extent as to practically be a whole new Creation Myth.

Thus, perhaps we can understand the lure of an imagined past. Most of us cannot let go of the tools of our lives, but we are simultaneously frightened by what gods lurk so close to our skin. Better we should hearken to distant principles, archaic mythic personalities, and benevolent Mother figures than encounter the sizzling, amoral electro-imps emerging from the petroleum pools that dog our every step. Yet, is the irrelevance of our gods not also the irrelevance of our avowed ideals?

Until we claim our lived values, until we wrestle with the responsibility for the world in which we live, we can never hope to find meaning and purpose in our lives. Hence, the time has now come to tell how, half a lifetime or more ago, I attempted to bring, kicking and screaming, my various beliefs into some accord.

24
A Young Lutheran Struggles with Prayer
Images of Devotion

I sit in a church basement classroom with a dozen or more other young Lutherans. The smell of oil soap permeates everything. We are all teenagers, 16 or 17 years old. For some reason, no Sunday School Teacher guides today's unfolding discussion on prayer.

Four years previously, just before beginning catechism, I started reading the Victorian Freemasonic books my grandfather left after his death. Someone should, I suppose, have returned them to a Lodge, but, in the tumult after his death, far more pressing issues arose. These leather-bound tomes proved rife with the creative mix of myth and quasi-history that constitutes the Masonic allegorical cosmology. My head spun with images of Hiram Abiff, Tubal Cain, and mysterious rituals hinted about or expressed in cryptic short-hand. With some persistence, I got past the hyperbole and learned about the Qabalah, Gnosticism, and Deism—or at least the Masonic scholars' glosses on them. Out of this esoteric crazy quilt of Templars, Assassins, Egyptians, Hebrew Tribes, Revolutionaries, and Medieval Guilds, one particular idea slowly bored its way into my mind: The Ineffability and Absolute Perfection of Ultimate Divinity. Combined with readings from New Age authors, Christian Science, Taoism, and my own curiously zealous and pious approach to Christianity, this doctrine of a Changeless and Perfect Principle of All Creation sizzled through my head—a long fuse in search of a hidden store of explosives.

Thus, back in the church basement, a thought is making its way toward my mouth—a blasphemous thought, intended to be the highest form of Devotion to the Divine. These young optimistic Lutherans are, literally, in their Sunday Best—boys in blue blazers and penny loafers, girls in Gunne Sax dresses and matching China flats. Although I cannot remember exactly, I wouldn't be surprised to find myself wearing a collar bar, a tie tack, and a pocket square, as well as a lapel pin. As with so many things in my life at this time, I overdo whatever I undertake with absurd tenacity. I have been the senior acolyte for four years. I approach my duties with the fervor of an Anglican Ritualist. Each month, in lieu of a simple schedule matching teens to services, I type page-long diatribes about devotion, reverence, and service. As any armchair psychologist could observe, I am likely overcompensating for the uncertainty and doubt plaguing me in every aspect of my life.

(Hidden in this overzealous pursuit of propriety and piety are the seeds of what will later become my idiosyncratic idea of 'apotheosis.' Borrowing a bit from Nietzsche, even in my mid teens I realize that ideas often hide their full implications beneath a veneer of anonymity, ignorance, or fantasies of moderation. Pursuing *reductio ad absurdum* as my central argument, I criticize capitalism, democracy, and even concepts of 'charity' as half efforts, which too easily conceal quite their opposite behind their good intentions. However, at 16, I do not have the subtlety to appreciate the nuances of deconstruction and, thus, find myself running headlong and obliviously toward a stance of empty nihilism. Nevertheless, in this morass, I have a glimmer of the idea of apotheosis as the ceaseless pursuit of an idea until it eats itself—rendering all further expressions or pursuits of it empty.)

The discussion, so far, has been lively but very polite. Mostly, each person has shared how and when he or she prays. I don't have the foresight to realize how uncomfortable the room is going to become with my question. I am about to assault something dear to the hearts of many of those gathered. I clear my throat and raise my hand. The discussion leader points to me.

'Why do we make requests of a God who knows all and is doing absolutely everything possible to help us? Are we not asking, "Dear Heavenly Father, You are absolutely Perfect, but could You be just a bit more Perfect in this particular way I've worked out for You."?'

Though I would never share it directly with this group, in addition to the bisque of esotericism simmering in my mind, I am hearkening to Richard Bach's *Illusions: The Adventures of a Reluctant Messiah* (1977). I suppose that, like many of his readers, I feel that this book speaks directly to my expanding adolescent mind. In Bach's work, on what are meant to appear as the oil stained pages of a pilot's notebook, he writes, 'The original sin is to limit the Is. Don't.' In my uncompromising logic, I see asking God for an alteration in reality as a way of limiting the Is.

But rather than the gentle, often folksy way Bach presents his message, I decide a snarky frontal assault is the best way to 'open minds.' As soon as I make the remark, four or five of the previously smiling adolescents look aside and drop out of the conversation. Most of the rest of them miss the point of what I am saying. In the face of the obvious discomfort, I push on.

'I mean, isn't it a sign of weak faith when we pray to have God change His plan? Don't we pray, 'Thy will not *mine* be done?' Shouldn't we pray for guidance to know His will?'

Suddenly the genteel tone is gone. Most are no longer engaged in the conversation now. They are having side conversations and ignoring a point that has little relevance to the way they think about religion. Three or four remain in the discussion as I teeter between overheated righteousness and crippling shame. I am genuinely looking for an answer but I am also aware that something isn't right. I want a means of solving this Calculus of God, but have not considered that a formula may not express the problem.

Can we have religion without a God who answers prayers? Years later, I will parody this theological impasse to my students with the premise 'Dear Baby Jesus/Buddha/Shiva, Please give me a pony.' After years of reading, I discover that this is one way to discuss the differences between Theism and Deism. Although the terms are quite slippery and change to meet the needs of polemicists, 'Theism' can be the concept of a personal Divinity whom the devotee can propitiate with prayer. 'Deism' is the vision of God as a principle, typically Rational, that is necessary for creation but beyond the scope of individual human affairs.

These, of course, are not the only two possibilities. Atheism, non-theism, panentheism, agnosticism, pantheism, strong versus weak theism, and a host of other –isms crop up in any discussion of the nuances of a topic rife from the start with logistical problems. Personally, none of these terms ever entirely satisfy me; yet, from an early age, I was fascinated with diving into the topic. Perhaps this is because, given the sharp contrast between my father's spiritualism and my mother's German Lutheran beliefs, I have never been offered the luxury of a simple faith.

Today, when I mock the idea of asking God for a 'pony,' in the midst of one of my stand-up-professor routines, I am not ridiculing religion or faith whole sheet. Quite the opposite, I think. I am holding out the possibility that a relationship to the divine and the sublime can be immensely more transformative and radical than submitting requests to a Celestial Supply Sergeant. I have never found a single word that sums up this possibility satisfactorily for me. Thus, even today, after all my journeys, I still come back to the same struggles and basic convictions I gave voice to in that Sunday School discussion. I suppose I should have thought twice about trying to give voice to the Ineffable.

Back in the church basement my screed continues. I am now unwisely comparing petitioning God in prayer to paganism. At this point in time, I know nothing about neo-paganism or the magical revival. I audaciously offer the idea that prayers of petition may even work, but perhaps we had best question who or what it is that has answered our prayers. I mouth Gnostic heresies veiled in what I think is unassailable logic.

My classmates have offered justifications for propitiatory prayer such as: 'it feels good' — to which I snidely reply that many things that feel good are not necessarily Holy in God's eyes; 'the Bible says we should' — to which I respond that I am only aware of Christ teaching us to pray what has become known as the Lord's Prayer; and other vexing oversimplifications.

Finally, Ryan Hanover speaks up. 'Because He wants us to,' he says. I am poised to snap that I am impressed at Mr. Hanover's access to the Will of the Divine, but something stops me. For some reason, I carefully conceal my initial derision. *How pathetic,* I think while maintaining a neutral expression, *He wants us to turn to Him with our hangnails, our Christmas lists, and our aunts-dying-of-cancer-after-40-years-of-a-two-pack-a-day-habit.* Even before having read much Freud, I know this sort of anthropomorphism. The Daddy in the Sky. Our parents will ultimately prove a disappointment, so we invent a transcendent Daddy/Mommy who will never let us down.

Somehow, through this thick haze of scorn, Ryan's statement echoes around my head. *There's something to this, something that works on multiple levels.* What if that is *all* He wants? What if this turning to God, this vector of our being, of Being, isn't so much a Desire of God, but *is* God Itself. I take a deep breath and furrow my brow. I remember C. S. Lewis' discovery that his adult yearning for a relationship with God was, itself, that very relationship.

In order to back out of the discussion and offer myself some time to think, I respond to Ryan, 'Okay. I'll buy that. That works…'

Several people breathe an audible sigh of relief that I am done with my theological tirade. The conversation turns to more pleasant topics and soon the class is over.

The idea, however, sticks with me. I keep rolling it over in my head. When we do this—this turning to God—something in us changes. Our heart changes if we free our own most 'prayer of the heart.' We open to what Paul and Luther both made central to their theology—Grace, that 'still quiet Voice.' Several years later, while studying Sufism, I will read a Hadith, a sacred Islamic saying of Muhammad, which speaks to this sentiment. The Prophet here characterizes Allah's stance toward humanity, 'Take one step towards me, I will take ten steps towards you. Walk towards me, I will run towards you.' What I struggle with is what this means, operationally, in our lives.

Around the same time as the church basement debate, my junior year English teacher guides us through the American literary canon. Hawthorne, Poe, Melville, and Miller all play strong roles, as well as John Irving with *A Prayer for Owen Meany* (1989). A year later, the teacher will retire from education to become a Presbyterian minister. Thus, it is no surprise that themes of atonement, penance, and penitence are central to many of our discussions. Near the end of the year, I put together an essay that is oddly free from the sort of Joseph Campbell-inspired archetypal mash-ups with which I have managed to skate through my junior year. I use the metaphors of light and shadow to illustrate the central question about penitence. I note that we inevitably cast a shadow, but do we stay stuck in the darkness or turn to the light?

(Today, this idea rings rather tinny to my ears, hokey even; but, at the time, the metaphor solved my theological paradox. Although God, as I saw Him, is Omnipotent, He endowed us with free-will. Therefore, we must choose to recognize the Divine Presence — to listen to the Voice within.)

In my essay, I take this idea and then ask: if it is as simple as turning to the Divine Light, then why doesn't everyone simply change their thinking or turn their heart? Surely, this is the central theme of all of these religious allegories? As I wrestle with this question, I have a minor epiphany that grows into something far more important than a clever argument for a term paper. What I realize is that these stories are not merely illustrations of ideas. The best of the religiously-minded authors of America were not simply creating narrative maps of theological territory. They were trying to convey the necessity of the *process* of transformation, the journey of atonement. The course of life itself plays out our penance — our return to a unified existence. It is not God that must change but us; and that transformation is a story.

As a psychotherapist, I had many chemically addicted clients who objected to Alcoholics Anonymous, stating that the whole 'Higher Power' thing just didn't work for them. Frankly, most of these objections were merely artificial hurdles that clients put in their own way to avoid responsibility for the carnage in their lives. (To confront this excuse, Seattle had at least one standing AA meeting that the organizers called the 'Four A' — Agnostics' and Atheists' Alcoholics Anonymous.)

Nevertheless, just as what you think will help has likely been keeping you trapped, so too will the one who hopes to get better never recover. Fascinatingly enough, my experience with alcoholic and drug addicted clients has been that the giving up of the idea that we have the ability to cure ourselves simultaneously clears the way for taking real responsibility for our lives. The small 'me' will always be subject to the vagaries of mood, whim, stress, and history. Something more abiding, something bigger must guide the process. And it must be exactly that, a *process* — not a destination, not a solution, but an ongoing commitment renewed with each new challenge.

Since my teens, the vocabulary I use to address these questions has radically changed. The metaphors may be quite different, but the realizations I gained from that time have continued to bear fruit. Life challenges us endlessly with opportunities to change, to turn, to reprioritize. These challenges are not created by some angel, or Architect, or Divine Committee that is busy sadistically pulling the strings to pose us with novel karmic puzzles; but rather because life itself is constantly changing, regardless of whether or not we notice it. The perspectives that carried us through one time in our lives will become the hobbles that limit our growth through the next stage. No level of 'accomplishment' can carry the day in the long-term. The only achievement we can hold onto is a lifetime commitment to refuse to stagnate—to always change and grow.

Nevertheless, these changes have to be guided by something greater than the little 'me' of any given situation. We must not only reflect and discern, we must turn to what we consider more important, more abiding, more true. Moreover, our principles alone won't solve our problems. At some level, in a way unique to each of us, we must let go. We must let go of 'my way' of doing things if we ever hope to continue to grow. This may even mean letting go of overarching principles, dogmas, and creeds in order that the story can unfold.

25
Why Magic?

As I noted in the story above, many people, perhaps most of us, are in a child/parent, boss/subordinate, or even pet/owner relationship with our realities. We keep waiting to see what we'll be given, almost as though we want to find out whether or not we *deserve* the things we want by being given them. Whether or not our parent/owner is a god or goddess, the Tao, karma, the Universe, our Will, or any other reified concept, the relationship is flawed. Job applicants and the prayerful alike both fall prey to a strange combination of the fundamental attribution error and the actor-observer bias in which they let their circumstances determine their worth. We are so used to a seemingly random world or our own contrived explanations that we conspicuously avoid actually assessing our own efforts, culpability, and efficacy.

Waiting to see if we deserve our will is like the lover who won't ask for what he or she wants and remains perpetually resentful and frustrated. We see again and again that the prize goes to those who try. If you want something, *do* something! (And assess your outcomes, then do it again with innovations based on your observations, then assess again, and innovate again …)

As far as I can tell, attempting this sort of deliberate magic (i.e., 'will-working') is the only justification for taking any notice of the structure of experience itself. To put it differently, genuinely making efforts at change *will* confront you with the structure of experience. Magic is the mechanics, the physics of the imaginal reality of each of our lives. As such, addressing the fabric of existence is liable to call into question many of our sacred certainties. Thus, it is probably best not to muck about in these fathomless waters unless you want to get wet.

Simply formulating your will may be enough to guide you toward effective action; however, as these volumes have frequently noted, we are often working against ourselves. The process of disentangling ourselves from the countless fictions that work against our aspirations also involves assessing those same aspirations. For many people in monotheistic religions, the act of praying about difficulties in their lives is a time to reflect on not only their desires, but the actions that they have taken toward dealing with these wants or needs. *Discernment* is crucial, yet the one attempting to gain clarity is too often the limited 'I' who is part of the problem. Thus, any attempt to *do* something effectively, if pursued adequately, leads us to a confrontation with the basic voids of life. Because we sense this inevitable slide toward what amounts to madness, we choose, instead, to remain within the confining certainties of a life of small problems, with small solutions.

Of all those people who are able to make changes in their lives in accordance with their will, the vast majority use what we can call 'other people's magic' — religions, philosophies, lifestyles, ethoi, political orientations, family structures, languages, and so forth. By their very continued existence, these systems have some sort of self-perpetuating validity to them. Usually, they work quite well. As mentioned previously, most of this relatively small class of successful people do not consider themselves mages. They make use of psychologies, marketing approaches, 'material' sciences, meditation, and prayer — that is, imaginal technologies. Effective, but with most of us, most of the time, not of our own invention.

Only a small sub-group of successful people actually acknowledge their will-working as some form of 'magic,' and of this minute population, most are still using, most of the time, 'other people's magic.' To be clear, I also want to restate, if you haven't guessed already, that I think most folks who self-label as mages, witches, sorcerers, cunning folk, and any other label, aren't even making use of these technologies with much, or any, success. Their efforts drown in the countless other forms of magic that permeate — or rather constitute — their lives. I think 'spirituality,' 'magic,' 'will-working,' and even a goodly amount of 'meditation' can simply be blinds we use to avoid uncomfortable truths. Thus, maybe it is only a coincidence when someone in the world of esotericism and the occult stumbles across something that actually works. Perhaps the wider range of 'other people's magic' is a surer path to finding efficacious technology.

Nevertheless, I have always been a little suspicious that using 'other people's magic' simply gets you something like 'other people's lives' — a prospect with which I am profoundly uncomfortable. Instead of listening to our own lives, reading the True Grimoire written in our lives' blood, we shape them toward other stories, other narratives. Thus, the first and foremost task with magic is to figure out what magic you are already doing and assess its success. The previous exercises, both in Volume One and in this text so far, were efforts to help in that process.

Regarding Sigils

Sigils, in the large sense, are everywhere. Any manipulation of language, text, or representation to achieve an effect is a sigil. Maps, graffiti, account summaries, the stock market, and books are just a few of the examples. Our bodies, too, are ensigilized. Tattoos merely make homage to the memories, histories, habits, and self-concepts wrapped up in what ends up becoming a vast unconscious landscape of flesh.

Sigilization is investment. It is the syzygy of intent, representation, and action. Sigils represent vectors of circumstance. Sigils are road signs that imply new maps, sometimes even new cartographies. As mentioned above, since magic always works, we must also say that every sigil works. But sigils, in their more narrow and traditional sense, have a secret about them. The key is that, often, the sigil that we see is not the ensigilization in its fullness. When we see a stop sign—a sigil of which I am rather fond—we see differently, we become differently. The stop sign sigil, in its fullness, is much more than a reality-altering octagon. The entirety of the sigilization includes roads, cars, drivers, pedestrians, and police forces as well as laws, insurance companies, and perhaps even road crews, the steel industry, the sign painters, and on and on. Thus, when we see only a 'sigil-as-seen,' we are apt to miss how it alters the specific 'me' and how I see. Moreover, we almost never go to the greater systems of which the sigil is merely an artifact. Seeing only the sigil-as-seen means that we have not yet entered the imaginal schematic of the alteration in reality that fuels the ultimate effect. If we are intending to make novel use of sigilizations, then we must change so that we see the truth of the sigil—we must change so that we realize how we ourselves are ensigilized.

All sigils and seals that would seek to will-work or change circumstances are, in truth, a singularity with the mage. More often than not, we do not stand in such a way as to rightly perceive this unity of purpose and, thus, we feebly attempt to portray our skewed perceptions through dimensions that we impose on the inscrutability of the moment. The moment of perfect Gnosis is when we see the sigil in its truth, for in that moment, the sigil has not changed, but we have. We have entered the imaginal.

Within mystical traditions, some sigils, seals, and mandalas seek to portray greater truths beyond mere situational will-working. As with all other sigils, the real magic is not in the symbol itself, but in the transformative relationship between the seeker and the seal-of-the-sought. In a way, all of these mystical sigils that surround and define our daily lives are forms of the point and the circle—byss and abyss. Because every symbol stands atop the sea of the imaginal, they all lead us to confront both intimate and expansive voids. Strangely, since all of life plays upon these depthless waters, all of our stories actually express, however distantly, these ultimate concerns. Specific sigils for specific ends are all mutations and forms of the point and the circle. The stop sign is a mystical symbol, since all of life is the mystical journey—often ass-first. All we have to do is scratch the surface of *how* the stop sign works and we suddenly confront the imaginal nature of reality as we know it. Yet, rather than allow true Imaginal Gnosis to bring us to the emptiness of the voids and allow us to choose our lives anew, we let the stop sign stop us.

Sigils come about through any intersection of power and expression. Most sigils emerge as extensions of current ensigilizations. We hold business meetings to develop mission statements. We meet with an academic advisor in order to pick classes. We go to the bank to sign loan papers. Within the imagination of magic, the process of creating a sigil has an ambience all of its own. Research into arcane texts, various forms of divination and scrying, and a certain amount of soul-searching will often go into the process. All the overtly magical methods of creating sigils—whether through word play, inventing alphabets, creating works of art, combining symbols, or all the other creative technologies—are marvelous ways to channel and play with our imagination. Nevertheless, we are all, self-declared 'mages' or not, thick with ensigilizations. Most sigils are far simpler than occult emblemata; signatures, text messages, corporate logos, and street signs name but a few.

Images and Method X

Archetypal psychologists will tell you that images are not *what* we see, but *how* we see. They mean to tell us that our habits of perception—in its narrowest sense—are merely a sliver of experience. Images bring with them their own prepackaged ethoi, logoi, pathoi, mythoi, teloi, mimesis, alterity, identities, and dualities. By reading between the lines of Jung's massive *Collected Works*, I have also found that, in addition to all these inherent qualities of images, we may also find a unique method, specific to each image, of undoing their thrall. Borrowing a term from Jung, I call this means of extrication Method X.

My doctoral dissertation focuses on the use of imagination by criminal profilers. My central thesis is that profilers use their own imaginations in much the same way as some Jungian-informed psychotherapists make themselves a receptive instrument for the images that emerge in the treatment space. I used Jung because his works are so rich in self-scrutiny and imagination, yet free from pedantry. Not only does Jung let imaginal evidence guide the direction of treatment, he feels that the very mode and means of treatment must be unique to the relationship with each patient. In a 1926 essay, he notes:

> Since there is no nag that cannot be ridden to death, all theories of neuro-sis and methods of treatment are a dubious affair. So I always find it cheering when businesslike physicians and fashionable consultants aver that they treat patients along the lines of 'Adler', or of 'Kunkel' or of 'Freud', or even of 'Jung'. There simply is not and cannot be any such treatment, and even if there could be, one would be the surest road to failure. When I treat Mr. X, I have of necessity to use method X, just as with Mrs. Z I have to use method Z. This means that the method of treatment is determined primarily by the nature of the case. (**Jung, 1926, 'Analytical Psychology and Education,' pp. 112-113 [CW 17, ¶ 203]**)

In my dissertation, I take this idea of Method X in order to emphasize the idea that neither criminal profilers nor psychotherapists can rely on some formula for success. For our purposes in this current work, which deals with a much wider range of imaginal/magical practices, we can extend the implications of this Method.

We cannot merely think our way out of real problems, and we cannot feel our way out of our stuck places, since our thoughts and feelings are so often part of the abiding problems. Analysis, more often than not, keeps you stuck firmly in the specifics of the image. The means of analysis is usually suggested or scripted by the image itself, its internal logic. This prepackaged logic will provide you with a limitless sense of understanding. You may even believe you have incredible insight. But a true Method X always undoes these dyads. Working our way out of our entanglements must be a journey, a story. Method X can engender journeys of many different shapes. It can lead us on an ever-ascending journey of apotheosis, or a dismembering descent of vitriol. Method X can just as easily manifest through the—ironical—'pursuit' of silence, stillness, or a host of other possibilities; however it is always dependent on the particularity of the imaginal territory in which it begins. How the journey unfolds depends on the image—the ensigilization—and what part of it you are. These fictions determine the story that we must play out in order to liberate ourselves.

However, I have to emphasize that the method will never be transcendent unto itself. We find the story that unfolds in the particulars of our lives, not in the imposition of some overarching formula or procedure. I always twitch a little when someone—or whole organizations—decide to imitate the actions of Crowley or Blavatsky or Gurdjieff or Castaneda. As Jung clearly informs us, this is a quick road to failure. Gurus tell the story of their journeys and we seize on and imitate the specifics rather than the process. Jung used his own journey as the source material for his Analytic Psychology, but he did not narcissistically suppose that the *specifics* of his method were transcendent, only the imaginal mechanics.

Nevertheless, setting aside these ideas of liberation, most of the time we don't want to leave an image—and shouldn't. Deciding to re-invent 'driving' while on the highway is questionable at best. Life is full of prepackaged fictions that we need not strenuously scrutinize in order to get through our day. But sometimes we might want to make other choices than those that we have made and which have been made for us. So, just in case you do, you might want to remember method X.

Every image is spiritual, is relational, is banal, is palpable, is an identity, is a body.... every image is an entirety of existence. Spirituality will never, unto itself, prove the means of undoing an image. 'Spirituality' may prove a pathway to a shift, but so too might banality, or materiality, or indulgence.

Nevertheless, as unkind as I may be to 'spirituality,' it is often the repository of that which has not has not fitted well into the 'material' definition of a person, society, culture, practice, etc. The problem arises when we believe that spirituality—some sort of 'otherworld'—is somehow *more* real or important than immediate experience. This will lead us to pursue habitually 'spiritual' solutions to our problems. Habitual spirituality is an entrapping addiction, which leads one to still deeper enmeshments in the very problems from which one would seek to escape. Spirituality is, unto itself, the ultimate futility, an aethyric tar baby that entraps its participant more and more deeply into its addictive stupor of ineffectuality.

As Christopher Hyatt instructed his readers, the vast majority of the time, the greatest magic you can ever do is to stop doing one of the millions of layers of spells we all cast about our selves every moment of our lives. You can conjure lightning, scry the lottery numbers, invoke Amon-Ra, and evoke Babalon Herself, but do you like your life? If not, stop doing the magic that makes it. This is, of course, not all that easy since you are asking 'you,' yourself, the very one who has been ensigilized by all these magical workings, to undo them. However, by seeking Method X, the backdoor of every spell, you may begin to have some success.

When you see a 'problem,' look at the whole picture of the problem—at everyone involved, everyone who grumbles about the problem, all the ways people have tried to 'fix' the problem (and created new problems), everyone who sees no problem, everyone who refuses to fix it, and how everyone talks in their own way about the problem. Then realize that all of this *is* the problem. Only when you can see the fullness of the system, all the ongoing rituals of ensigilization, will you be able truly to extricate yourself from the imaginal structure.

Method X and Banishing Rituals

Even outside of the world of self-avowed mages, most people naturally know how to begin a ritual. They pour a scotch, they turn on particular music, they let out a deep exhale, they chug vast quantities of coffee, they stand up, grab a dry erase marker, and say 'Okay, let's get started,' sometimes they even light a candle. And all of these techniques work, usually due to the power of repetition.

In the imagination of magic, some sort of initial ritual is performed, and this is often in relationship to the elements. Earth, air, fire, and water are rather popular. Jung associates these with his functions: sensing, thinking, feeling, and intuition. Archangels, elementals, colors, tones, and a host of other images show up in these rituals with the intention of creating some sort of sacred space.

I'm a big fan of these opening rites. Sometimes it's the most powerful part of what ends up being a rather disappointing evening of lifeless, lackluster, formulaic 'magical' rote. But I am never quite sure what the spell-casters intend. In the Watchtower Ritual—probably one of the oldest and most repeated opening rites in the West—the mage calls to each of the Guardians of the Watchtowers of each direction to be present, and welcomes them. So, are these Guardians of the Watchtowers *protecting* the space? Yet, if they are the denizens of the elements, aren't they always already there? In which case isn't it *we* the workers who are making the shift? In which case, the rite has little to do with Them and everything to do with us. It is we who turn. It is we who *orient*—an appropriate word since, as noted above, it means to turn to the East.

Should not opening rites hearken to Method X if they are to truly accomplish any intentional magic? Shouldn't we become proficient at *undoing* before we begin any important undertaking? I believe that great benefits can be had from a move toward trying to temporarily undo the endless spells we cast upon ourselves day and night. For most mages, in most traditions, the habit of repetition makes most any opening rite work successfully. But if we don't learn to undo (i.e., become proficient at Method X), we unwittingly accomplish spellwork in that now-sacred space that is merely a dressed up version of what we are doing all the time, because we never stopped doing it.

Let's take a step back from the imagination of explicit magic and apply this to those parts of our lives that don't always feel so magical. How many committees have you been on that are simply an opportunity for people to bring their own agendas to the table? Wouldn't it be nice to be able to process an argument from a fresh perspective, free from resentments? When we find ourselves stuck and want new insight, how do we clean the slate? Because we, in our material devotion to progress, feel compelled to always *do* something, we rarely develop the skills to undo or not do.

Devoted meditation practitioners who get beyond the dogmatism of their practice know that the real power of meditation is in not-doing. Settling into meditation becomes an ongoing practice of Method X. The *via negativa* or apophatic mysticism, the constant undoing of imagery and eventually ideas, is the long-term application of Method X. *Neti neti*—'not this, not this'—is the mantra of the Nameless Path. (With a strong dread at treading into territory I know not nearly well enough to hold forth on, my understanding is that this 'clearing' is part of what many Zen traditions, especially as they have evolved in the West, seek to accomplish.)

The fantasy that we can cast a circle and banish all the world's influences is a seductive one in the imagination of magic. Our lives, however, follow us wherever we are. Just as, for the devout Christian, penance is a journey of realization and transformation after confession, so, too, is any real extrication from the images that possess and entrap us in their predefinitions. We learn from count-less tales of ghosts, tortured heroes, and the films of Tom Cruise, that we must undergo a journey, a process, to free ourselves from hauntings, our past, or our father's legacy, respectively. Therefore, some ritual to mark this developmental milestone may be important to begin or end this unfolding liberation, but gains its power from the *process*.

Hence, as a final note, if you are casting circles because you are afraid that objectively, transcendentally real 'demons' will foil your workings and ravage your soul, I have some very special instructions. Kindly:

1) set down this book;
2) douse it in lighter fluid;
3) place it outside your elaborately constructed ritual circle; and
4) into a lovely triangle of evocation of Michael; and
5) burn this evil, evil book.

That procedure will, for some time, feel rather good. If it doesn't, buy several more copies of this book at full price and try, try again.

26

Application 7
Corporate Logo Contemplation

Corporate logos are incredibly powerful sigils. At their best, they are seamless integrations of intention, representation, and action. (At their worst, each of these vectors moves in its own direction and yields a logo that is more of a cipher for a vast corporate unconscious.) Multi-millions of dollars, pounds, euros, yen, and rubles worth of focus-groups, design firms, branding, and executive whim go into each stroke of what the corporation hopes will become an iconic sigil. The best ones are recognizable on a subliminal level—that is, consumers need not engage in any higher cognitive processing in order to recognize and orient their behavior in response to this symbol.

Grant Morrison does a fine job of highlighting this phenomenon with his term 'hypersigils', and this idea is well known to archetypal psychologists. Consider *McDonald's, Mitsubishi, Apple, American Airlines, Starbucks, Microsoft* and a host of other multinational corporate entities who need only show you a color palate or typeface for you to recognize their branding. You might not even need to know anything about the company in order to learn something about it simply from a well-crafted logo.

If you have spent any portion of your life examining expressions of the imagination of magic such as the Tarot, the Goetia, the I Ching, Runes, or any other visually powerful occult symbolism, you might do well to move up to the big leagues and take on corporate sigilizations.

For this experiment, pick a business's public face: a sign, letterhead, emblem, webpage, what have you. Study the emblem/logo, fixate on it, scry it, breathe into and through it... and then see what is revealed to you. Without resorting to their propaganda or reports, ask: 'who are they?'; 'who am I to and with them?'; 'what is their actual product—that which they replicate throughout the world?'

Journal carefully your responses.

And banish, frequently, with locally-produced, sustainable goods.

(And you thought playing around with *ancient* demons was scary!)

Part 6
Emptying the Vessel

There is no rationality in the world. There is no finality.
There is just a set of interactions. The world is adrift.

Humberto Maturana,
'A Question of Desire,' Interview by Omar Sarrás Jadue

27

Of the Amish and DeMolay
Images of Engaged Living

The old Amish man and I walk down a grassy hill. It seems insulting to use the word 'spry' to depict him, but few words exist to describe his aged agility. At this point, he is in his late 90's and I am 14. We stepped out of the sugar maple woods that separate the farm from the gravel road to find the late February afternoon sky clearing. We had been checking the taps on the trees. This will be the last year that they use the sugar shack to make syrup.

The ground is muddy and we squish our way down to the dirt lane that leads up to the house. For several years, I have spent one day a month with this Amish extended family. It will be several more years before I realize how unusual these experiences have been and how lucky I am to have had them. Regardless, I enjoy the time.

The previous summer, I get my first buggy ride. The family has a boy about my age, and he received the first wagon of his own the day before we arrived. He is visibly proud. We hook up the horse and climb onto the plank that passes for a seat.

Our mothers stand arm in arm in front of the house on the hill. His mother sighs as she says what every other mother says as her son drives away in his first used car: 'they grow up so fast.'

The boy gives the reins a snap and we are off like a shot. We rip down the lane at what feels like a far faster speed than any car I've ever been in. I grip the bench seat and wedge a foot against the buckboard as we hit ruts that nearly bounce me out.

On that day, I begin to feel less like a visitor and more like a friend.

Back with the old man, we make our way around the property, checking gates and doors, the smell of manure pungent as we pass the cows on the lowest level of the bank barn.

I have an absurd question stuck in my throat. The man is the nearly complete embodiment of 'wise elder' to me. When called upon to visualize 'senex' or 'wizard,' his, and later my mentor's, faces are the wizened ones that come to mind. Hence, I suppose it is only natural that I should feel compelled to seek this Amish elder's advice. But my query is ridiculous because I want to ask him if I should join the Masonic youth organization, DeMolay. I want to ask the old man what I should do. On a cognitive level, I am very clear that a 90-something

Amish Bishop cannot give me direct insight into what I fantasize to be my official entrance into the world of Western Esotericism, but the urge to ask is not abated by this logic.

Perhaps further driving this strange urge, I inexplicably have a distant sense that there is some sort of choice set before me, between a life with the Amish and what DeMolay has come to represent in my fevered imagination. This dichotomy is even more ridiculous than asking the old man for his advice on the topic. For a thousand reasons, I could never be Amish. Nevertheless, I love and respect the Amish for their integrity and tenacity. The vast majority of them live their values. I want that. In the rest of my life, I can see a thousand compromises all around me—maybe this is the developmental task of all teenagers, to see the hypocrisy of the world that they will inherit. But so much of what the Amish live addresses what I already see as wrong with the world around me.

I have no illusions that I could ever realistically become Amish. I could never really give up music. I would probably grow unbearably bored with their way of life. As much as I respect the Anabaptist impulse, the theology would likely make me break out in a rash. But this simple, close-to-the-earth life holds and embodies a call for me: a call to integrity; a deep engagement in life; and a profound and functional sense of community.

We finally make our way up to the main house. As we open the door, the middle-aged spinster daughter, as well as my mother and father, greet me with broad smiles. The smell of kerosene lamps, followed quickly by that of freshly made elderberry pie—the perfectly flaky crust made with lard—washes over me. We all enjoy a generous helping and this moment embeds the tangy and floral pie as my favorite of all time.

Five years later, I am a junior in college. The old man has, by this point, passed away. He was 104.

I sit next to one of the Masons who sponsor this chapter of DeMolay. The argot of DeMolay calls them 'Dads.' We are in the first floor banquet hall of a Masonic Lodge in a suburb of Cleveland. It smells of wax and old books. I joined DeMolay three or so months previously and completed my initiations a month ago. We have just finished the first initiation of a new member. I played the organ for the ritual, sneaking in strains of *Carmina Burana* and a few film soundtracks.

For my part, this brief courtship and period of initiations has been dominated by an overwhelming feeling of 'okay, when do we get to the real stuff?' (Looking back, I will realize that I, more or less, missed the point of the initiations.) In the interest of trying to uncover 'secrets,' I ask this Dad about a symbol I saw on a Masonic bumper sticker, something like a crooked stick with a large dot on either side.

He puts on a hoary, avuncular tone and says, 'Well, that is a symbol for one of Masonry's mythic founding fathers.'

I furrow my brow and review what I know from my seven years of research.

Oh gawd... it's a rebus.

'Oh,' I interrupt the silence in disappointed realization, 'you mean Tubal Cain — "Two Ball Cane"?'

I groan at the pun. The Mason invites over another Dad and conveys my realization in an impressed tone. The other Dad notes that I am carrying a copy of Albert Pike's *Morals and Dogmas of the Ancient and Accepted Scottish Rite Free-masonry.* He feigns having never seen it before and asks if he can borrow it. In effect, he repossesses it into the Lodge's collection. I will never see it again.

After being active for six months or so, I stop attending meetings. Essentially, I am disappointed. I should have joined DeMolay a bit earlier in life. My fellow members are kids, three to six years my junior. The group serves different ends than those I sought. Middle-class, future pillars of their community, these are good folks, albeit devoid of any real passion for esotericism.

I think my real moment of disillusionment comes when I see, in a catalog, an advertisement for Masonic barbeque aprons. Soon, I make the horrified discovery that this Secret Brotherhood, that I have idealized since my youth, also gave rise to the fez-wearing, tiny-car-driving-in-parades Shriners. I don't doubt that we need frater-nal organizations committed to charity and moral rectitude, but I am left wondering, who really pursues making the rich symbolism of the West relevant to life?

When, on my 21st birthday, I receive the letter inviting me to join Freemasonry, I have to ask myself, 'What am I really looking for?'

During my senior year of college, I finally finish reading Umberto Eco's *Foucault's Pendulum*, a book I have been reading in fits and starts over a period of three years. The ultimate insights of the book, I suspect, were waiting for me to catch up to them before they would let me finish the text. In it, Eco wrestles with the accumulated detritus of Europe's love affair with all things occult.

In the dramatic climax of the novel, a horde of occultists, esotericists, and illu-minati gather in the indoor courtyard of a museum, in which swings a massive Foucault Pendulum. The gathered ritualists discover one of the protagonists spying on the mysterious proceedings, to the horror of his still hiding friend. The occultists lift their victim up and wrap the line of the pendulum around his neck. As they release his body, the gyrations of his death throes create an eccentric oscillation in the pendulum's course. From his still hidden vantage, the remaining protagonist realizes that this vibration perfectly describes the shape of the Qabalistic Tree of Life. In that moment of dread realization, he discovers that the Secret of Secrets is life itself.

I am many years away from having any glimmer of how to live this realization, yet I still recognize the implication of Eco's moral. I tuck the letter from the Freemasons, with its beautifully ornate letterhead, carefully away with the rest of my grandfather's volumes.

'Okay,' I say to myself, 'I get it. This needs to be my life. Not a formula. I need to get about the business of living. This must be my own story.'

But how powerfully I want my story legitimized, supported, sanctioned, endorsed, even sanctified by some secret society, some hoary tradition! A part of me narcissistically still hungers for this kind of exclusivity. I sit in my dorm room alone, feeling lonely, and think of the Amish. I distantly sense that the pull, toward both the esoteric and the Amish, finds its origin in a longing for real integrity, for which the various traditions are simply blinds, distracting me from the much more difficult work of living my own story.

That's the point, I realize. *It has to be my own journey, seeking a life that is both holy and immediate.*

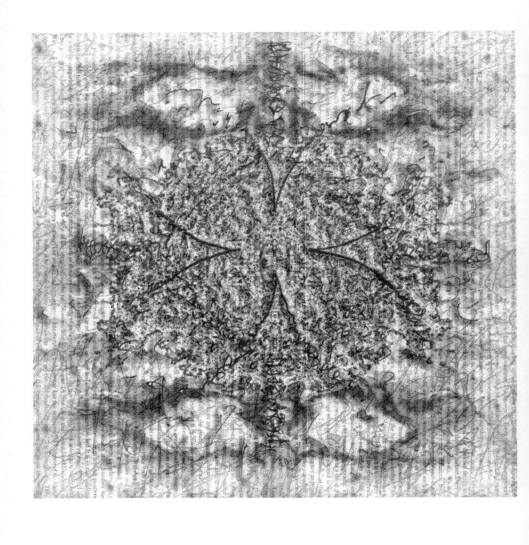

28
Nothingness
The Fifth Void

So-called 'objectivity' is a labor-intensive process in which we (dis)animate our world into thing-like entities possessed of a dead (but reassuring) permanence. This procedure yields an absurdity that we can only deny with strenuous effort—but succeed at with a liberal application of booze, distractions, scientistic technobabble, and the hope of sex.

The journey toward appreciating the reality of nothingness begins with the fundamental shift away from a reality built on *what* we observe, toward a focus on the immediate reality *that* we observe—that we are, in fact, simultaneously in the acts of observing and cobbling together our lived world.

Experience is not... is nothing... is not a thing; and, as any Chaos Mage will tell you, nothing is true. (The phrase 'Nothing is True, Everything is Permissible' is popularly attributed to Hassan i-Sabbah, the richly storied founder of the 'assassins.' Although sources as far back as the 14th and 15th centuries—in particular, the Egyptian historian Al Maqriti (1364-1442)—link this saying to some leader of this Islamic secret brotherhood, the persistence of the myth in the imagination of magic is now far more important than its origins. Nietzsche quotes it, having likely read it in the work *Die Assassinen* (1818) by Joseph von Hammer-Purgstall. Thus, by the mid-20th century, it had become a password in secret societies seeking to hearken to the heretical, deadly, and 'orientalist' resonances of this now-mythic order. The Chaos Magical order, the IOT, adopted it as a motto and, today, gamers the world around know the phrase from the *Assassin's Creed* series of videogames. Regardless of provenance, that this phrase has multiple layers and potentials for meaning is frequently lost in a haze of antinomian fantasies.†)

Existential phenomenologists use *very big words* to explain this not-thing-ness, but it is as apparent as can be. The only way we 'know' something is a 'thing' is through the flow of experience. When we awaken to this way of being, we find that our experience is now more primary, more fundamental, and more real than those abstractions about some aspect of experience that we choose to partition off into some category of 'thing-i-ness.'

---

† Thanks go to Steve Snair for his fine legwork in tracking down the provenance of this phrase.

The implications, however, of this simplest of shifts in observation are so phenomenal that the very nature of the mind itself resists this adjustment. Consciousness is, as the phenomenologists remind us, always consciousness-*of.* To remove the seeming permanence or even viability of the very *things* of which consciousness is aware, also indicts the permanence of the consciousness itself. That is, we must also realize that each of us is also not a thing.

Nevertheless, 'I am nothing,' is amongst the most uncomfortable of statements. Hence, with great confidence, we can say that we are indeed afraid of nothing. To further this glibness, we can also say that our lives are neither here nor there—or perhaps more accurately, 'never there, and always here.' Spatiality itself shifts given the various fictions we live. Nevertheless, once we ignore experience and fall into a thing-mindset, we find ourselves in vast meaningless wastelands into which we must arbitrarily place absurd and trite artifacts in order to advance the nonsense of this brittle expanse of a material 'reality.' We are left desperately trying to find 'where it's at' since we constantly sense, however dimly, that we are nothing, nowhere.

The Phantoms of Nothingness

Thing-ness is a very functional aspect of many magical orientations. Most magical systems, whether overt or covert, create and rely on some sort of fundamental materials or substance. Through this sort of reification, we can convince ourselves that certain substances, entities, vibrations, or locations are constitutive to everything else. Chakras, aethyrs, atoms, elements, DNA, spirits, memes, souls, identities, grammatical constructs, quintessence, gods, natural forces, brain structures, quanta, and a host of other powerful imagery provide 'objective' components from which we can construct a reality. For example, by appealing to 'matter' and 'spirit' we can guarantee that the two must go to extraordinary lengths to affect each other. And, as with so much in life, we are usually very grateful for that paradigm.

But whatever sort of 'things' we create, we are, simultaneously, stuck with them and dogged by their fictionality. This functionality/fictionality duality is a dicey business. We think of things as self-sustaining; but, of course, they aren't. Their thingness is an assertion on our part, an act of imagination, not a passive perception. Thus, we must constantly re-invest in their 'permanence.' This becomes incredibly neurotic. Soon we are treating ourselves and others as things as well, simply to keep this thing-racket going.

In one of the most popular thing-paradigms—let's cut to the chase and call it 'materialism'—the rest of our non-thing experiences stand a very good chance of becoming unconscious. You could say that they slip into another dimension if that sort of language floats your canoe. But that dimension, or unconscious, or shadow realm becomes an increasing presence in every moment. In a screaming indictment of our increasingly limited 'reality,' these marginalized experiences sadly shriek in a language to which we have given ourselves no access. What this means, essentially, is that although they are right in front of us, all those aspects of experience which don't fit our materialism are epistemologically inaccessible. *How* we know what we know—our epistemology—makes us functionally blind to the vast majority of experience in a materialist world view.

And this would be all chuckles and cakes if it actually worked.

But it doesn't.

So, we are posed with phantom worlds and dimensions. Materialism, being the most popular spell-working system, tends to be responsible for the largest shadow realms, but any system that creates rigid 'thing' categories will induce these compensatory other worlds—these pressing indictments of our 'reality.' Because all experiences are whole, every second faces us with experiences that we must shatter, or face a complete undoing of some of our most basic functions.

We do not experience things. We *are* experience. Experience is made of images. 'Things' are fictions that help our various storylines along—'props' and 'MacGuffins' really. Sadly, because we claw for a type of permanence to ease our anxieties, we tend to latch onto these useful fictions and soon find ourselves thing-i-fied, as well. We are not things, although the more we treat ourselves as such, the more our 'I' becomes thinglike.

Unfortunately, for many of us, the 'thing'-mentality becomes incredibly pervasive. Regardless of whether we are in a materialist, spiritualist, animist, or other thing-system, the compensatory shadow realm will carry with it a power by which most of us are profoundly undone: nothingness. Not-thing-ness.

Philosophers, novelists, and artists have struggled with the creeping power of nothingness for close to two centuries now. In the West, we seem to be convinced that we will be able to buy enough crap, look lovely enough, or snort enough drugs to outrun nothing. Even Western intellectuals seem to think existential and postmodern ideas addressing nothingness are out-dated, and thus of marginal relevancy. Of course these defenses only bring us, ass-first, closer to the yawning abyss of nothingness. Lovecraft may be one of the more popular examples of an author who despaired for our thin reality's incapacity to defend against such assaults. But for those who find Lovecraft's depictions of characters' madness-inducing encounters with nihilism compelling, I suggest an inspection of Thomas Ligotti's prose poetry stories. In a collaboration with David Tibet's Current 93, Ligotti's *I Have a Special Plan for This World* (2000) presents a series of visions, each one out-stripping the last in their zealous devotion to ineffability and annihilation. In this passage (Section XI), Ligotti has a voice reveal to the narrator the essence of the insurmountable chasm between our inadequate language and the desiccated husks of a reality around which we can only blindly stumble. In these stories, the reader can easily hear resonances of Zen doctrines of emptiness:

> It was twilight and I stood in a greyish haze of the vast empty building
> When the silence was enriched by a reverberant voice
> All the things of this world it said
> Are of but one essence
> For which there are no words
> This is the greater part which has no beginning or end
> And the one essence of this world for which there can be no words
> Is that all the things of this world
> This is the lesser part which had a beginning and shall have an end
> And for which words were conceived solely to speak of
> The tiny broken beings of this world it said
> The beginnings and endings of this world it said
> For which words were conceived solely to speak of
> Now remove these words and what remains it asks me
> As I stood in the twilight of that vast empty building
> But I did not answer
> The question echoed over and over
> But I remained silent until the echoes died
> And as twilight passed into the evening I felt my
> Special plan for which there are no words
> Moving towards a greater darkness

Ligotti presents devastating insight into what the indictment of our flimsy thing-worlds looks like. In this and his many other works, Ligotti demonstrates that nothingness has some serious teeth, or tentacles, or creeping madness that it brings to bear as it erodes the color, sensibility, and permanence out of our cheap façades of matter and our selves.

Otherworlds

Longstanding rigid paradigms, such as materialism, tend to engender a parallel permanence in their shadow realms. When we lived in tinier islands of predict-ability — caves, walled villages, towns, collectives, etc. — the otherworld was as close as the darkness of the forest or wilderness beyond our kenning or campfire. Today, access to these realms may be down a dark alley, a peep show, or another country or culture.

The truth, of course, is that the otherworlds, 'the land of the Fae', 'the mundus imaginalis', 'the dreaming', 'al mithral' whatever you call them, are all here and now; yet we split ourselves off so that only a portion of our selves can be in them. These vast realms support and sustain our small world of appearances, yet we deny their fundamental reality. At best, we consider these otherworlds to be quaint suburbs of 'reality.'

Nevertheless, these otherworlds are not ideal, derivative, or secondary in any way. These are not worlds we 'should' live in if we plan to effect change in our lives. These are worlds in which we *do* live. Only through millennia of practice have we so narrowed our gaze as to miss them.

Small wonder, then, that our species is cursed with a love of other people's fantasies. Far better that we allow ourselves to 'play', in the smallest of senses, in these seemingly 'created' worlds than that we should realize we are always already there. Films, graphic novels, horror fiction, role-playing games, magical paradigms, religions, psychotheocosmologies, and fantasy novels allow us to briefly access, in a safer way, the architecture of being. But beware: Their seduction is strong and we may soon find ourselves walking paths that lead to far larger realms, and far darker territory than we bargained for at the checkout line!

If we do persist in braving the emptying harrows of these encounters with nothingness, our experiences deepen. We see more, feel more—in essence, *live* more. In fact, one can go about it the other way around. By living more richly and deeply, by engaging experience more fully through the invitations of the senses, we may come to effect an un-thing-ing, an emptying of our bloated 'realities.' The next exercise speaks to just such an effort.

29

Application 8
Multi-Modal Ritual Construction

In order to effect a return to the moment, rather than face the painful consequences of resisting nothingness, we must reacquaint ourselves with experience itself—the sensuality, the immersion, and the richness of every unfolding instant of life. When lost in 'things,' perception becomes a mere machine that may be accurate or inaccurate. But with a reawakening to experience we become acutely aware that, rather than a regrettable mediator between subject and object, 'perception' is the very essence of reality. Not the subjectivist or solipsistic nightmare of 'everything is whatever we make it'; but the imaginal flow of shifting fictions that gives birth to, and subsumes, subjects and objects at every instant.

The best rituals absorb us in all the senses. Although a dominantly visual species, we still operate through the many other senses. Vision, audition, gustation, olfaction, and tactition all integrate seamlessly with proprioception, kinesthesia and the vestibular senses. In the brutal efficiency of a mass-production world, the philosophy of 'function over form' has too long focused on what blueprints look like, rather than the realization that, for a sensorially integrated creature, form *is* a function. As a species, humans absorb and record the overall tone of situations. Thus, no particular sense can successfully substitute for the gestalts in which we operate.

Whether in the workspace in which we best function, the sacred space in which we worship, or the wilderness in which we rejuvenate, the secret lies in the whole, not any one aspect. Nevertheless, each of us tends to emphasize, or rely, on certain senses, perspectives, or functions over others. One popular example is the VARK model from Neuro-linguistic Programming (NLP). VARK stands for 'Visual, Auditory, Reading/writing, and Kinesthetic' and represents the four dominant learning styles. Some students and pedagogs use this model as an excuse to explain classroom failures (e.g., 'that instructor only uses Auditory teaching techniques and I am a Visual type'). However, this model is more of a call to recognize your comfort zone and growth areas, as well as a call for teachers to teach with a wider range of styles. (It turns out that simply moving around a classroom as you teach tends to improve the performance of kinesthetic learners.) Moreover, students who take time to actually assess their learning style often discover that they have been trying to exclusively force themselves into a style that doesn't match their strengths.

In a similar vein, Jung developed his four functions model, which the Meyers-Briggs Type Indicator (MBTI) made famous. Jung's four functions are thinking, feeling, sensing, and intuiting. The names don't translate terribly well from the German and thus the English terms are somewhat deceptive. 'Thinking' involves the logical connections we make when we move from A to B to C to D. 'Feeling' centers around liking or not liking, or assessing something as 'good' or 'bad.' 'Feeling,' in this case, is not really the same as emotionality. 'Sensing' types deal in what they consider hard evidence, direct experience, or 'facts.' 'Intuitive' types make leaps from A to Q, often skipping over B through P. Whether deliberately or not, Gene Roddenberry's original *Star Trek* series portrayed the four functions quite well with Spock the thinker, Bones the feeler, Scotty the sensate, and Kirk the intuitionist. (Beyond the four functions, the MBTI integrates Jung's ideas about the attitudes of introversion and extroversion and adds a novel scale to determine judging or perceiving 'lifestyles.') In general, one tends to be relatively strong in two of the four functions with the other two settling into an underdeveloped, unconscious 'inferiority.' These inferior functions often show up in the language of our dreams, as well as in complementary or antagonistic relationships.

Of course, these 20th century inventions are far from the only typologies. The Enneagram of Personality has a strong New Age following, as do countless other categorization systems that have been invented in order to give a scientistic face to an urge for systematization as old as astrology.

I have been somewhat surprised that no authors have seized upon Theodore Millon's Clinical Multiaxial Inventory (MCMI) to categorize people. Perhaps because the test is notoriously pathologizing, it would seem inappropriate; but, honestly, I think sorting people into narcissists, histrionics, schizoids, avoidants, and many other dark cubbies seems immensely more descriptive to me than Virgos, Cancers, and Capricorns.

Putting aside all these various systematizations, it should be clear that we are polycentric creatures. We are, of course, all thinkers, feelers, sensers, and intuiters, just as we all, with the exception of those with sensory disabilities, are visual, auditory, readers/writers, and kinesthetic learners. Beyond simply our strength areas, we all interact, navigate, and predict our world through all these capacities. Thus, multimodally engaging ourselves on all these levels, although sometimes overwhelming, tends to have a much more profound impact.

The Passover Seder is a prime example of a marvelous time-tested ritual that taps into all of our functions, senses, and styles. Recitations, readings, actions, and strong and marvelous scents and flavors, all swirl into a multimodal masterpiece of tradition. So, too, the Roman Catholic Mass has the potential to engage the congregants and celebrants on many levels. The real secret is that all of life is already happening in this multimodal way, even when we habitually rely on a limited range of senses or ways-of-being to encounter it. Great rituals may evoke a wider array of experiences in the participants, but we need not turn to the bells and smells of hoary rites to expand our sensoria. A freshly cleaned bathroom, a public pool, a visit to the seashore or the city—all of these experiences are pulling us in hundreds of directions at once.

Therefore, this exercise can go in many directions, of which I will only suggest a few:

First, pick one of your favorite pleasurable experiences, one which you think won't be harmed by a bit of scrutiny. Go through it slowly and deliberately. Perhaps film yourself doing it and review the tape, or do it in front of a mirror. Now go through it once again, even more slowly. What all goes into making this experience 'just right'? What are the thoughts, feelings, sensations, reactions? Of course, many experiences lose their luster when we analytically pull ourselves out of them, but through doing this we can also discover that we rarely give ourselves license to genuinely enjoy ourselves. Learning our pleasure style, our modes of engagement, can give us a deeper appreciation for what our needs are. (Tantric coaches and sex therapists actually suggest applying this exercise to your sex life in order to raise sex out of its dominantly unconscious landscape of imitating porn, habitually repeating early experiences, and shame.)

Perhaps an overall experience doesn't suggest itself for the first exercise. Regardless, take activities such as drinking a fine tea or wine. Slow it down until you can feel the various phases of sensation. The nose, the first wash of flavor, the expansion into the sinuses, and the finish. Note how long the experience lingers. Try interspersing new flavors, and compare and contrast them. Finally, ask yourself why, most of the time, you avoid these experiences so conspicuously? (A warning in advance on this exercise: if practiced consistently, it will likely ruin the experience of eating fast food for you.)

Go to an art museum with enough space for you to view paintings and sculptures from a variety of angles and distances. (I find this experiment easier with abstract modern art, but you can choose any type.) Approach an artwork as closely as the security barriers will let you and then slowly begin stepping back. Look for the vibration of the colors and patterns, the rhythm and vectors. Note how your eyes move. Try to observe how your eyes feel differently. Judge the shifts in the experience at various distances from the work. In what ways are you altered by this engagement?

Seek out businesses that sell clothing, carpet, lumber and any other products that feature texture. Take time to run your hands across a wide range of surfaces.

Allow your reactions to come to the forefront. Let words like 'rough' or 'smooth' fade into the background and try to get in touch, once again, with this most primitive and intimate of senses.

If you practice any sort of physical exercise, martial art, stretching regime, or sport, take time to slow it down every so often and listen to your body's communication with the activity. Solidity, weakness, firmness, burning, and any number of other contingencies are merely the first level of a massive reservoir of information flowing, shifting, and transforming in our embodiment.

Find as many other types of experience as you can imagine and address them with the same curiosity. You may discover that journaling elicits a different set of descriptions than verbally reporting your discoveries. Persist until you arrive at a level of awareness where you realize that you are allowing yourself to experience aspects of your world that you have always experienced, but refused to acknowledge. Then, try to gain some sense of the subtle feelings that come from the transition from repression to receptivity.

When we want to construct a ritual, whether it be a dinner party, a date, a wedding, a work retreat, or the more deliberately magical exercises of invocation or evocation, how fully do we engage styles, modes, functions, and senses? Many people do not understand the difference between 'not liking' an experience and 'not being comfortable with' it. Experiences that challenge our habits can quickly lead us to those most uncomfortable confrontations with the voids. Thus, many of us develop a narrow inventory of acceptable experiences, which we endlessly repeat in order to reinforce our pseudo-stability.

One oft-repeated bromide defines insanity as repeating the same actions over and over, expecting a different result each time. Yet can we not speak to that different sort of insanity in which we repeat the same actions over and over, content with the *same* results? Sensation, let alone pleasure, is inherently intimate, but this intimacy does not dissipate through ignorance. Our flesh, the True Grimoire, records our styles of embodiments and makes these our intimacy. Thus, as you become more familiar with your styles of life, ask yourself the same question that we have posed throughout this work, 'is this what I want?'

30
Marching Until All is in Shatters
Images of Decimation

Munich. A spring evening in the early 1990's. Munich Bayern just beat Liverpool in 'fußball' and the Marienplatz is a sea of ecstatic Bavarians.

I am one of a group of 16 undergraduates on a Grand Tour of Europe. We have each come for our own reasons; but, primarily, I think the 'wouldn't it be cool to spend a semester in Europe?' reason dominates. I am still victim to a version of this, in the form of 'everything about Europe is amazingly cooler than America.' This impression endures until, several weeks later, I have to run for my life from street punks at two in the morning in Rome. To a certain extent, the whole trip is a sort of running—hoping that the new sights, sounds, and flavors will drive away the agitated depression that has increasingly dogged me throughout my senior year.

After a long day of train travel from Amsterdam, we are all a bit shell-shocked to be in the thick of this throng. One of our three professors-cum-chaperones has decided to take us on a late evening tour—more of a 'forced march' really—of Munich's historic central pedestrian artery.

The smell of beer is strong and it combines with the crowds and humidity to create a sense of claustrophobia, odd in such an expansive space. Good-natured but still jeering sports fans surround us occasionally, assuming from our English that we are Liverpool F.C. fans. The professor panics for a second, his eyes bugging out as fans in white and blue encircle us.

He yelps, 'Follow me!' and we begin to make our way across the square. Even over the din, I can hear a loud crunching and feel my feet grinding into something on the bricks and cobble. I take a second in our dignified scurry to realize that the jubilant fans have covered the pavement in shattered beer steins.

Crunch, crunch, crunch, we weave between conga lines and spontaneous street parties. We finally escape into a quieter diagonal side street and encounter three lederhosen wearing men, arm in arm, beer steins in hand, replete in Tyrolean hats, singing, staggering back and forth across the alley. The image is so clichéd that I worry it is some kind of joke. Somehow, this added ludicrousness throws our professor over the edge. Going to his comfort zone, he begins to narrate the architecture and notable sites, having us lean in close as he describes, over the roar of revelers, the finials, street layouts, and fascist insurgencies of this city's thousand years of history.

Finally, after still more trudging over fields of glass, our professor releases us with a vacant look in his eyes. In his mind, he has done due diligence to prepare us for our next day, free to wander the city. After our schlep, most of the group is hungry, so three of us strike out once more into the sea of partying Germans. We quickly find a basement buffet and ratskeller.

After an hour, in which I discover the unexpected delight of a Rattler—beer and Sprite in Olympic quantities—we emerge back onto the Marienplatz. Just as I stumble up the stairs past eye level with the cobble, I see the last two coverall-clad street cleaners descend through access panels into tunnels below the avenue. With massive green brooms, they have swept clean, practically sterilized the bricks and cobble in less than an hour.

I am flabbergasted but also shudder with the efficiency. I am well aware that the ponderous Greek and Romanesque Revival architecture surrounding me is inexorably linked with the ascent of the Nazis in this, their Bavarian homeland. My head spins just a bit, and not just from the beer. I feel an inexplicably empty ache in my gut. I cannot attend to the various emotions and shut them down in a smog of intellectual association with the images of the evening. In the midst of these fascist resonances, a phrase boils up into my mind, *Wir marschieren weiter wenn alles in Scherben fällt.*

My German is a useless hodgepodge of musical and philosophical terms, but somehow this phrase, with my dim sense of its meaning of marching on and breaking things, seems important. Thus, as we head back to the hotel, I ask a classmate if she knows what it means. She crinkles her nose, certain that I have made it up.

Bleak, dark, and anxious dreams will plague me for the rest of the trip. In one in particular I am homeless and destitute, wandering hostile streets, all the time knowing that I have done some terrible thing that has condemned me to this fate. In the dream, however, I cannot seem to remember what my transgression is.

My impetuous teen temperament, combined with my collegiate neo-Romanticism has blossomed into a deadly admixture of self-loathing and arrogance. Later, I will realize that this is the schematic of clinical narcissism—a somewhat different creature than mere egotism and condescension. At the time, I am desperately running from, and simultaneously re-enacting this pattern in my relationships, work, and the rest of my life. In short, while busily struggling with a sense of victimhood and inadequacy, I can be a royal ass to those who care to be my friends.

During that first night in Munich, something of this bile threatens to overtake me and only with intellectual misdirection can I avoid the consequences.

Two days after the night of shatters, we take a rather more relaxed tour of the city that finishes at the famous Rathaus-Glockenspiel — a multi-tiered tableau of automata. While waiting for the next procession of clockwork knights, dancers, and assorted royalty, I recount my story to the professor. I ask him if he recognizes the phrase. He takes a stab at the meaning, but I already have the sense of it. There is something more to it, I feel certain.

He takes me over to our guide for the morning. She is a middle-aged frau, in a cardigan with her glasses on a chain. She has coifed her hair so perfectly that it bespeaks her having stopped keeping up with fashion sometime in the late 50's. She smiles easily and clearly enjoys her work. I repeat the phrase to her. She blanches and steps back.

'Where did you *hear* this?!' she says, her disbelief wrestling with something like concern or misgiving.

I tell her the story of how it popped into my head.

'Do you speak German?'

'Not really,' I admit.

'This phrase, it means "We march onwards," yes? "Until even everything is in" — "shards"?'

'Shatters?' I offer.

'Yes... "broken," "ground down," you see?' She grinds the butt of one palm into the other like a boot heel.

I nod. She clearly has something else to add.

'But you see, this is from a song. This was a Nazi propaganda song — the Hitler youth, they sang it. The chorus is famous, I think you know it, yes? "Wir marschieren weiter wenn alles in Scherben fällt; Denn heute da hört uns Deutschland, Und morgen die ganze Welt." — "We march on even if everything in shatters falls. Today, Germany listens to us, Tomorrow the World".'

I shudder again, just as I did at the efficiency of the gnome-like street cleaners.

'How did I learn this phrase?!' I wonder aloud in disbelief, also attempting to defuse any worries about some hidden neo-Nazi affiliation.

'This was a popular propaganda song from before the War,' she explains.

I thank her and walk away.

This marching on in shatters has horrific resonances to the pogrom Krystall-nacht — the Night of Broken Glass. Surely the parallel is no coincidence. This relentless, blind force of destruction and malice haunts me for the rest of the day. I cannot look at a statue, a bridge, or an edifice without thinking how this all figures into the nightmare of World War II.

In spite of being enamored of Joseph Campbell and Carl Jung, I find myself unable to make a necessary personal connection to this emergence of the unconscious. Thus, instead of engaging in the necessary further personal scrutiny, I eventually become somewhat proud that *my* psyche could be so clever. Today, the irony of such pride is palpable.

By the time the Grand Tour reaches Florence, I begin to remember the source of my little fascist phrase. I had copied this line, I realize, several years before, as part of a poem. I can remember copying it onto a graph paper pad—my preferred journal stock at the time.

I think I copied it from a novel. It begins with an absurd line, something like 'we are the chin chopper and the golly whoppers,' but I recall I liked the poem for its absurdity and a sort of matter-of-fact brutality.

Was it from *A Clockwork Orange*?

Over the next several years, I tell the story relatively often. Enough so that my various partners along the way learn to step away and enter into other conversations when I begin to dramatically hold forth with my Munich Tale. That I am trying to 'work through a personal issue,' as the self psychologist Heinz Kohut would say, is lost on me, and apparently only distantly apprehended by my significant others.

I will have to wait a decade before the internet catches up to my research needs.

When it does, I discover that the line was from a prefatory poem, 'We are the Centuries,' at the beginning of Walter M. Miller, Jr.'s *A Canticle for Leibowitz* (1960). I read it as a sophomore in High School. I hadn't enjoyed the novel much at the time. I suspect the teacher assigned it in an effort to interest the young men of the class in literature. Nevertheless, at the time, substitute baby Jesuses emerging from tumorous growths in a post-apocalyptic desert monastery were a little too bizarre and blasphemous for my embattled teen mind.

I am 31 when I finally find the reference. By this point, I have spent enough time on both sides of the therapy couch to realize that all these 'uncanny' events need to be brought home to a day-to-day relevance. Staring at the words of the poem on a computer monitor, I recognize that most of the things that have repulsed me over the years have held vital lessons that I refused to learn. Thus, like all forms of resistance, the lesson haunts me in progressively more brutal forms until I finally give in and listen. Munich was just another opportune irruption of my creative unconscious attempting to confront me with its tutelage. Leaning back in my office chair, considering the poem and the novel, I am finally ready to begin considering the implications of this message.

Introduction to Psychology, as I teach it, includes a rather expansive third unit dealing with the History of the Human Species. Beginning with the evolutionary half eye-blink that is the presence of *homo sapiens sapiens* on earth, I make my way through prehistory, the agrarian revolution, the creation of world religions, the emergence of the bourgeois, the Renaissance, the Victorian Period, the birth of 'psychology,' and the postmodern condition. (The unit is supposed to take a couple of weeks but often ends up becoming a quarter of the semester.)

When we get to World War II, I try to emphasize the horror of this apocalypse. I discuss the decimation, the war crimes, and the effects of a generation of traumatized returning veterans. At some point, I ask the students, 'who won World War II?' By this point in the semester, my students already know the easy answers won't satisfy me, so I get answers like 'The Soviets' and 'The Working Class.' I also hear responses such as, 'The Atom Bomb,' 'Radar,' and 'Computers' which starts to get to the heart of the matter. I take the stance that 'technology' won World War II—not that technology merely helped the allies win but, rather, that Technology itself was the victor. We have become technologized, colonized by the industrialization that became our lives during the war. The Atom Bombs dropped on Japan were merely the awakened Technological Beast opening its eyes in horrifically sentient triumph. War would now no longer be a necessity in order for Technology to annex the rest of the world. 'Progress' and technology would become inexorably linked, indistinguishable in the imagination of the world. 'Today, the warring nations listen to me; tomorrow, the world!'

The so-called 'Military-Industrial Complex' has become a power center of its own, unprecedented in its dominance and control of all aspects of production, society, and government.

The problem with all this Luddite protesting, of course, is that it sounds like I am raging against the toaster. The classic counter-argument is to ask whether I am not grateful for penicillin?

However, that's really the point. How can I be grateful for a *thing*? We are at a point where we think things have inherent value. The technological triumph is practically the apotheosis of materialism—materialism becoming so dominantly our only narrative that we no longer see it as a collection of values, but as Reality itself. Everything else becomes interpretation, poetry, or fantasy.

Nevertheless, in its empty nihilism, materialism—and its Messianic child Technology—march on until every newly reified *thing* is itself in shatters. Empty matter eats itself in an autophagic orgy of destruction. Yet, the mystical cannot be adequately suppressed beneath this leaden overlay. The very self-devouring quality of materialism is the manifestation of the ouroboros—the snake biting its own tail. But, the ouroboros calls for renewal and regeneration. Materialism, cut off from the animating Imaginal, is left without rebirth and can only accomplish the black, vitriolic arts of destruction.

I like to think of that episode in Munich as something like a calling—a vocation trying to sear through the haze of my self-possessed young adulthood. But rather than being simply a personal outrage at the horrors of the Shoa, or some sort of neo-Amish reaction against technologization, it was a less convenient, less comfortable sort of calling—as I suppose any real vocation must be. I too was infected with a sterling dream of automated perfection in the vain hope of avoiding toxic levels of shame. I could also mount brutally inhuman/dehumanized arguments against the values of those for whom I should have cared more than I did. The calling demanded a revolution of psyche. Nevertheless, in my early 20's, I ignored the more life-altering implications and focused on the uncanny synchronicity and social commentary, carefully avoiding any personal resonance.

As a student of mine often ironically points out when discussing Hollywood's various cinematic discharges, 'It's okay to hate Nazis.' Not only is it 'okay'; it feels good, *really* good. Through our socially-sanctioned hatred, we can blithely (but only temporarily) relieve ourselves of guilt, self-doubt and scrutiny, and give in to the mass projection of our shadows. We are all, after all, marching on. But simply disavowing technology, or materialism, or whatever other 'evil' plagues the world won't solve the problem. To throw another metaphor into this mix, I have to quote Walt Kelly's *Pogo*: 'We have met the enemy and he is us.'

Our lives are the ever-unfolding journey of trying to overcome, rather than trip over, our own foibles. As we persist in our stuckness, ego-intoxicated with our reassuring 'realities,' we grind down and destroy ourselves, and those around us. Desperate at the carnage, we must find others to blame: 'conservatives,' 'liberals,' 'terrorists,' 'fascists,' the 'gubmint,' 'kids today,' 'immigrants,' 'anti-immigrant activists,' and anyone else who will temporarily hold our shadow in escrow, relieving us, however briefly, from the dread realization of not only our own culpability in the world's problems, but how our seeming 'personal issues' drive all of the world's ills.

Although our hatreds may give us pre-packaged meaning, they will never give us 'meaningfulness.' Without adequate examination, our hatreds' meaning-frameworks lead us to the precipice of meaninglessness, unprepared for the liberation and responsibility this encounter demands. Nevertheless, even in the shattered remains of a materialist work bereft of any significance, this emptiness calls us to awaken to the moment, to the pervasive, sustaining reality of the journey unfolding.

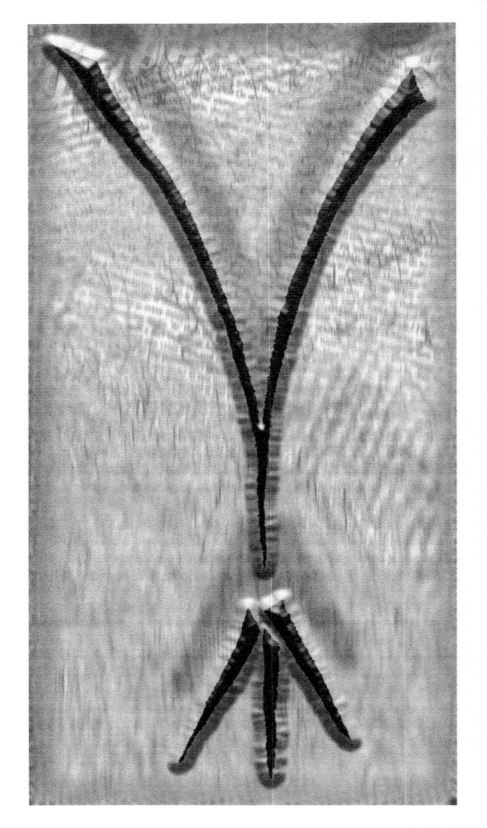

31
Meaninglessness
The Sixth Void

The world is, unto itself, purposeless and completely devoid of any inherent meaning.

Have a nice day!

Come on, though, you all knew this one, right? You understood that you had to come up with a completely bizarre rats' nest of implausible, make-believe suppositions that became increasingly experience-distant in order to give the world a meaning unto itself, right? *Right?*

It just feels different when you start dissociating into 'spirituality' or 'materiality' or whatever other elephantine scatology you use to try and bankrupt the moment. That whole distant ache of angst that tells you, 'whoa, I feel wrong in such a deep way that I don't think I know what "right" feels like anymore.' That's the same sensation that tells devotees of the imagination of magic that they had best chase after some supernatural explanation, get another initiatory degree in the hierarchy of *The Sublime Order of the Goat-worshipping-Templars*, or engage in another bracing spate of 'chemognosis' for this life to work for just a little bit longer.

That's cool. Magicians are no different from everyone else in this regard. Most people change relationships, jobs, location, hair color, or whatever else helps them carry on. As noted in the story above, probably the best way to avoid the meaninglessness of this world is to be outraged. Hence, many people feel deep hatred for some political alignment or the other and blame 'them' for everything that is wrong with the world. This hatred provides focus, purpose, and freeze-dried meaning. But observe carefully the depression that sets in about a year after their plucky alternative candidate takes office. Frankly, in this way, the media unwittingly serves a very fundamental existential purpose: it supplies a steady flow of items that reassure us that, even (or especially) when things don't go the way we want them to, the world still operates within defined meaningful parameters, most of which we can do nothing about. So sit back, and enjoy your righteous indignation!

It works, you know. The problem is that we're always left with that nagging distant feeling. And the alternative—abandoning the whole construction of inherent meaning—takes an awful lot of getting used to.

This introduction of the idea of meaninglessness is one of two places where listeners tend to give up on discussions of existentialism—the other being 'death.' Most people seem to think that existentialism is speaking to some form of what this text has called 'empty nihilism.' Empty nihilism is a form of ineffectual abdication from the responsibility for meaning-making in our lives. Existentialists most definitely do *not* advocate for this resignation. True existentialism places the responsibility for our lives firmly in our own laps, whether we accept it or not. Those who accuse existentialists of empty nihilism are still stuck in the things-as-meaningful mindset that cowers in terror at the inherent meaninglessness of 'things.' This text gently extends existential ideology to a type of 'mystical nihilism' in which we realize that the various passing meanings of the moment are the threads of a greater fabric of our unfolding stories. Mystical nihilism sees all meanings as fictional, but all meaning-making as fundamental acts of the *homo imginalis*.

We all want there to be a point to life—a goal, a telos. But, the idea of a linear endpoint to life enslaves existence to an endless con built on pre-packaged *teloi*, whether they be success, redemption, enlightenment, box seats, or whatever.

The sad truth of it is that experience does not reveal meaning. Experience is the making of meaning itself. As such, genuine experience is intolerable to most people. Even though we are each responsible for making meaning in our lives, because of the popularity of 'external' meaning, we don't know what our own meaning would look or feel like. That sidelong glance that is necessary in order to see the shape of life, rather than its seeming contents, goes against a thing-based world and its attendant comfort of certainties.

To put it more bluntly: each of us is always already making the very meaning that we seek in the world. Even when we adopt the pre-packaged meanings of others, this is still our own act of taking up that meaning. In order to awaken to this imaginal level, we must transcend those of our philosophies that begin with *things* and move to explanations that begin with *how we see*.

Epistemology: The Regent of All Knowing

How we know is more important than *what* we know. To put it in a high-flown metaphor, epistemology is the regent of all sciences and philosophy. Epistemology is that mad science that informs us that where a door leads depends on what key you put in the lock. Thus, different questions yield different answers—and different sorts of questions yield different sorts of answers.

Without question, hermeneutics has its value. As the study and practice of interpretation in which what you see depends on where you stand, the pursuit of hermeneutics can lay bare the shifting perspectives that bedevil us in even the simplest of interpersonal transactions. However, stand wherever they might, hermeneuts cannot see epistemology, because epistemology is the unconscious of hermeneutics—the ocean upon which it floats.

Epistemologists know that you will always prove your assumptions, because in your very way of knowing you embed the means of confirming your assumptions. Thus, not only is the answer usually in the question, the answer is in *how* we ask the question. 'Things' are a product of a thing-assuming, thing-seeking epistemology otherwise known as 'materialism.' But similar accusations can be leveled at all the other forms of literalism.

A decent grasp of epistemology, if only intuitively, can get you far in life. Sad to say, but in most cases, especially in academia, the seemingly brightest people are those who figure out how to give others that for which they are asking. Unencumbered by ideas of 'the truth,' these geniuses simply listen to the question and figure out what *sort* of answer would fit nicely into the awkward silence.

Truth can only be contextual in the small sense and structural in the larger. That is to say, 'answers' are always specific and particular. You can never make anything clearer with details that are more abstract, because context itself is the only specificity. Universal precepts are useless if they do not draw you back into the moment itself. Within the moment is the only place in which we can determine our orientation, and orientation defines status within context. Otherwise, we are just blathering about the hypotheticals that comfortingly distract us from the discomforting uncertainties of life as lived. To put it differently, the abstractions of your intentions and aspirations can easily blind you to what you are actually doing right now. If you want something more like a 'solution' instead of an 'answer' you will have to dive into your story in all of its specificity. You will have to resort to Method X. Method X grows from an epistemological awareness that refuses to leave immediacy.

When you are in the tightest fix, when nothing makes sense, stop and ask, '*how* do I know this?' But do not take the route of the skeptic's call for better evidence, or the spiritualist's escape to metaphysics. Ask the epistemologist's question: how is it that I have come to such a stance that I know what I know in such a way as to know that these circumstances are, supposedly 'in fact,' my circumstances? Your liberation depends on your asking these questions habitually. It is in the *knowing*, not that which is known, that we find the means of our liberation.

Regarding Oracular Consciousness[†]

Within the imagination of magic, the divinatory arts occupy an ambiguous yet central position. Their place is ambiguous because self-declared mages are trying to discern the future and, simultaneously, to change it. For many people who do

[†] For the attitudes that inform this section, I owe a deep debt of gratitude to Dianne Skafte for her incredibly insightful works on 'Oracular Consciousness.'

not align themselves with 'magic' per se, a trip to a fortuneteller is a time tested and relatively safe venture into this territory. Of course, it is best that these palm readers, Tarot interpreters, and psychics be somehow out of the way, whether at a carnival, a rural cabin, or even a second-floor apartment just above the comfortable familiarity of a thoroughfare. We need to venture at least a step or two beyond our daily trances to allow for the sidelong glance at life-as-we-know-it that these modern oracles provide.

Divination, scrying, and other 'mantic arts' are marvelous ways to temporarily convince yourself that you don't know the answer to most of your life's questions—and simultaneously *do*. We frankly don't want to have the kind of awareness it would take to already know these answers, so we make choices that obscure this oracular consciousness, but offer us day-to-day answers to smaller questions.

Is it any accident that so many divinatory systems are simultaneously cosmologies (i.e., alphabets of desire)? As noted in Volume One, the Tarot links with the Western Qabalah's Tree of Life diagram. The I Ching has a rich Taoist and Confucian worldview behind it. But even the less elaborate divinatory systems bring their own shift in consciousness. That our palms could reveal our fate speaks to our alienation from our storied flesh in such a way that only others can read our own True Grimoire. At their heart, whether or not the psychic readers or the querents appreciate it, all inquiries that abandon the 'givens' and 'knowns' of our daily lives will stand upon and bring us closer to the structure of the moment.

'I' am usually part of whatever problem I face in life. So too is how 'I' 'know'—the epistemology that, at each moment, reveals and conceals. Thus, asking yourself in a day-to-day sense to come up with the answers to vital questions often proves futile. Only no-one, not 'I,' will have access to a different way of knowing, an alien epistemology, an imaginal epistemology. Therefore, we must dive into the waters of oracular ritual and imagination, an indigenous tongue of no-one.

The tools of divination temporarily bridge the false dyads of inside/outside, matter/spirit, and a host of other silliness (i.e., 'binding fictions'). Thus, neither 'I' nor the cards, bones, twigs, numbers, or snips of text have the answer; but the 'between' does. Divination is, after all, an experience and a process, not an answer. To be clearer, divination does not so much discern the truth, but liberates us to our responsibility for meaning-making by offering us an elaborate ritual in which we can surreptitiously exercise this birthright.

Oracles speak the language of Dreams. When we enter into divinatory or oracular space, we enter the dream that informs 'seeming.' The ancients surrounded themselves in oracular trappings. These temples, street peddler carts, and dark alleys kept this mantic frontier of epistemology closer at hand than today's materiality allows. Still, with rituals as common as checking a newspaper horoscope, reading a fortune cookie, or breaking a wishbone, we maintain a furtive contact with the Fates.

One ancient form of mantic technology is augury. Classically, this practice involved observing the flight and behavior of birds. One could easily move to clouds, fires, or streams of water as alternative foci. The point is to move the observer into a relaxation of the habits of self-identification and into the oracular stance.

As an aside, I have seen a few brujas who performed something like cineromancy (i.e., divination by ashes) with the accumulated remains of a cigarette that were never flicked away. The smoker was the querent and the question had to be relevant to him or her. The bruja then viewed the patterns within the column of ash for letters, symbols, and paths. I particularly liked the practice for several reasons: many people already use smoke breaks as a time to dwell on the questions that linger; the 'smoker's gaze' can be quite oracular; and many traditions consider tobacco a sacred plant.

Another form of divination that has proved tenacious over the centuries is bibliomancy. Sometimes querents use an actual bible, but any text will do. This procedure involves closing one's eyes, holding the text, either clearing one's mind or imagining the question, then riffling through the pages until a page seems 'right,' and finally either pointing to a passage or having a formula for the paragraph and sentence to which one should hearken. I think bibliomancy's popularity owes itself in part to its metaphoric power. In a way, all oracles are bibliomancy, since all of life is text. Cultivating the bibliomantic, oracular gaze within these strips of phrase and sheets of scribble that form the snap-shot palimpsest of our experiences gives mythopoeia its due. All oracles are, after all, poets. Even the ineffable, whether divine, sublime, or both, must stand in contrast to language — the effable. What is beyond language is the frontier of the text of our lives, limiting and defining. Our in-texted-ness concurrently isolates us from and points to the voids surrounding and indicting our fictions.

Building on this constant presence of meaning-threads, we encounter one of the most telling of oracular practices. It is cocktail party divination: the *kladon*. The kladon is a procedure by which a piece of conversation, language, text, or imagery suddenly catches a querent's attention, without him or her having consciously tried to enter into a divinatory transaction. The unsuspecting questioner, pursuing the uncanny snippet, then investigates the source a bit more deeply. Finally, he or she must decide whether to accept the oracle. In ancient Greece, you needed to declare openly whether or not to accept the oracle that had emerged. This could be as simple as the process of raising your arms to Olympus and declaring, 'I accept the kladon!'

A kladon is inseparable from the idea of Kairos. A kladon pulls us out of our complacency and demands that we, however temporarily, wake up to the moment. These seemingly happenstance coincidences remind us that, although the world itself will never yield inherent meaning, we suffer from an overabundance of meaning in our *life as lived*. Experience is meaning-making in the thick of the tangled ropes of all the fictions that make up our lives.

Although classically drawn from some form of overheard conversation, today, kladons can be billboards, song lyrics, text messages, and any other scraps of meaning convergences. Whether a phrase stuck in our head or an image that receives an extended gaze, these seeming happenstances actually hold disowned shards of our experience in sizzling escrow, yearning for us to claim more fully the wholeness of the moment. Through the various partial fictions that we hold to defend us against the voids, we are constantly living out these incomplete forms. Our missing pieces scream out with every second, but the very fictions that leave us so bereft also deafen us to our own cries. Nevertheless, the shape of the unfolding moment brings us endlessly into confrontation with the voids. This yields a stream of 'inconsistent' information that stands out as these sorts of uncanny events. The kladon reminds us that answers emerge all around us; but we must decide whether we accept these answers, whether we seize the Kairos by the forelocks.

Then again, if you believe there is a 'right' answer to life's questions and your job is merely to discern the meaning, I can't imagine why you have persisted so far in this book. The contrast between our delusions and the structural truth of the voids creates Derridian *différance*, vital interstitial spaces of contrast that save us from the homogenous hegemony of extra-personal Meaning. Each inconsistency, each break in the tyrannical Mass Narrative is an opportunity, an invitation to meaning-making.

Perhaps the divinatory discipline that contains the best warning is haruspicy or extispicy. This famous practice, which has gone by many names, involves the observation of the entrails of a vivisected animal. A powerful lesson lies here: more often than not, our quest for knowledge kills the vitality of the moment. Examine enough, analyze and vivisect, and you encounter the lifeless fictions of 'facts.' Better to drift with dreams and speak their liberating argot than sink to certainties' mortifying termini. Ultimately, only a world that is meaningless can liberate us to make meaning in our lives. Rather than inspect the rotting corpses of disanimated matter, it is our own life's blood and even our very names that ring with a hunger to lay claim to our narrative authority.

Application 9
Your Name

When entering into the imagination of magic, it is common for practitioners to take on a magical name of some sort. (This is just as common with conversion to or rites of passage within religious communities.) There's a wide range of means used to create these names. Some are a reflection of aspirations, others come from a defining moment, still others are wordplay based on magical mottos—much as Niel Estes' name came from *nihil veritas est*. Unfortunately, as personal as these names may be, many magical types seem stuck in the hackneyed argot of fantasy and gothic romance novels with creations such as 'Lady Trifenia Treesilver,' 'Lord Darkling Sanguinius,' and 'Sheepjuggler the Oathwelder.' (Which would be fine if these people *lived* in those realms; but I worry that these overblown monikers simply help them to perpetually feel disappointed that their ears aren't quite pointy enough to pass for an elf.)

In addition to taking on magical mottos and names, many mages create some sort of sigil to represent their magical selves and aspirations. This is all well and good when the mage in question is still trying to stoke the fires of those non-mundane parts of themselves that they partition off from day-to-day life. Of course, in the process, the rest of the mage becomes increasingly banal. This particular disconnect can continue forever or until mages finally reach a crisis in which they realize that they haven't done a damned thing about their life but have succeeded in becoming the high priest(ess) of a bunch of other maladjusted messes—or garnering a daunting accumulation of experience points in an MMORPG.

The practice of taking on a special name for a particular purpose stands on the inherent power of naming—a God-like power granted to Adam in Genesis—and to our names themselves. Myths, fables, and folklore are rich in examples of the power of a name to control various demons, bogans, and other creatures from beyond. Even wizards are apparently subject to such strictures, as Jim Butcher's mage-noir hero, Harry Dresden, reminds us by never giving away all his names with their proper pronunciation and inflection.

To learn from these mythic lessons, we need to think once more about the audacious power of language. This ability to call something—to both refer to it and to cause it to come forth—gives us a magical command of the imagination. Is it any accident that the imagination of magic is so entwined with language?

The names of creatures, the proper words of control, the carefully inscribed runes and sigils—all speak to this fundamental vector of being. 'Civilization' occurs, in large part, because of language. So too does consciousness. As mentioned above, consciousness is always 'consciousness-of' and is, therefore, always mediated by language. As this text has repeatedly presented, language becomes about still more language, rather than a return to the experience to which it promises to refer. Thus, what can we say about our own names, the first and most direct way in which we are called?

Consider that powerful sigilization of magical will: your day-to-day signature. For many, it is a bizarre piece of scrawl little resembling the letters that fed into it. Signatures are supposedly unique and, thus, broad swathes of society center on this uniqueness—contracts, checks, and a host of other commitments rely on this most personal of scribbles.

Ever stared at yours?

Try it. Look at it: each stroke, each loop, each chip of ink. Keep staring until you aren't sure what you are looking at. What does this gateway to byss reveal to, and about, 'you'?

Record your results carefully.

When I was little, perhaps starting at the age of three or so, I remember occasionally hearing my name when no one had called me. I soon realized that the voices that called me had a different quality than any I could hear around me. Eventually, perhaps when I was four or five, I had several episodes where I heard several overlapping voices calling my name quietly, pleasantly even, but insistently. With each repetition of my name, I felt a slight surge in my head—not painful, but distinct. As the voices persisted, I started to see, in my mind, silhouettes in black and dark purple, against a background nearly as dark. Each dark form, I realized, was calling out to me in a voice that was haunting, to be sure, but not frightening. Once I reached grade school, I cannot remember this happening ever again.

Later, as I took various developmental psychology classes, I wondered what this experience might have been about. I had no hallucinations, or any other psychotic symptoms through the rest of my youth and, thus, I have to assume this was a relatively 'normal' event, even if my childhood was not itself entirely normal. What it has led me to wonder is how a child comes to associate a certain combination of sounds with the need to turn his or her attention toward the call's source. Moreover, how does that response eventually become part of the ground for our sense of self?

Self-identification is essential, yet it remains an inscrutable mystery to us all. We simply cannot see through this occluded glass. But our own names become so common as to veil even their referential valence and power.

In more fanciful moments, I like to imagine that those voices were other-worldly and fey creatures calling me to run away to their realms. Perhaps they succeeded and I am merely a changeling, given these memories to hide my real origins? But, with a little examination, I recognize that my personality matches my origins far too well for that to be true. Thus, I am left with this strange memory. Even today, I can feel my hair stand on end if I call up the memory of just that particular inflection of those voices calling a name that had only just become the magic ensigilization of all that was to become me.

How do we tap into this strange force, this nominative power? Perhaps our pin numbers are more intimate analogs of our selves than any name. Today, many of us use alternate names on social networking sites, themselves playing out completely new shifting demarcations of public and private. So, too, do our videogame avatars have elaborate lives of their own. Yet most of us still turn when we hear our birth names called.

Once you have a sense of your signature as sigil, see if you can discern the ways in which people speak your name. With the last vestiges of strict rules of title and manner of address rapidly fading, our given names are not as intimate as they perhaps once were. Nevertheless, our parents do not address us the same way our co-workers, friends, or children may. As an extension of Volume One's Application 3 examination of 'your many selves,' ask yourself these questions: What are the various names by which people address me? How do I feel when a form of my name comes from someone who I would prefer not use it? Or in a tone I prefer not to hear? What happens when a soon-to-be lover first uses my name with that pulse quickening tone for which I will come to yearn?

Where do you feel these names in your body? We embody our identities and, thus, it is not surprising that many people have unique bodily reactions to being called. When you hear someone else with your name, what do you assume about them? When people look at you, do they have a consistent guess for what your name would be? (I am impressed by the number of people who have assumed or guessed my name to be 'David.')

A firm grasp of the various threads, which extend from this early childhood achievement of self-identification, may yield a much greater power to claim the technology by which we shift, refine, or recreate who we are.

Part 7
Awaking to the Dream

This nature of ours is the source of all dharmas, all thoughts, even all objects. But we turn this cornucopia of magic into a quagmire of delusion when we separate ourselves from dharmas and thoughts and objects, and dharmas from dharmas, and thoughts from thoughts, and objects from objects. Thus, Hui-neng urges us to take refuge in this triple-bodied nature of ours and in the ten thousand realities that arise from it and that lead us back to our nature because they are our nature.

Red Pine (2006)
The Platform Sutra: The Zen Teaching of Hui-Neng

Armchair psychoanalysts always search for one defining moment in the childhood of newsmakers or historical figures by which they can explain all the trials and triumphs of that person's life. Frankly, we all grunt a satisfied, 'aha!' when we hear of that particular trauma at age seven, or of the death of a parent, or of some other formative challenge the child overcame, such as polio, or pleurisy, or the loss of a limb.

Film, television, and literature bank on this conceit. Many of us can tolerate clunky storytelling and shallow characters so long as we slowly approach that one salient detail, that crucial moment, the revelation of which, just at the story's climax, provides us with a satisfying catharsis.

Any psychotherapist worth his or her salt knows that this idea is ridiculous in the extreme. Holding onto this idea is actually dangerous for a mental health professional. They can find themselves undertaking what I bemoan to future therapists as 'archeological expeditions' or 'fishing trips.' The danger is that we miss the life that the patient lives right now. The past can so easily occlude the present. This is not to say that clients don't sincerely believe that some single event defines them. Many do. Moreover, one particular moment may poignantly sum up a whole series of events in such a way that only this snapshot is necessary to convey the whole story. But, in the end, no single episode makes us who we are.

Nevertheless, we are storied creatures. Images, which create the centers of gravity for the meaning we make in our lives, lend themselves to emblematic representations. And so it is that I come back to a particular ritual my father and I developed so early in my life that I cannot remember its origins.

I am six or seven. It should be past my bedtime, but I am allowed to stay up to see Dad come home. I sit five steps up the stairs facing the foyer in order to be at eye level with him. Dad has spent another evening with the Atlantean Brotherhood (AB), a group that centers on the psychic Francis T. Lazarus. Lazarus, my father carefully explains, makes himself available in deep trance for the transmissions of 'the Porticans.' These spirits use this name because they sit on the Portico of the Godhead. Thus, the information they impart is of the highest quality.

Dad has filled the pages of another yellow legal pad with information from this evening's trance session. He uses a blue erasable pen, which leaves a waxy ink easily smudged by my father's left-handed writing. Perhaps once on every page, I can see the blurred smear where he has erased and overwritten a different term in his precise and unslanted cursive. The Porticans speak to a wide range of subjects. Reincarnation, Atlantis (and its Pacific precursors, Mu and Lemuria), vitamins, healing, and the schematics of the after-life are just a few of the topics they present.

A few years ago, Dad began the tradition of reviewing his notes with me listening. I sit on my step as soon as I hear the garage door open and, once he has hung up his coat, he flips through the pages, still standing in the entranceway. For him, this information is vital, and his passionate exhortations often over-whelm me. When he hits upon a particular piece of information that he sees as crucial, it can be like staring into a laser. The details sear into me with a mythic power—a secret cosmology I am far too young to reject with any kind of incre-dulity. Other children have Santa Claus, the Easter Bunny, and fairy tales that they will outgrow, or at least come to understand with a nuanced wisdom. I am offered no wink, no 'as-if' to these stories—these are Divine Truths.

These revelations provide proof for my father that the world and its reli-gions are mistaken—these earthly institutions have corrupted the fundamental messages once contained in the Bible and in other ancient sources. It will be well over a decade before I discover that all these verities are standard New Age and spiritualist cant, warmed over from Theosophy and the New Thought move-ment. The basic cosmology is a classic New Age neo-Gnostic gloss: once pure spirits that co-created along with the Godhead fell into their own creations, becoming entrapped in gross matter. Reincarnation is, hence, a lamentable means of trying to purify the soul of this erroneous prison. The Fall happened in a series of ever-more terrestrial Golden Age civilizations that descended into greater darkness due to their own hubris.

I have tried to express to my Sunday School teacher how Jesus actually was talking about reincarnation in one of the Bible stories she shares (with the help of felt cutouts). My spiritualist evangelism is poorly received. Thus, I know that the sort of truth my father is sharing is best not discussed with everyone, at least not by a precocious second grader. In contrast to being a Lutheran, which needs no explanation in the Midwest, I have no name for the facts—not 'beliefs'—my father reveals. These and other friction points with 'the rest of the world' give me some sense that something isn't quite right with these super-natural insights, but I am too young to sort through my feelings and untangle the situation.

Misgivings aside, I enjoy these times with Dad. These are not like the often-uncomfortable dining room rants where my father subjects some unsuspecting guest to an indoctrination session. As I sit on my step, he is sometimes receptive to my questions and occasional observations—there is a pleasant parent/child enmeshment as he feels the pride of passing on something unique and valuable to his son.

In a progression going against classic initiatory imagery, I will gradually move down the steps over the next several years, as I grow taller. But the tradition endures until my teen years when my father leaves the group, believing the messages of the Porticans have become 'colored' by Lazarus's own personal material.

Today, when I eventually get around to explaining this part of my background to friends, I usually get some form of an uninflected 'oh...' or 'ah.' My contentiousness around spiritual matters suddenly comes into sharper focus. As noted in the introduction to this volume, because of these early experiences, I can never have the sort of epiphanic conversion or awakening so many people experience when they encounter alternative, New Age, or spiritual beliefs. The metaphysical metaphors that, for others, open up possibilities and give voice to unexpressed impulses and intuitions ring hollow and grating to me.

When I encountered the likes of Richard Bach or Mary Baker Eddy in my teens, they didn't so much 'blow my mind' as reassure me that someone else held the same sort of strange beliefs with which I was being raised—and with which I was, underneath it all, struggling. It wasn't until, at the age of 14, when I read Benjamin Hoff's *The Tao of Pooh* (1982), that my misgivings became partially conscious. In Hoff's presentation of Taoism, he brings everything back down to how we live our lives each day. In deceptively approachable presentations—who could get hung up on a conversation between Pooh and Piglet, after all?—he makes 'ideas' just another aspect of how we live, the things that go on in our heads while we go about acting in what we think or hope is a commensurate fashion.

Suddenly, I was posed with a problem. As obvious as it seems to say, I had never allowed myself to consider the potential disconnection between ideas and action—not just hypocrisy, an idea with which I was painfully familiar, but the concept that holding a particular idea could engender actions quite different to those that the idea had originally purported. The implications of Hoff's observations proved to have a long burn for me.

Lee Patrick, starring as Sam Spade's Girl Friday, Effie Perrine, says, 'Look at me, Sam. You worry me. You always think you know what you're doing, but you're too slick for your own good. Some day you're going to find out.' Pat and I both smile broadly and exhale plumes of smoke from our respective couches. The room is thick with the haze of the unfiltered cigarettes we have chosen especially for this viewing. The late afternoon sun cuts through the broad-lathed louvers and creates planes of light and shadow in the smog that renders the room as black and white as the *Maltese Falcon* (1941) playing on the VCR.

I'm 18, on summer break after my first year of college. Pat Capitan has invited me over to enjoy some film noir. We take a break halfway through and I make my way to the bathroom. On top of his refrigerator is a pharmacopeia of epic proportions. Pat was diagnosed with schizophrenia and dropped out of college long before I met him when I was in junior high. The meds have made him put on considerable bulk, which only makes his shaved head and stubble goatee all the more intimidating, but ultimately he is a teddy bear of a guy.

After the film finishes and we adequately extol its virtues, we get to talking a bit about reality. Having experienced dramatic psychotic breaks, Pat is less than flexible about the issue. His argument comes down to a fundamental distinction, which he explains with a corny Bogart accent.

'You can shee things all shorts of ways; but when you shtarts to shee things that nobody elshe is sheein', that ain't reality. Shee?'

I tell him that I don't believe that there is anything outside the window — passing on an aphorism from the Porticans. Pat blinks at me several times. To date, I have been levelheaded enough around him that this declaration truly floors him.

'You're telling me that you don't believe there are cars and buses and people and shit going up and down that street out there?!'

'Prove it,' I respond.

He stands up from the couch and demonstratively bulges his eyes to indicate what he sees through the window behind me.

'Well you see, you just changed the situation. *Now* there are,' I state.

Pat sighs, 'And people say I'm the crazy one.'

I take this moment to heart. A recovering schizophrenic has just questioned my sanity. Several years before this, a biology instructor pulled me aside, worried at my somewhat confrontational attitude toward the natural sciences. He didn't understand that it was only because I liked and respected him that I was trying to test my mettle against him. I pulled the same line about there being nothing outside the window and he incredulously asked, 'you don't *really* mean that, do you?'

The biology teacher's exasperation took me aback and I regrouped, equivocating, 'not really, but it helps me think more clearly,' (whatever the hell that was supposed to mean).

Back in the chiaroscuro haze with Pat, I consider the two episodes and decide that my theories need a bit of refinement.

Because I only really had my father to speak to about these ideas, and he was mostly interested in asserting their facticity and reality, I struggled to understand what to do with them. My mother and brother maintained their Protestant convictions, but I was offered no such clear option. My Christian piety, these New Age certainties, and the archaic mystique of Western esotericism battled out their incompatibility throughout my teens. I was oblivious to the possibility that this conflict expressed my personal misgivings, struggles, and shame. The supposed metaphysical priority of these various 'truths' blinded me. Although I used my realization from Hoff of the ideas/actions-reciprocal-relationship to criticize others, I could not bring it to bear on my own problems.

My father quoted one particular Portican declaration more than any other: 'All cures must be achieved first in the spiritual.' My father, to this day, says this with a hoarse conviction sometimes bordering on tears. It resonates so power-fully for him. For my father, this sentiment is concrete and practical. It translates into the need for visualization, laying on of hands, guided imagery, and, for a time, distance healings by the psychic, Lazarus. My father once acknowledged that the 'spiritual' *might* involve a personal journey or transformation, but the psychological nature of this explanation made him mutteringly uncomfortable.

As with so much of life, the way I see it, the ultimate challenge is really, 'so what?!' Perhaps it speaks to an overly psychotherapeutic bias, but what I want to know is if a person is any less of an asshole, not whether they're going to live to be 120. Although people may become free of disease, genuine *healing* is exceed-ingly rare. Healing involves realizations that change how we live. This focus on the human capacity to change led me to practice psychotherapy and eventually to become a teacher. What I realize, reflecting on both practices, is that I can reveal all the secrets of life and the universe, as I know them, and they will have no effect on my patients or students. This is not so much because my audience is 'resistant,' 'unready,' 'benighted,' or 'asleep'; but because the 'secrets', as I reveal them, are only *my* discoveries as I made them. The real secrets must be lived and inscribed in the True Grimoire of our flesh. Real secrets, genuine mysteries, must be lived.

When I am eight or so, having moved down to the fourth step of my home's staircase, my father gives me my own erasable pen. However, it is not the robin blue capped version like his, but a newer white clickable style. I am disappointed. It isn't what I want. I want one like his, *exactly* like his. In some sort of Oedipal fantasy, I want to possess this ritual tool—to be part of this process—to own something of the power I see him holding. Perhaps I want a late-in-coming transitional object. Sadly, my distant sense that my father's spiritual revelations are not satisfying to me further fuel this desire. In fact, although I don't realize it, these 'truths' are a psychic irritant which drive me hopelessly in search of some means of integrating them into my muddled psychotheocosmology. This dissatisfaction manifests itself not in resistance, but in an overzealous pursuit of these ideas in an apotheotic quest to see them to their end. But even at this early age, the quest is not going so well. I cannot adequately effect the conviction, the certainty, that I see so powerfully etched on my father's face. In an effort to bolster my faltering faith, I want the symbol, the empowerment. I want that erasable pen.

Children do not merely imitate their parents, although they surely do that. Children also embody the unconscious of their parents, the uncontainable, undesirable, unspeakable, and unresolved. Children can become the ghosts of their parents—haunting the world and attempting to tend to the 'unfinished business' left in the wake of their parents' incomplete lives. Even the best of parents leave these fractured legacies.

Parents say a whole lot of asinine things to their children and children take it all in trying to make a cohesive whole picture—trying to maintain a consistency where none exists, but driven nonetheless. My childhood may have been a bit stranger than some, but more than anything I am grateful for the curious level of diversity and contrast my parents offered me, sometimes quite by accident, but often by design. The gaps, juxtapositions, and disparities have not only driven me, but also offered eyes with which to see what many others don't, or won't.

In the end, you really can't erase pen, can you? At best you can smear and fade the waxy ink. The result is like life, a palimpsest, an overlay of image upon image. We so dearly want to go back, to perfect, refine, and 'get it right.' We want to pick and choose what stories are told, what parts are important. We desperately struggle to separate and edit our lives, rather than address them whole sheet. But the unfolding moment is always in motion and leaves us no opportunity to undo—only a chance to move on and make better choices.

Maybe I wanted that erasable pen so much because I wanted to be able to change things I had done? Perhaps, as a magical tool, it is part of an effort to deny the famous lines from the *Rubiyat* of Omar Kayyam:

> The Moving Finger writes; and, having writ,
> Moves on: nor all your Piety nor Wit
> Shall lure it back to cancel half a Line,
> Nor all your Tears wash out a Word of it

Nevertheless, I think what I really wanted was some magical implement to grant me the zealous certainty of belief with which my childhood eyes saw my father burning. Even then, I knew these ideas, these supernatural explanations didn't quite work, but maybe that pen was the answer. Those ideas were larger than life—and that was the problem. In the end, what I needed were ideas neither small and banal nor overblown and paranormal. For me, the quest has been to find life-sized ideas that cannily speak to me.

By sixth grade, my previously miserable academic record rapidly improved, thanks, in large part, to a teacher who took me under his wing and encouraged my budding skills as a writer. Suddenly, the power of the pen was no longer a hunger for a totemic fetish but an actual power to create. I filled notepad after notepad with my stumbling efforts. I imitated. I innovated. I created twist endings that would have made Rod Serling roll his eyes.

Nonetheless, regardless of the product, I knew that this was what I wanted to do. There was something about the architecture of a sentence, the flow of images and ideas, and the ability to play with expectation that offered me something unlike any previous experience. Ironically, I had no language for it. I realized that writing allowed me to escape the narrow poverty of certainty and explore the rich topography of possibility.

Thus, as I think back on my father's erasable pen, I know that, at six or seven, I had no sense of 'meta-fiction,' 'intertextuality,' or 'narrative authority,' but perhaps that pen, clearly capable of creating histories, theologies, and cosmologies, called to me with the possibility of something far more precious than spiritual truths: a path of liberation.

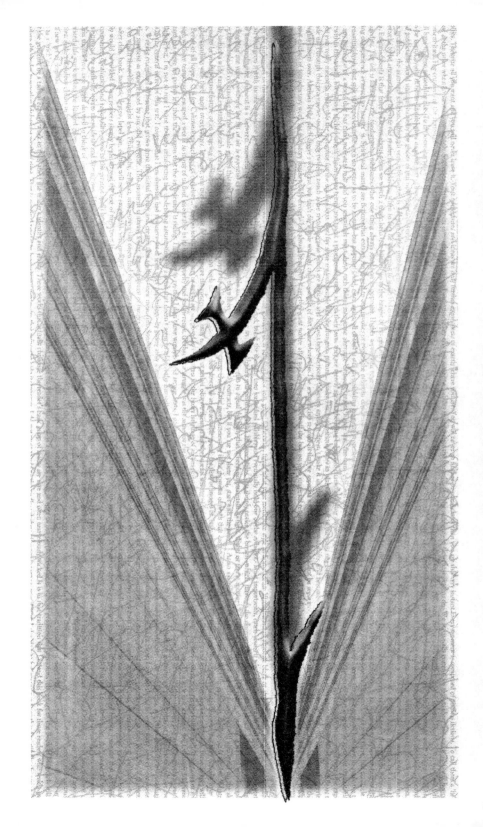

34
Freedom and Responsibility
The Seventh Void

In each unfolding moment, we define existence by the choices we make in relationship to our lived world. Again, various prepackaged 'causalities' may attempt to protect us from the terror of complete responsibility for our lives. Of course, a narrow sense of 'consequences' might emerge from our choices. Moreover, other people react to our decisions and we often do not achieve our imagined ends. Nevertheless, claiming our freedom and ferreting out the specters of 'inevitability,' 'restriction,' and the myriad ways we hand to others responsibility for our feelings, actions, thoughts, or choices is an ongoing struggle. Nonetheless, whether we simply claim our freedom or exercise it to its fullest, we are still accountable to the reality of each moment.

Responsibility is not about 'culpability.' Responsibility centers on the process of acknowledging the world in which we find ourselves. Etymologically, the word, in this sense, is about *responding to life as it is*, rather than the various limited perspectives that entrapping fictions may offer us. Only with some apprehension of life-as-lived can we actually be free to act, rather than react. Only through properly calibrated responsiveness can we be our own most unfolding selves, rather than playing prescribed roles. Thus, freedom and responsibility inexorably form the foundation of all authentic choice and action.

Regarding Choice and Agency

We are always exercising our freedom of choice—and thus responsibility—whether we claim it or not. Regardless of whether we feel forced, or are unclear on the options, or think ourselves to have been deceived, we still make choices with which we must live. Interestingly, more often than not, we willfully choose to retreat into scenarios in which we feel as though we have more abundant and easier choices than we actually do: vanilla or pistachio, party A or party B, coffee or tea. These illusions of choice are far more common than the conscious exercise of genuine agency, standing as it does on an unblinking acceptance of life's limitations. Sadly, regardless of how aware of our choosing we are, we are still responsible for our choices and the world in which we make them (even if it really *is* all your mother's fault...).

In the same way, if we cobble together enough affectations, we imagine that our personalities are strong enough to withstand their fundamentally fictional nature. Well, maybe just one more tattoo and an anachronistic hat will help. Our various eccentricities give us not only a (brittle) sense of self, but also make it seem as though we exercise more choice than 'conformists.' The mystique of the 'alternative' esthetic, favored by many enamored of the imagination of magic, promises to liberate us from the banality of conventionality and (this is the real magical thinking) liberate us from responsibility for the current state of the world. With enough piercings we can imagine that we are no longer part of the problem since the 'real people in power' would never allow us into their boardrooms looking like this.

Although our identities are always fictional, any convergence of experiences with which we identify still entails the freedom of choice and the contingent accountability for those choices. Unfortunately, since we typically construct our personalities to defend against a full realization of our lived world, we will inevitably struggle to *recognize* those choices. That is, we are always responsible for our lives, but we rarely have the necessary perspective and awareness to assert any degree of agency.

The process of liberating yourself toward increased agency is amongst the most complicated of journeys since so many technologies exist to convince you that you have greater agency, and thus different choices, than those you actually face. To say it a different way, why go looking for real choices when so many of us feel like we are drowning in too many (meaningless) choices?

Dependence? Independence? What's the difference? Liberation is far more elusive, subtle, and rare than simple pigeonholes. We all know 'bold individualists' who try to live by their own terms. Maybe you've had the bad luck to try to date one of them. Many adherents of Ayn Rand's brand of libertarian rhetoric think they can pick and choose that for which they are responsible. They believe they'll be able to be truly free by mowing over all those weaklings who don't know how to shove their way to the head of the line. Good for them! They're free from having to make the real, difficult choices since they just need to live life like a giant cliché!

Sadly, more often than not, bold individualism and rebellion both support those very structures they claim to strive to overcome or unseat. A defense always bespeaks and enforces that which it would resist. Genuine rebellion demands a vision beyond the definitions of the entrapping structure. The true anarchist (free from the archons) rebel must be an epistemological guerilla—or gorilla, for that matter.

Regarding Intention and Ethics

Identity will always be vulnerable to the deception of 'intention.' As noted in Volume One's brief conversation of the unhappy couple in Chapter 10, 'Undifferentiation' ('I didn't *mean* to hurt you.' 'But you *did* hurt me!'), too often, intention blinds us to what we actually do, and to that in which we participate. True ethics means a deconstructing and deepening of intention. Nearly everyone has good intentions. The true difficulties lie in assessing the effects of your choices, which often involves letting go of your intentions long enough to see actual consequences. Moreover, regardless of what we intended, we are still responsible for the actual, lived consequences of our choices. If we are to give up on the contrivances of responsibility-eschewing 'cause and effect,' then we have to admit that the actual consequences of our actions are all the things that happen during and after our actions.

There are no ends, only means. Becoming wedded to 'ends' corrupts. Then again, being rigid in one's *choice* of 'means' breeds blindness. The ethical ambiguity of every moment, tangled in intention, identification, and interpretation, leaves us with the moral paradoxes that make freedom so intolerable. This is why we love to moralize to others, blame others, legislate against others: it feels good to know that some other person, over there, is *wrong*. For that brief instant, we can feel relieved of our own complete responsibility for our lives.

If you don't want to play into that game, then don't worry about what the next yahoo is doing. You can trust everyone to play exactly their chosen role.

In the end—which is right now—there are no truths, no lies: only gradations of fictions with their contingent lived worlds. What fictions are you living?

Regarding Violence

In our ongoing quest to blame others for our own moral discomfort, we often look at certain individuals who commit intolerable acts of violence and find it feels (temporarily) good to hate them—like the Nazis in my Munich story. For just a little while, we can imagine that these assholes are the real problem with the world. Then our lives become mere exercises in getting on with life and trying to avoid these people and the disaster zones of pain and hate they leave behind. How blissful it is for us to blame others for our misfortune, to be the victim of 'those people,' and thus relieved of culpability, free from guilt, and absolved of the need to discern!

Unfortunately, these strategies have limited shelf lives. Every perpetrator of violence I have ever met has justified his or her actions with some degree of 'victimhood.' Truly living free from violence is no easy thing, and should this be your chosen path, more power to you! If you are genuine in your efforts and honest with yourself, I bet you would make a pretty good neighbor. I, myself, have struggled more to ferret out the why's and wherefores of violence itself—mostly in an effort to understand its pull on me (and many others if we are to take film ticket sales for splatter-fests and shoot-'em-ups as any indication of the state of the collective unconscious). One idea in particular keeps coming up for me: violence is a failure of the imagination. (I wrote this phrase before reading Alan Moore's brilliant *Promethea* in which he declares that war is a failure of the imagination, echoing the sentiments of Adrienne Rich.)

A lifetime of violence is a sign of a disease of the imagination: *imagopathy*. In studying serial killers while writing my dissertation, I coined this term and found three characteristics that point to an imaginal foundation for their sickness. 1) Rigid, repetitive, yet simultaneously unsatisfying fantasies; 2) A lack of empathy, a quality rooted in imagination; and 3) A rampant need to project intolerable feelings—usually 'victimhood'—onto others.

If we want a world in which violence is the exception and not the rule, we must consider how to cultivate the skills in our children that will lead them to creative solutions for their conflicts, rather than the insidious self-replicating legacy of violence. As countries like America strive to assert technological supremacy in the world, mathematics and science dominate curricula. Yet, in imagination we find the seedbed of all innovation, leadership, creativity, and compassion. Play, pretend, collaboration, and paradox all foster the growth of the imaginal core of experience: the *imaginatrix*—the organ of imagination according to Henry Corbin. It is not identity, not the self, nor some spiritual essence that we must foster. It is the capacity to imagine, the very essence of wonder and experience. As we are busy trying to make our children into someones, we might pause to consider whether they might need to practice being the sort of no-ones that can imagine a future for our bleak, bankrupt, and benighted world.

Ethics in the Imagination of Magic

Within the imagination of self-declared mages, witches, wiccans, pagans, and the like, labels and their definitions have tended to provide a fecund font of logorrhea. 'I'm not a wiccan, I'm a witch,' 'I'm not a witch, I'm a cunning man,' 'I'm not a pagan, I'm a heathen,' 'I'm not a sorcerer, I'm a High Magician,' and so forth. All of this strikes me as only slightly less silly, but far more useless than deciding whether you will play an elf, dwarf, or knight in your next nacho-cheese-drenched evening of RPGing.

Since the advent of Wicca in the 20th century, one particular piece of ethical imagination has played out in a variety of ways. Fundamentally, the distinction is between what others might label as 'good' and 'evil,' but which, within the imagination of magic, could never be quite so simple. Sometimes apologists use the words 'white' and 'black' to explain this distinction—which has inevitably led to 'grey' and 'green' to further nuance (or muddle) the discussion. In this systematization, 'white magic' deals with healing, light, goodness, growth, and may even extend to a sense of selflessness, and perhaps sacrifice. Thus, 'black magic' harms others or at least puts one's own advancement ahead of all others. Although I have heard this distinction used less as of late, its underlying naiveté remains prevalent well beyond the world of neo-pagans. Bound to a shallow interpretation of 'karma,' this explanation of 'magic' relies on overt and intentional acts of magic for its definition and rarely intersects with the lifestyle choices of the practitioners.

Some aristocratically-minded writers distinguish 'high' and 'low' magic. In this vision, 'low magic' centers on folk traditions and the accomplishment of terrestrial aims such as wealth, healing, or love. 'High Magic,' on the other hand, leaves behind such petty concerns and focuses exclusively on the enlightening practice of meditation, conversation with celestial creatures, and a general accumulation of arcane knowledge. It becomes easy to see the wholesale begging of the question, when one can only choose between 'pettiness' and 'irrelevance.' These labels originated out of a late Victorian neo-Romanticism in which magicians either were endowed with family trusts or could mooch off those that had them. These High Magicians could thus ignore the proletariat and their quaint custom of worrying about whence their next meal would come.

Other commentators begin to catch on to the inanity of these overly convenient labels when they explain that any sort of good/bad distinction simply cannot be made. These writers explain that such dichotomies are a holdover from Christian ethics, inappropriate in a practice styled as 'pre-Christian.' I find these arguments, though historically suspect, are at least worthy of further examination since so much of the imagination of magic is, in fact, a thinly veiled reworking of European Christian ritual and ethics.

Nevertheless, in the thick of all these distinctions, few labels have been as simultaneously provocative and confounding as the dichotomy of the 'right-hand-path'/'left-hand path' (RHP/LHP). Commentators appeal to Tibetan Buddhist and Hindu terms, writers cite Edwardian and Victorian fantasies of evil secret conspiracies entwining the Tree of Life, and moral relativists try to contrive some sort of 'internal' versus 'external' foci as the salient defining features. In the end, as best I can tell, the distinction in actual practice has more to do with fashion and aesthetics than ethics. Each camp defines the other to their advantage. Thus, exponents of the RHP explain that LHP practitioners are deluded slaves to unspeakable forces that entrap them in grossly physical thralls. LHP writers accuse RHP adherents of being afraid of their shadows.

In an effort to vex fans of both and neither of the camps, here are a few thoughts to consider. No act is neutral and all acts are magical. Every act is, thus, ethical in its own way. Growing from this foundation, it becomes increasingly difficult to define what is 'high' or 'low' magic, other than by some sort of aesthetic or socioeconomic judgment. Moreover, even distinctions between a meditative (internal) or action (external) focus for magic become tricky as well, except in the shallowest of descriptions, since meditation changes our lives, and, reciprocally, changes to our lives change our mentality. Therefore, all magic is 'results' magic, regardless of whether one labels it as such or whether one is cognizant of the results. (Academics and scientists who work in 'purely theoretical' areas or the 'basic sciences' might do well to consider this perspective.)

Far too often, magical groups, and the commentators thereof, have tried to distinguish traditions by what amounts purely to their choice of imagery. Groups that like sunshine and squirrels are in one camp and practitioners who have too many tentacles and horns are in another. Even descriptions that cut to a deeper level, to ideas of 'personal freedom', 'enlightenment', or 'reverence for the gods' still fall short of addressing the actual results these groups achieve.

Certainly, the question of 'true will' and 'harming none' come into this discussion as well. Crowley's ethical mandates for Wicca ('An' it harm none, do what thou wilt') and Thelema ('Do what thou wilt shall be the whole of the Law; Love is the Law Love under Will.') receive extensive lip service but scant examination. Has anyone *ever* 'harmed none'? Moreover, in their most sober moments, does anyone believe 'Will' is synonymous with 'whim'? In short, these statements are likely far better Zen koans than they are mandates, and attempting to distinguish the ethical stance of a group based on their cherished bromides is suspect at best.

This topic deserves far deeper, and far more tenacious investigation, but I will finish with one archetypal reverie. Solar worship is relatively prominent in the world of esotericists, occultists, and magicians. Many groups that would define themselves as 'White Light' or 'Right-Hand Path' orient themselves in a solar fashion—although they often balance this orientation with a certain lunar reverence. Death and rebirth, enlightenment, growth, freedom, and rationality are just a few of the attributes these new Freemasons can claim. I am inclined to agree that these descriptors apply well. Nevertheless, it may be either appropriate or ironic to note that the Sun itself has a shadow. Every time I hear a Solar Ode or view yet another Solar Phallic Symbol, in the background I see the unforgiving light of a nuclear blast. The apotheosis of the *Sol Invictus* (i.e., the 'Unconquered Sun') is the mushroom cloud, demented and inevitable off-spring of solar worship, shining on and ON and on. Bearing in mind that the Nazis did not succeed in detonating an atomic bomb, it is still worth noting that the Swastika is a Solar symbol.

The sun-worshipping hippies wanted to co-opt the sun with no shadow. The hope was to get all of the freedom and none of the responsibility. Today, our unbridled pursuit of technology and progress represents just such an immature and enslaving meta-fiction. The aesthetics and intentions of our ethics must fall a distant second to the actual consequences of living from these perspectives.

Suffering and the World

This world was, is, and will always be a horrific freak show. War—covert and otherwise—even after its active pursuit of carnage, leaves horrific legacies of landmines, unexploded cluster bombs, famine, violent revenge, orphans, and bizarre 'peaces.' Genocide, whether popularly acknowledged or denied by revisionists, appears throughout human history and is sometimes extolled as part of a people's founding mythologies. Colonialism, in existence long before Western Europe's ascension to dominance, has created occasionally beautiful syncretisms and mutual aid, but has usually yielded appalling exploitation, cultural if not literal genocide, and slavery—both the literal forms and its de facto economic manifestations.

Over the last 500 years, the Western world has progressively—and desperately—insulated ('in-SOL-ated'?) itself from the effects of its actions. The wars, abject poverty, exploitation of natural resources, and slavery that fueled the advancement of capitalism's triumphant modernism needed to be exported since, eventually, the consciences of some vociferous citizens became inconveniently pricked. Thus, when a government bans slavery in its own territories, it must export its means of production to a place where slavery still exists in one form or another. Furthermore, capitalism relies, albeit disproportionately, on a general elevation of the standard of living for its host country. This goal is far from benevolent. An increase in the standard of living simply means that a broader swath of consumers will buy more things. Thus, this system must rely on an exploited working class to produce ridiculously cheap goods and services upon which 'successful capitalists' build their wealth.

Moreover, when the internecine and regional wars of Europe proved too costly a means for securing resources, colonial wars became easier and more profitable. In short, any illusion we may have of an enlightened and progressive *Pax Moderna* is merely a deluded testament to the success of this exportation of the bitter cost of our excessive lifestyles. When pieces of the legacy of the Western world's various exploitations come too close to the 'first world,' whether in the form of the drug trade and its business wars or in the form of terrorism, the Western world feels all the more justified in perpetuating the same strategies that created the hostilities in the first place.

Why this brooding tour into globalization and world politics? Because so many occultists and neo-pagans have half-conceived, and under-researched visions of

'Golden Ages.' Frankly, most of us do—whether it be some matriarchal proto-Europe, or a Merry Olde England, or the 1950's of American cruising culture. We hold out these ideals and perhaps we even imagine that we live in some form of an ideal. Yet we do not see the interconnections—the cost of the life we live. You can never live enough 'off the grid'; you cannot adequately reduce your 'carbon footprint'; you will never create enough of a sustainable community to extricate yourself from the ills of the system of the world. These efforts, as effective as they may prove, neither isolate nor insulate the practitioners from the legacies of a world bleeding out from its suffering. Ignorance of the anguish in the world comes at a horrific cost of disconnection from our lives. It is a refusal to acknowledge the responsibility we already hold for the entirety of the present moment.

And so, I have to state again what a freak show this world is. Not that there isn't beauty, love, and the sublime, as well; but any portrayal or understanding must include the constant and relentless beat of appalling depravity. Any other idea is a fiction that denies the suffering to which we all are party. The essence of morality is to awake to that in which we unwittingly participate and then take responsibility for it. This is not the ineffectuality of a guilt-ridden, self-loathing, hand-wringing wallow in impotent pity. Rather, I suggest the sober realization that no one aspect of our lived world can entertain some sort of dissociative freedom from the complete systemic interconnection of every other aspect. This responsibility *for* our lives is a responsiveness *to* the world.

The denial of pain, which every single one of us perpetuates, yields far greater suffering for us. How many people seek out esotericism, meditation, 'spirituality,' religion, hobbies, promotions, addictions, and initiations in order to somehow rise above their pain? How many of us desperately seek these distractions, imagining that, in our ritual robes or wearing our lapel pin, we are no longer 'part of the problem'? The great iron—universal law of life that it is—is that, eventually, any true initiatory path will confront you with suffering of a specificity and intensity you could never imagine. Really, Western Esotericists, what did you imagine made that Rosy Cross so red?

As noted above, I am not advocating that we acknowledge the pain in the world and ourselves and then simply wallow in it. Nor am I calling for an immediate universal suffrage to overthrow some culpable power responsible for the pain of the world. I am proposing that the only effective action, individually, familially, culturally, nationally, or planetarily will proceed from a frank assessment of the disastrous state in which we find ourselves.

One example of the scope of real responsiveness in today's world is decidedly unpopular. How do we address responsibility in a world 100 years past its capacity to sustain its population? In 1910, with a population between 1.5 and

2 billion, the world could only just feed its inhabitants. The introduction of artificial fertilizers facilitated the ludicrous boom in population of the 20th century. Now, with a world population nearing 7 billion and a projected increase to 9 billion by 2050, fundamental assumptions of the morality that carried us to the industrial revolution may no longer prove valid. How do we speak to ethics when the very act of having a child, previously an archetype of hope itself, becomes the source of our suffering? Pollution, extinctions, war, famine, drought, global climate change, and poverty are easily linked to our current obscene population levels. Yet, for now, we seem to be able to bemoan ozone layers, hold famine-aid concerts, coo over baby penguins and pandas, and hate terrorists at a sufficiently engrossing level to ignore the fundamental dynamics of a world population long past merely 'unsustainable'. However, until the colonization of other planets becomes a viable reality for multi-millions of humans, genuine, real responsibility must confront population growth.

Other examples of genuine responsiveness involve overcoming our own defenses and denial. In the midst of some free-flowing discussion in my Introduction to Psychology classes, I will often have to halt the progress and ask the students, 'Okay, so given where we're going with this discussion, how do we account for a minimum of 26% of women and 17% of men being raped or molested by the time they reach their 18th birthday?' (Perhaps this explains how I earned the nickname 'Dr. Downer.') I don't ask this question out of some morose desire to depress everyone into a guilt-ridden funk. I challenge the students to look at how we have constructed a series of intermeshed systems that both reveal and conceal. I ask the question so that students remember that we can hide behind our intentions and ignore the effects, both tacit and direct, of our choices.

Notwithstanding that the Old Beast Crowley tells us that what makes us happy makes us wise, our pain and the pain of the world is often far more instructive. Frankly, a whole lot of what people call 'happiness' is merely the temporary success of their defenses against their pain — a thin sort of happiness, really. This defensive happiness tends to shove the pain elsewhere — onto others, for instance. Worse yet, we grow experienced in ignoring suffering in others and the world. I would contend that addressing our pain makes us wise and compassionate. Truer happiness comes through a genuine acceptance of others, and specifically ourselves. In short, only through the sacred marriage of freedom and responsibility do we achieve any modicum of our humanity.

'Help' and the Kingdom of Heaven

A clearer sense of the suffering of others and ourselves may move us to action. Nevertheless, striving to alleviate the suffering of others, as noble a cause as it may be, is neither simple nor easy. Being 'nice' may make pain temporarily more bearable, but it certainly doesn't do a thing to alleviate the underlying conditions. The simple solutions inevitably miss far more pervasive and insidious suffering and tend to further bury these patterns, thus increasing overall misery. To help another is incredibly rare, since we are more often 'helping' ourselves. Too often, we cannot bear the suffering of another and merely seek to temporarily make the annoyingly-pained-other less difficult for us to behold through some form of palliative bandage help. These misgivings are part of the reason that I tell my counseling and psychotherapy students that, in their future careers, they will never 'help' anyone. We spend the better part of the semester simply puzzling through the implications of that idea.

Figuring out how our attitudes, actions, and assessments contribute to our own pain and that of others will always be the most fruitful path. In a world full of diagnoses, pharmaceuticals, procedures, and treatments, every medical, mental health, and chemical dependency professional will always admit that *lifestyle* is the most important factor in prognosis. That is, how we live, eat, exercise, sleep, drink, and relax will always have a far more pervasive impact on our well-being and health than any intervention. Yes, terrible diseases *do* happen to people who exercise, eat right, practice moderation, have fulfilling relationships, and manage their stressors. Nevertheless, people who pursue those healthier life choices generally develop far fewer disorders over their lives. This doesn't mean they have alleviated suffering in the world, but their lives alone serve as a testament to better ways of living.

Given the challenges of actually achieving real change, I am compelled to say that, like the various labels neo-pagans may adopt, 'optimism' and 'pessimism' are labels for feeble minds unable to deal with reality. Nearly everyone has good intentions and hopes for the best — to the best of their ability. See how much good that does them? Try spending your time *living* rather than slapping a new coat of paint on your life. Get that under your belt before you go around trying to change things. If you can actually begin to take in hand your lived values, your underlying patterns, and let go of your certainties, then maybe you can address the idea of making a change or two to the world.

Throughout the Christian Gospels, the Evangelists give Jesus a series of sayings about 'The Kingdom of Heaven.' The essence of these statements redirects the apostles from their politically motivated questions about a Hebrew Messianic revolution and toward a far more radical vision of reality. Taking the idea of the being-vector-toward-'Heaven,' the Rabbi from Galilee offers a vision of life in which both creation and the end of days are all *now*:

> Once, having been asked by the Pharisees when the kingdom of God would come, Jesus replied, "The Kingdom of God does not come with

your careful observation, nor will people say, 'Here it is,' or 'There it is,' because the kingdom of God is within you." **(Luke 17: 20-21. *New International Version*)**

So, if you will forgive me a return to my childhood roots in the Lutheran Church, let's take this idea seriously and give our discussion of responsibility a more mythic sweep. Following the statements attributed to Jesus, we can say that Heaven and Hell are now. If you want to be present to your life as you live it now, then hearken to neither a Golden Age, nor the New Aeon, nor an Apocalypse. The Four Horsemen are already here, and the Garden of Eden is under your feet. As soon as we become aware, the fictionality of our existence plagues us and so we tend to push the most amazing of stories about ourselves out into the world, the distant past, and the far future. This misdirection into the 'mythic,' however, does not make the stories any less true about right now. The 'sanity,' 'rationality,' and responsibility-eschewing 'explanations' of this world do not withstand the pervasive madness of the moment—the Folly of Heaven. We need neither ask, plot, nor ensorcel 'when' the Kingdoms of Heaven and Hell or the New Aeon will be. Heaven and Hell are now.

The term in theology for this parallel between creation, the apocalypse, and us is 'realized eschatology'—that is, the realization of the Eschaton, the end of the world, *as we have known it*. This idea receives ample representation within the additional Gospels that comprise today's Gnostic Bible. Yet mainline Christianity bears adequate witness to this realization. Drawing as it does so strongly from the *Book of Revelation*—a visionary apocalyptic account of the Second Coming of Christ and the End of 'the World'—the Roman Catholic Mass is a ritual of this realized eschatology in which the opening of Heaven, and the end of this world, can be a daily event.

Many of us have a strange and uncanny feeling that 'something is coming.' We watch films about world-destroying events, alien revelations, and massive government plots and feel strangely soothed or validated. However, perhaps the resonance is not so much an intuition of a forthcoming apocalypse. Perhaps we deeply resonate with a portrayal of a world infinitely more decimated, stranger, and more alien than our habitual explanations can ever account for. Perhaps images of the end of days resonate with us not because 'something is coming' but because the Event is already—and has always been—unfolding *now*.

So too can we look to Hindu ideas about reincarnation to see further expansion of this idea. If one cycle of reincarnation takes 28,000 lifetimes, but, as some Hindu scriptures indicate, time is itself an illusion, and divisions of 'you' and 'I' are also wrapped up in misapprehension, then reincarnation can just as easily yield the realization that all times are now, all events are occurring concurrently, and we are all each other, reincarnated and reincarnating. This includes mythic ages, the birth and death of gods, and the dissolution of the world as we know it—all is *now*. Reincarnation can be, after all, a nightmare. Scientology's dogged efforts to rid its devotees of their various past-life traumas are testament to this potential. Perhaps Nietzsche's cryptic 'eternal return' can only be redeemed if we participate in a different sort of time; not an endless sequence of cause and effect, crime and recrimination, but of Kairos. John Caputo asserts as much when he links Kairos with the Event of Christian theology in his *The Weakness of God: A Theology of the Event* (2006).

Specific causalities and the time-perspective of cause and effect may help us to narrow our responsibility to an absurd micro-accountability. On the other hand, we can strive to achieve a chaos-based responsibility in which we realize, whether we think we 'caused' it or not, that we are the entirety of where we are. Thus, any convenience we hope to engender with our limited causalities, isolated identities, and limited perspectives quickly fades in the light of our responsibility, accountability, and enmeshment with everything.

With that last blast of bombast, let's end our meditation on responsibility and look to some of the ways in which we can learn to read the myriad languages in which our lived worlds are written.

Our lives are texts, intersections of texts, expressed through generative texts, and saturated with intertextual references. Where no words or symbols exist, we co-create them. We, those meaning-makers who are made of meaning, drown in letters, words, and phrases whose signification, far from being fixed, drifts with each use toward unknown seas of reference. (I have always imagined that this intertextuality is why so many of Tom Stoppard's works bear the visual signature of pages blowing across the stage.)

Have you ever noticed the strange autochthonous languages that surround us? The bold ancient Asiatic lines of Worm-eaten-woodish? The delicate arabesques of Branching-spring-buddian? Perhaps the Pali resonances of Upper-storm-cloud? We see stories in stucco, countenances in concrete, and wildernesses in water-stained walls. Graffiti and corrosion confront us with a secret language more alive with gravitas than any occult alphabet. Rather than merely 'projecting' onto these ciphers, are we not really *intersecting* with a lived world awash in meaning vectors?

Throughout this work, you have seen the sigils and symbols that try to carry some of the intent of this grimoire. Text made of text, they are palimpsests of layer upon layer of intention, construction, and happenstance. A form of automatic writing went into much of the source material in which I constructed the overall sigil intentionally and then filled it in with rapid 'writing' while mouthing the intent, discovering new poetry contained in the implicate image, and coming to a stand in new places. Then I let go of the meaning, in many cases 'forgetting' the original intention. At this point, my able graphic artist wife morphed, mutated, and manipulated the symbols into their current form.

Glossolalia, or speaking in tongues, is a common enough practice; but, too often, we miss that all language involves invention, misinterpretation, and the novel configurations born of intersecting meaning-makers. Speaking in tongues relies on our innate capacity to generate meaning and reference. Similarly, but less engaged in the production of 'nonsense,' automatic writing—or psychography—too often relies on one's native tongue. Many 'channelers' and other psychics use automatic writing or typing as a means of accessing the 'akashic records,' past life experiences, or paranormal intelligences. Nevertheless, in their hunger to have an 'inside track' on reality, these creations are typically allegorical reflections of the world in which the psychic lives.

In all these practices, nonsense is vastly under-rated. Through a perhaps Dadaist or surrealist approach to these exercises, we have a chance to access the *how* of meaning-making, rather than the *what*. That is, when we give up on the deliberate production of information, we may come to know better the mechanics of our meaning production. Most of us intersect with far more potential text in the visual, than we allow ourselves in the auditory realm. Thus the habit of linguistic meaning-making can be well exploited if we can only find a means of access.

For this exercise, you must embrace nonsense. In the process of realizing or creating your own alphabet of desire—a language of symbols with which we construct our lived sigils—you could do worse than to start filling pages of your journal with scribble. Your language may follow the direction of your day-to-day sentences, but perhaps you want to try other directions or dimensions? Follow this practice, which must be taken up as a waste of ink and paper if it is to break through your barriers of 'effectiveness' and 'conscientiousness,' with a half-lidded scan of the page to discover what has emerged. Decrypt the secret language of your alien script.

Then, once this practice becomes a habit, look to your lived world and see the choking over-abundance of texts crowding every vista. The danger with this exercise is the potential for 'ideas of reference' (IOR). This psychotic symptom shows us, in an uncanny sense, the significance of page numbers, weather reporters' tie choices, and the random activities of the stock market. IOR are the delusional shadow of oracular consciousness. To banish IOR, read a well-written novel, garden, or take a trip away from your accustomed haunts and habits.

We like to think that 'words get in the way' of our experiences. Yet words—fictions—are the way we *have* experiences. Therefore, rather than seeking language-free sublimities, this current text suggests we take command of the myriad languages of our lives. In order to live our lives more fully, we need to gain a working knowledge of the means of making meaning. Otherwise, we merely live out unexamined fictions. Whether through the subtleties of identity, the negotiations of relationships, or confrontations with the inexpressible, only when we become aware of *how* we live can we ever hope to claim our lives as our own.

36
Shadows and Forms
A Final Image

The drumming is throbbing and insistent. Shadows play across the concrete walls from the growing bonfire. With the circling dancers dark with make-up and soot, the silhouettes and bodies blend. The walls of this grotto bear arcane marks in black, umber, scarlet, and azure. Embers from the fire shoot up and blend with the stars that are visible behind a thin veil of wispy clouds.

Clothes are indistinct and the normal limits of propriety slip easily across sweat-lubricated lines. This is my first celebration with a Wiccan coven and, in my intoxicated early-20-something mind, it easily blurs the Wiccan Sabbat and the Witch's Sabbath. Before the sunset, one could walk 50 feet and discover that we are in a decommissioned hilltop military bunker in the San Francisco Bay area. Some 500 feet down the hill toward the Pacific, a bank of Nike Missiles sit ominously, although disarmed and purely for historic purposes. They have a surreal quality that, rather than suggesting a particular time during the Cold War, seems to convey an ancient quality, like Greek ruins, or prehistoric monoliths. Now, an hour after a mid-summer sunset, any mark of modernity has faded in a wave of smoke and incense.

The drumming shifts to a slower, more accented rhythm. I, and several others sit back onto cushions and watch as a half-dozen of the women begin to belly dance. No fan of the commercial gaudiness of Moroccan restaurants, I am surprised by the power and precision of what I see. No gaudy bangles or neon colors adorn these priestesses, or if they do, they are transformed by the ancient provenance of what animates their bodies. At one point they carry fire in their hands—the effect is palpable as those gathered hush in awe. Near the end of the series of dances, the High Priestess Mora performs a slow hypnotic piece. Her eyes surrounded in blackness, her hair piled on her head in plaits, she carries a strange metal loop and shaft in each hand. I realize with surprise that she has perfectly taken on the form of an ancient bas-relief of Inanna. Rather than some intellectual reference that suggests the form, these tools serve as an expression of something deeper and more fully present than mere detail can convey.

The performance ends with a raucous circle dance, which soon involves most of those gathered. From our cushions, I lean over to the High Priest Peter and comment, 'You know, this could be any time.' I struggle to find the words. 'I mean, this could be 5,000 years ago!'

'Come with me,' he responds with a smile.

We step away from the group into the darkness. We stand at the edge of the hill and overlook the valley that gives way to the ocean.

'You see over there?' I follow the shadow of his hand.

I see another bonfire on the opposite side of the valley, perhaps half a mile away. Then I scan and see two more, one up the hill from the first, and the other just visible on the beach.

'Those are all covens celebrating the Sabbat.' He names them one by one.

I am stunned.

One of the dancers has joined us looking into the darkness. She has over-heard the description. She laughs for joy, 'It's so beautiful!' She sobs in her delight. Later, I hear her explain to a friend, 'It's just like in Starhawk's *The Spiral Dance!* — it's happening!'

After another glass of wine, I am pleasantly buzzed but the night's revelries are only warming up. Everything here tastes of spice and wood and moss. I feel relaxed and happy — at ease. I hear the sound of tires crunching on gravel. I turn to see three or four cars and a motorcycle quickly turn out their lights. Out of them emerges a throng of leather, spikes, Mohawks, and piercings. Several of the Wiccans shriek with glee and run to greet the newcomers.

'Ah! The Crowdads have arrived!' someone drolly notes with a chuckle. I quickly learn that this is the affectionate name for a local group of followers of Crowley's Thelema.

Introductions are made. They are a pleasant and lively lot sporting marvelous hybridizations of anarchistic punk and Thelemic regalia. Their leader hangs back and speaks with Peter. I am told he is a psychologist. He has an academic's trimmed beard and an aura of authority.

One of the Crowdads greets me and begins asking me about how I've come to be here. I explain my brother lives on a boat off Alameda Island and I moved up here to be closer to him and hopefully get some experience in the mental health field. My leather-clad interlocutor nods with a thoughtful furrow beneath his spiked bleach blond hair.

'Ah… your brother, he knows the Deep Ones then,' he observes. I pick up on the Lovecraft reference, but, for my life, can't tell if he's kidding or not.

Finally, my sense of timelessness breaks through into something else.

It's not just that this could be any time in history. It is more — we are in a place in which our timelines have intersected throughout the history of man. We are firmly in the Imaginal now.

I narrow my eyes, look at the Lovecraft referencing Crowdad, and nod with equal sagacity. A smile breaks over his face and he slaps me heartily on the shoulder. I realize that we are re-enacting the classic welcoming-of-the-'other tribe' to the celebrations of the village. We have done our ritual confrontation and can now share in the festivities.

This is not pretending, because we have no script. This is a genuine irruption of the Real.

Another conflagration of dancing breaks out, this time even more throbbing and infectious since a DJ has brought her turntables and has added African tribal and Middle Eastern beats to the mixture.

I lay back, munching on grapes and bread. The dancers whirl and spin in their circle. In an instant, it is a Fellini *hora*—a circle dance of every character of the film, impossibly gathered together in one place. The overabundance of reference and resonance engulfs me and I cannot think, only feel the power.

I think I briefly fall asleep or pass out. I dream of my first night in Florence. I wander the narrow medieval streets of the city, overwhelmed with wonder. Few streetlights disturb the 1000-year echoes of the place. I make my way toward a café I see two blocks away, but halfway there, I catch a glimpse down a long narrow alley that stops me in my tracks.

Staggered up both sides of the alley are small, squat tables, each with their own antique oil lamps sputtering dirty, ruddy flames. Shades dance and loom up the walls. I venture one or two careful steps toward them. They are tarot readers, heads wrapped in scarves, eyes heavy with kohl. Men and women, I suspect they are Romani. I cannot believe what I am seeing and take several deep breaths to help embed this moment in my mind.

I never want to forget this. I want to live in this. I want this. I want this.

I awake, my mouth thick from wine. I still feel the tingle of the dream and realize it is the same as I feel here, tonight. I don't want to leave our time, the contemporary world. I am not a re-enactor or a sentimentalist. What I want is to live in the imagery—so fully, so deeply that I can taste the blood of each second, to speak its language and dive into the richness of the imaginal that informs and animates, creates everything. I realize this night, that this is what I mean when I say 'sacred.' These moments that break through, sear through our expectations and complacency are something worth living for—they are what I think 'living' actually means. I do not know the word for it, but I will come to believe that this is another sense of the time of Kairos.

I breathe a heavy sigh of happiness and make my way to my tent.

Two decades later, Professor Lesh and I chat amiably in the center of the Great Room. Clutches of professors circulate and kibitz. Ostensibly, we are here to meet parents visiting their students partway into the Fall semester. In reality, we take this agenda-free time to catch up with each other.

Balancing a cup of tea and a plate of danishes, I explain what I am writing about, with a bit of difficulty. Lesh teaches biology and, to some extent, my current work is an indictment of the inherent limitations of the natural scientific method. He is, to my surprise, highly receptive to my descriptions. Frequent smiles animate his thick hedge of a beard.

More than my topic, however, the writing process itself is what engages him. Lesh has several textbooks to his name and makes a decent living as a writer. His success, and passion for his work, both intrigue me. We end up interrogating each other for the better part of an hour about our work styles.

Lesh is ardent about his personal journals, as am I. We discuss favorite styles and he shows me his current notebook, a gorgeous Venetian piece with a soft leather cover and marbled endpapers. I remember seeing this type of notebook when in Venice years ago. I drooled then and am duly impressed as I flip through the pages and hear the distinct sound of rag paper.

We weigh the merits of lined, blank, and graphed pages. We discuss styles of pens. In short, we geek out on the trappings of the writer's craft. I enjoy the conversation immensely.

I describe that I often struggle with nicer journals, worrying what thoughts would be worthy of such artful receptacles. He scrunches his face and, in his quick bursts of excited phrases, he explains that his publisher has similar misgivings. He explains that he got over those limitations early on in his writing career. He writes anything in his journals, even in his Venetian masterpiece: grocery lists, meeting notes, book ideas.

I am, at first, aghast — a sure sign of this being a significant moment. *Grocery lists in a journal with hand marbled end leafs and gilt pages?!* I get no chance to examine the idea further. Our topics progress, and soon the 'coffee with the faculty' time ends.

Two days later, I receive notice that I have a package waiting for me in the campus' mailroom. Assuming that it is another publisher sending me a desk copy of a text that I will likely not adopt for a class, it takes me two more days before I make my way across the street to pick up the parcel.

I am confused as I note that the return address is from an online book dealer. To my surprise, I discover two journals of my favorite sort: stiff covers, thick blank sketchpad pages, and small enough to fit in any of my bags, but large enough to accept 20 lines of my handwriting. I am puzzled until I read the gift receipt:

Aaron, It is always pleasant to find a co-fetishist... and remember: no thoughts are too mundane to enter here!

I laugh out loud. In my mind his line echoes a passage from Crowley's *Gnostic Mass*. After communicants take the wine and host, they turn to the congregation, arms crossed in a suitably Osirisian pose, and intone, 'There is no part of me that is not of the gods.'

Crowley's phrase has always struck me as significant but a bit overblown. Somehow, Lesh's book dedication brings home a message I have needed to hear. 'Mundane,' of the world, the mundus. But rather than being synonymous with 'banal,' 'mundane' can point to the *unus mundus*, the one world. Not a material world separate from concepts, spirits, or feelings, but one lived world of grocery lists, books, danishes, and the sublime.

I don't claim to be a scholar of Plato, but I have read more than my share of passages from his works in addition to the countless, obligatory summaries of his ideas one must encounter in the course of a liberal arts education. Because of my Jungian studies, one particular set of Plato's ideas has always come to the forefront: the 'Forms.'

For Plato, the Forms are the Real of which our world is only a faint silhouette. According to his philosophy, most of us are chained slaves who can merely look at the flickering dances of muddled shades and never apprehend the eye-burning majesty of the True Forms.

For my part, I have found this idea to be dangerously close to a denial of life. I have always suspected that this idea of the Forms was merely intellectual self-justification. 'Oh, you pedestrian sots! I pity you and your obsession with the fleeting world of appearances. How you all chase after such ephemeral nonsense! If only you could merely glimpse the slightest hint of the Verity of the Timeless Realm, beyond the heavens where reside the Pristine Forms!'

Then again, I suspect that my obsession with the Imaginal looks indistinguishable from Plato's ideas to many people. I suspect that Plato and I struggle with the same problems, but I feel that I come to a very different solution. I do not claim that the Imaginal realm is perfect—far from it. The Imaginal is, however, the realm in which we actually live, regardless of our pedigree, social class, degrees, or initiations. The world of 'appearances,' is actually more of an 'idea' than the Imaginal. Moreover, the Imaginal is constantly in flux behind the seeming permanence of our various 'things.'

Philosophizing aside, when we do fully open our eyes to the sublime power of the Imaginal, something changes. Real moments of insight reorganize our pasts and our futures. Moments that pierce through 'seeming' and penetrate us through with reality are beyond the vain efforts of our religions, philosophies, or sciences to classify, categorize, or even capture. Reality can indict 'me,' regenerate my lived world, and give me moments of consciousness-destroying clarity. These realizations can also make us run shrieking in eldritch terror if we have no ability to open ourselves to the mystery.

Thus, when I have been able to receive these moments—I think they must always be trying to burst forth—I suddenly feel every moment from my history reconfigure. I feel my future suddenly ring with sympathetic power. I feel a contact with the ineffable—the syzygy of dreaming, memory, hope, and perception.

Years of talking about, struggling with these ideas are no substitute for the experience. Thus, several years into my teaching career and midway through writing this work, I had gotten a bit lost in the weeds. Whether he realized or not, Professor Lesh and I let our topic flow through us. I was held up in comparison with the images that reverberated beneath us as we spoke. Out of this Moment came the oracle I needed.

I open one of the journals and smell its new pages. My head spins for a second and I smile broadly until laughter overcomes me. Jarred back into the moment, I look around me. Although there are no whirling Wiccans or tarot-reading Romani, this here-and-now hums with the same electricity. Lushly romantic settings may make for pleasant awakenings, but every moment carries the same potential. The magic is the irruption, the burning away of the barriers.

Still laughing, I step outside the Student Center and raise my arms to the gods, 'I accept the Kladon!'

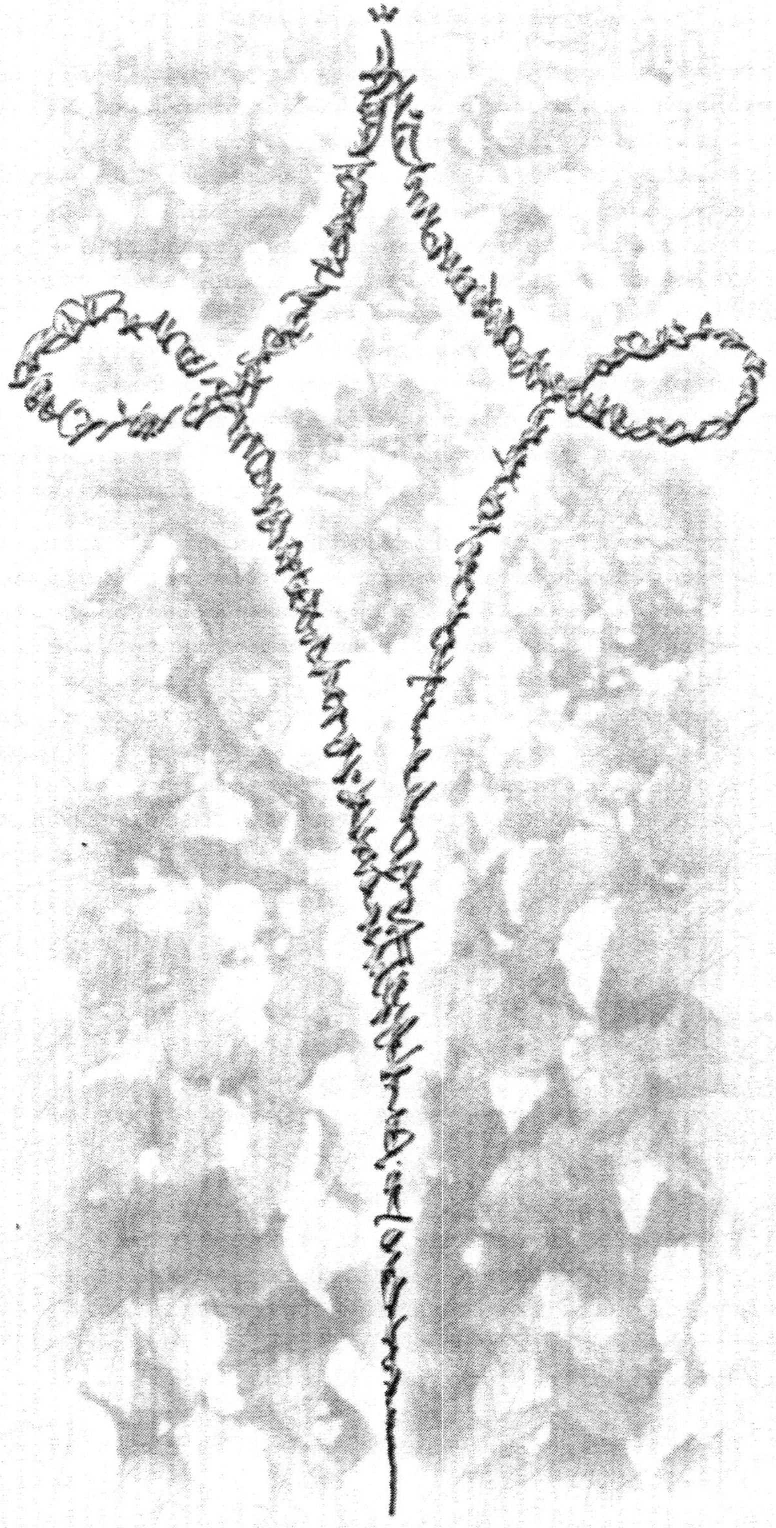

37
Change and Finitude
The Eighth Void

Though 'the moment' is omnipresent—to the extent that anything is 'present'—*this* moment is also endlessly in motion and finite. These two qualities are indistinguishable from each other. 'Eternal' and 'Infinite' are beyond the scope of lived experience and thus, when it comes to the prospects of life, are irrelevant and distracting. All experiences end. Change is the only constant (thank you, Heraclitus).

'Consistency' is illusory and an imposition upon the moment that leads to possibilities that are more restricted. Death bounds and leads to the reanimation of every experience. The convergence of experiential vectors we call 'I' ends with each passing moment. The process that is death underpins and fuels change. Far from a massive cosmic downer, however, *Momento Mori* is the motto of joy, beauty, pleasure, and the sublime. This transitory nature of life is what fuels our responsibility and justifies the resoluteness necessary to grow throughout the unfolding moment.

Change and Sacrifice

Nature is indifferent but full of undeniably pervasive patterns. Perhaps Her greatest lesson is to remind us of constant change and the necessity of death. We need only look at our current food chain to realize that resisting these deaths fuels a butchery of unimaginable depravity. Because most people can no longer bear the thought of killing animals to survive, we construct mass abattoirs of unspeakable cruelty that create half-lives for animals, all so that the blood and slaughter are at a comfortably deniable distance from our dinner plates.

We fear sacrifice and dismissively imagine ourselves too sophisticated for it. Thus, of course, we no longer allow death its due. Yet death has not gone away. It has only become more twisted and anonymous as all things do when left to ferment in the shadow. As an example, we can take a mythic perspective on the current state of warfare. From here, we can see that through no longer sacrificing to appease the gods, the gods have given us new wars so that we might murder our young at a dissociative distance through the video-game-like controls of drones, missiles, and high-altitude surveillance. Nonetheless, as Volume One describes in its presentation of Giegerich's meditation on 'Killings,' most of the

world's religions at least ritually acknowledge that only through the sanctification of death do we achieve true sacrifice (i.e., 'to make sacred').

Growing out of the elaborate images of alchemy, the imagination of magic has
inherited a love of multi-layered mottos, acronyms, and acrostics. One central
magical motto speaks to the necessity of death and regeneration: I.˙.N.˙.R.˙.I.˙..
Supposedly the legend born on the placard hung above the crucified Jesus' head
by the Romans to indicate he was 'Jesus of Nazareth, King of the Jews' (*Iesus Naza-
renus, Rex Iudaeorum*), few mottos have as many alternate and fanciful meanings.
One meaning in particular is germane to the current discussion of the resistance
to finitude: *Ignis Natura Renovatur Integra*. That is, 'through fire nature is reborn,
whole.' This is the motto of the remarkable chaparrals—plant seeds that depend
on the heat of wildfires to open them. It is also the essence of the Rosy Cross,
that balance point midway up the Western Initiatory Qabalah. Christianized as
it is, the Western Qabalah superimposes the crucifix over the lower half of the
Tree of Life, putting the crown of thorns and this acronym firmly in the center
of the Tree. Sacrifice, the nourishing blood of willing surrender to the mysteries,
provides the axis of this model. That the Christ—the Christener, the Sanctifier,
the Sanctifying Vector of Being—Himself occupies this pillar offers profound
mythopoetic insight into the nature of change, transformation, and rebirth.
Neo-pagans, suspicious of such rhetoric, nonetheless adhere to these resonances
within the imagination of change; they thus substitute Odins, Dionysuses, Sacri-
ficial Kings, and various resurrecting chthonic Divinities.

Nature needs destruction and renewal. Not the toxic decimation of the half-
deaths offered by human society, but the floods, volcanoes, wildfires, stampedes,
predatory culling, and a host of other devastations that nourish and strengthen
the ecosystem. Humans are no different on the existential level.

(However, unlike some occultists with a penchant for fascistic ethoi, I cannot
quite bring myself to advocate for the culling of the human species, no matter
how murderous I may feel in traffic jams. This jackboot and substitute-swastikas
crowd often has a tongue-in-cheek or dark satire agenda with their overblown
goose-steps and SS references. The message seems to be a call for us to recognize the uncomfortable parallels many of our contemporary attitudes have to
regimes such as Germany's National Socialism. The joke, however, often gets
away from these tricksters and we soon find ourselves in the sort of conversations
that would not tolerate the light of day and thus remain fixed in subterranean
realms and their internet equivalents. I have often wondered how these fascist-
esthetic-loving rebels think they would fair under an actual totalitarian regime.
Personally, I always assumed these impulses were misdirected efforts at resolving
Daddy Issues.)

Society and the Denial of Death

The patterns of nature, though often brutal, are nothing compared to the ruthless desperation of humanity. Putting aside intention and rhetoric, societies are self-sustaining distraction machines, designed to facilitate the genocidally-fixated, raping, and planet-destroying agendas in which we all participate.

We can invest these societally manufactured distractions with more numinosity and sacrosanct pomp than most religions can muster for us, but ultimately the effect will be one of (often welcome) deadening—like most people's experiences with religions. Deadening is a far more primary experience than most of us will admit. We prefer the experience of deadening to the alternative of living in a world in which death is a reality. Thus, we doggedly seek out these distractions with their initial promise of novelty. Yet, every defense betrays its denied core and our distractions continue to confront us with distorted representations of the death from which we would run. Television programs full of vampires and serial killers, endless news portrayals of 'distant' wars, and films steadily increasing the gallons of blood spattered per minute are just a few of the examples.

Nearly every pattern will continue, because it has to this point continued. Patterns persist beyond necessity, origin, context, or even meaning—if they ever had any. All that they require is perpetuation. What *is* is what has continued to be through replication, or the failures of decay. Perhaps this is what Richard Dawkins intended with his *memes*—patterns that continue because they have the capacity to replicate.

No pattern or idea is so benevolent that it does not seek to dominate—not 'love,' not 'charity,' not 'insight,' not 'enlightenment.' The luxury of labels blinds us to actuality and effect. Labels carry the same sort of misdirecting delusions as most 'intentions.' All patterns seek to emerge, manifest, and individuate. This is the archontic nature of patterns and ideas. We must exercise tenacious insight and strength of will in order to extricate ourselves from these inveigling patterns—and most of the time we will fail should we be audacious enough to imagine ourselves capable of such Quixotic aspirations.

Patterns are autonomous and autochthonous—that is, they self-regulate and emerge from themselves. Ultimately, they do not come from anywhere since any image of 'creation' is merely a representation of their depths. They do not, unto themselves, end, since eschatology—whatever apocalypse it preaches—is merely their prepackaged telos.

The root meaning of 'angel' is messenger. Thus, perhaps we can make a contrived play on words in order to address the ways in which we become wrapped up in thing-sets and information generating patterns. These autochthonous patterns do not have content, but rather generate content-mindsets in their victims. Their messages are their messengers: autangels, autonomous/auto-chthonous angels. Billboards, doctors, technicians, ministers, marketers, tracts, texts, coupons, and on and on. Messages are not *whats*, but *hows*. Don't worry about what your master television tells you, listen to *how* it tells you—how it assumes you are, and subsumes you as its willing slave.

Vitriolic Descent

I have hinted at two potential vectors for mystical change throughout this text. These two possibilities can both be a means of Method X—a path of extrication from entrapping patterns. One is the process of ascent through apotheosis, in which we tenaciously pursue one idea well beyond its logical ends, often in a refined form of deconstruction. The other possibility is vitriolic descent, a path of dissipation, debauchery, and antinomian rage. This latter path is, in many ways, the libertine's mysticism, a neo-Romantic howl of bitter disappointment with a world that fails to support its simplest of assertions. Thus, brace yourself for it, that swiff of robes on marble you just heard is the sound of another esoteric reference bent on justifying the slow desiccation of your life with arcane studies, instead of learning something useful!

As with I.˙.N.˙.R.˙.I.˙., the alchemist ancestors of magicians offered us another gift when they encoded a secret in their name for sulfuric acid. V.˙.I.˙.T.˙.R.˙.I.˙.O.˙.L.˙. *Visita Interiora Terrae Rectificando Invenies Occultum Lapidem.* 'One must journey to the center of the earth to rectify the hidden stone.' The stone of which they speak is the Philosopher's Stone, the secret elixir of life, that which can transform lead into gold. The stone is also, initially, the stone of matter itself being transformed, rectified from mere leaden matter into the vitalized gold of life. Better yet, if you'll forgive some appropriate vulgarity, we could also gloss the motto to instruct us that, 'you've got to dig pretty deep into this steaming pile of shit to find your stones again.' This is the journey Dante took in his *Inferno*. (Since Dante precedes the advent of European alchemy, it is suspect to use the idea of alchemy to analyze the Florentine Poet's work. Nevertheless, if V.˙.I.˙.T.˙.R.˙.I.˙.O.˙.L.˙. describes his descent in the *Inferno*, then I.˙.N.˙.R.˙.I.˙. well describes his ascending self-scrutiny and penance in *Purgatory*. Near the end of his gradual climb up that mountain of purification, he passes through a curtain of that rectifying fire, transforming lust into Love, and entering the renewed whole world: the Garden of Eden.)

More often than not, we become so enmeshed in our patterns that we will never be able to extricate ourselves in some sort of bootstrapping ascent to apotheosis. Thus, we must journey more fully and deeply into the current state to see it in its fullest. This vitriolic journey will not only be a descent but also a death since the one who undertakes this journey will not be the one who completes it. No-one completes this journey. Vitriol is sometimes the only Method X that is available.

Nevertheless, we live in an era in which even the awful decimation of the descent, the long dark night of the soul, has become market fodder. The black nobility of vitriol is so easily overtaken by ironic self-ennobling fecal wallowing, which is never vitriol but simple masturbatory self-congratulation by the chronically impotent. Heroin, intolerably formulaic music, and an aversion to sunlight mark this breed. In the past, I have been tempted, no doubt by my close proximity to and fear of identification with this crowd, to snark at these self-enobling zones of self-destruction, 'Brood more, maybe that cute Byronic loner by the bar will notice you this time, wanker.' (When the Beat Generation left its Zenny wonder at life-as-it-is and descended into reveries on the authenticity of drooling alcoholism, they reenacted this failed vitriol. So often, what may have once been a true descent of self-undoing is sabotaged by the emergence of syphilis, addiction, or other brain-rotting disorders.)

Iconoclasm is indeed a powerful path, but unto itself bespeaks either a deeper ethos or an unsated patricidal bloodlust. As countless poets and Goth Rock Stars, since Yeats onward, have noted, ours is an age of walking upon broken idols. The liberation afforded by iconoclasm is initially heady, but ultimately empty, until we seize our own lives. To be blunt, unto itself, iconoclasm is as empty as slavish worship. Simply dig up the laudanum-soaked corpses of our iconoclastic ancestors to find evidence of the limits of this method.

Rise up or sink down, apotheosis or vitriol, usually there's little difference. If you don't want to descend, you can always extrapolate, theorize, abstract, and transcend—just don't stop. Keep going further. Ask where you stood to ask the question. Then ask it again about that last question. Keep going without letting words like 'absurd' get in your way. As ideas reach their fevered pitch, tenacious monomania should be your guide. This process is the unfolding of apotheosis. Or complete destruction.

At times, only you will be able to hear the attenuated strains of that haunting melody you knew lay within the noise everyone else heard. Listen closer, learn the scale, the logic. Attend to its tutelage so that you may become its fanatically devoted priest. There's only one rub: when the idea runs out, dies spectacularly, or deposits you on the shore of an unknown land, be ready to move on.

Apotheosis only works as Method X if you never relent. Otherwise, you are in the same ditch as the vitriolic iconoclastic asshole, but it smells of a library or a temple rather than a bar or an Emergency Room. Academics know to never push apotheosis; they'll never get tenure. Scientists know not to push it; they'll indict their reality. Theologians know not to apply it with any vigor; they'll become atheists. Apotheosis eats itself. That's the point. Apophasis—the *via negativa*—is the truth of apotheosis.

Growth, Development, and Initiation

We are the entirety of our lives all at once. That is to say, you are the possibility of all the things you have ever been. Growth is not 'and then…' but 'and also…' I cannot count the number of times a client desperately asked me, 'will I ever feel differently than I do now?' only to have me tell them, 'No. But you may have the option of other feelings as well…'

All experiences are whole experiences. Identity and epistemological limitations may shrink our awareness. This does not change the fact that the experience was whole. Where do the other pieces go? Who sees them? No-one. Moreover, the seeming multiplicities of levels of reality are all now. The inability to reconcile them is a product of our specificity and choice of limitations.

Thus, from this perspective, initiations are supposed to impart privileged access to increased inclusion, and the reconciliation of previously disparate levels. An initiation that limits perspective is cultic enslavement. Sadly, in the early levels of far too many initiatory pyramid scams, the initiations actually divide and limit in order to store up the 'good stuff' for later degrees—with commensurately higher membership fees.

In the contemporary imagination of magic, the dissipated legacies of archaic holdovers from Victorian social clubs have driven many would-be mages to pursue 'self-initiation.' In order to be genuine, self-initiation must be built on the shift from everydayness, to oracular consciousness, to initiatory consciousness, and then—dazed and hung-over—usually back into everydayness. However, self-initiation must be a surrender to a greater process, not a comforting spate of imitating irrelevant procedures, finishing with the acquisition of a new tattoo or ring. When it comes to real initiations, remember: The one who approaches is never worthy.

No-one passes through the gates.

In all of this, we really must ask ourselves, why should I endure all this labor? The questions that began the first volume of this work still hold true: why should I strive for what is always present?

Every moment is the same in its structure. In this sense, nobody has experiences that differ in any fundamental way. What we can do is live them more fully, more deeply—to hearken to the depth and silence that underpins all of this noise. To live well is to embrace the moment given to everyone. Not to long for it to be otherwise, not to despise the lived world as a prison, and not to fracture the wholeness into a million more palatable shards. When we open to the fullness of experience, we are not stuck in the rigid trances of our identities—we become no-one.

What differentiates those who would truly live most fully, from those who are having their lives lived by others? The courage to embrace possibility. This embrace begins when we each acknowledge—and stop defending against—the imaginal truth of the moment. Through a gradual process, living in the unfolding moment, we may come to find the distractions, deadenings, fears, and false hopes less and less fulfilling. We may choose different potentials, different paths. We may choose something *new*.

For most people, this development never occurs, because it is sabotaged by false enlightenment and expensive simulacra. But for those who have turned toward the moment, the choices become easier. The practice of noticing how we fall into the habit of forgetting becomes more frequent. Because fall we must. We fall into everydayness in order to accomplish remarkable tasks with the magic we can't see as magic: materialism, communication, and a host of other technologies. But we must be able to remember, at the end of the day, that these are all spells and dreams.

With this work, I have tried to 'unmoor' my readers—and myself—from the penurious certainties of all the competing literalisms with which we try to defend ourselves from the Voids that underpin and animate our every moment. Adrift on these Imaginal seas, we often find ourselves doubting our compass, hung up in the irons of our previous logics, and deathly afraid of the depths that threaten to swallow us. We have learned to look away from the stars that might guide us. We have become so accustomed to 'destinations' that we scarcely see the journey for what it is—the whole of our lives. Thus, if we are truly to learn the languages of these open waters, we will need to abandon our land-born metaphors and develop the navigational sensibilities native to these depths. Although the entirety of our lives speak these tongues, one third of our lives are spent not speaking the pidgins, creoles, and patois of the waking world, but the ancient mother tongues of dreams.

Putting aside linguistic and sea-faring metaphors, a fundamental paradox underlies the shift away from literalism. Once we undertake the labor of dreams, we realize that we dream all of life. Thus, rather than developing some 'theory of dreams' we are actually cultivating an imaginal sensibility. Toward this end, we must, first and foremost, disabuse ourselves of the notion of 'dream interpretation.' The hackneyed platitudes of one-to-one symbolic ratios that we find in the New Age aisles of bookstores are drivel. Dreams speak in the unique language of each of our lives. Although certain images tend to have particular archetypal resonances for a broad swath of the population, their significance cannot be found in some allegorical translation. Don't interpret dreams—work with them.

The literature growing out of the imagination of magic has tended toward those formulaic dream interpretation primers. Confronted with the awesome and often terrifying objective reality of psyche and the imaginal, I am not surprised that commentators in magical literature feel comforted by a retreat to such concrete assertions. Nevertheless, these mechanical approaches, as reassur-

---

† The attitudes and perspectives for which this exercise advocates are products of my education at *Pacifica Graduate Institute*, in particular, my classroom experiences with Professors James Hillman, Mary Watkins, Ginette Paris, Steve Aizenstat, Lionel Corbett, and Allen Bishop. In order to pursue these ideas, I strongly suggest that the reader attend the workshops and acquire the writings of these luminaries.

ing as they may seem, will tend to smother psyche in leaden convictions instead of liberating potential.

Below are a series of questions and perspectives that will tend to open up more possibilities, rather than fewer. Undertaken in collaboration with a skilled dreamworker, these practices can become even richer, as well as life-altering. So, too, can groups devoted to working dream material with each other. But, experience has shown that a personal process of 'dream tending,' as Aizenstat calls it, can prove incredibly powerful.

The classic means of beginning a course of dreamwork is to set a blank journal and writing instrument beside your bed. Perhaps you want to pick just the right tools and even engage in a simple ritual of dedication for them. Make it as easy as possible to sketch out the basic shape of the dream. If you have corrected vision, you may not want to have to grab glasses, so choose a large format journal and a bold pen. Typically, a simple self-hypnotic suggestion as you drift into the hypnogogic state before full sleep will prove effective in eliciting the right dream. 'I will remember one dream from tonight that will... [insert open-ended statement of intention that best reflects your personal unfolding process, realizing that *any* statement will ultimately orient you toward this journey either nose or ass first].'

(I had one client, who was so anxious to do dream work that she managed to induce insomnia for a week when she woke up after every dream to record it. Since she was obviously somewhat susceptible to suggestion, I stared her squarely in the eyes at our next session and told her, 'You will bring me *only one dream* per night and enjoy a refreshing night of sleep.' Psyche was amenable to the request.)

To address a few common concerns: with the tiniest fraction of an exception for those with disabling disorders, everyone dreams. Many simply don't recall their dreams. If you don't remember your dreams, but are interested to, the journal by the bed and hypnotic suggestion may be enough. If not, you may need to resort to more drastic methods, as advocated by many professors and ably illustrated by Schulz's Snoopy in *What a Nightmare, Charlie Brown!* (1978). In this classic, Snoopy consumes five pizzas and a milkshake and soon finds himself dreaming of being a mush-dog in a trans-Alaskan, mid-winter run. Eating foods near bedtime that come just short of heartburn will tend to slightly disrupt sleep enough to allow for better dream recall.

Another misgiving leveled by would-be dreamworkers is the idea that they don't see the dreamwork getting them anywhere. Setting aside the problems of applying concepts of 'profit' and 'progress' to the expressions of psyche, dreams do not need to be 'understood.' Oftentimes, they merely need to be witnessed or heard. The gradual transformation of repetitive dreams, once hearkened to, bears witness to this phenomenon. To put it more clearly, *dreams respond to dreamwork* although, being a mere character in our larger dreams, we may not have access to the necessary vantage point in order to appreciate the planetary motions at work.

A final concern also needs a brief comment. If you either do not remember your dreams or do not find the work viable, dreams are neither the only, nor necessarily the best, means of coming into a richer relationship with the dynamics of psyche. Jung famously notes that fantasies are a far better means of accessing imaginal material and may well respond to these suggestions.

And so to those questions and perspectives.

Recount the dream in present tense. In order for the Dreaming to be more fully present in the recounting, speak of the events as unfolding as you tell it. This practice will allow details, implications, and feelings to emerge more easily.

How does the dream begin? Like the teaser at the beginning of a television episode, or the background action behind the opening credits of a film, these first images may yield rich insight into the 'theme' of the dream. Dreams are not, in all likelihood, linear. This sense is probably an imposition by the ego-function, desperately trying to reassert its dominance over the unconscious onslaught that takes place during its weakest phase. Thus, dreams are more like spirals or hazes of images, all centering on one particular imaginal gravity center.

'I am alone,' 'It's dark and I am scared,' 'I'm with my family,' 'I'm in some sort of classroom.' You don't need a psychoanalyst to tell you that these are powerful archetypal images. Skilled cinematographers present these configurations to great effect on a regular basis. Even if you don't remember how the dream began, wherever you begin recounting the dream will provide a fine starting-off point. After all, many films begin with us already in the thick of the action.

Sit with these opening images and see if playing with the framing of this snapshot may yield better insight. Referring to the previous examples, we might shift slightly to a more generalized perspective in order to see: 'When I am alone...' 'When I can't figure things out, I become scared...' 'When I am with my family...' 'I am trying to or supposed to learn something here...'

This technique of gentle abstraction borrows from Mary Watkins' technique of 'dream neck-lacing.' Following Doctor Watkins' background in phenomenology, this method slightly generalizes the themes of a dream and then links the images one to the next and eventually links the final image of the dream to the opening image. This is done through the addition of phrases such as 'when I (a)... then I (b)... and when I (b)... then I (c)... and when I (c)... then I (a).'

Who is the dreamer? Are you with your family as they were when you were a child but you are now an adult? Are you alone? With others? With 'friends' but can't quite figure out whom? One of the more uncanny aspects of dreaming is how our identity can shift and reconfigure. A clearer fix on your dream identity and perspective can provide as much information about a central theme or juxtaposition as the opening image.

Where are the transitions? Do you step through a door into a surprising new setting? Go down a flight of stairs? Turn around and find yourself in a completely different dream? These transitions are common and can be seen as completely separate dreams. However, you can also view them as a new director taking over the dream-film and addressing the basic themes with a new genre or idiom. Therefore, a dream with three transitions could be four different meditations on the same central image.

Where are the incongruities? 'It's my mom but not my mom...' 'It looks like a spoon but it actually is some sort of key meant to open up a storeroom I forgot about...' 'I turn around and suddenly there is my Uncle Russ—but he would *never* be in a place like *this*...' These particular images present tension and juxtaposition. They will probably yield more insight if you work them, play with them, give them more language. Which leads to the next suggestion.

Play with the language. Lacan sees dreams as primarily linguistic undertakings. Thus, instead of looking at the visual figures, he advocates for an intense focus on the words used—and often misused—in the retelling of the dream. Homophones, slips of the tongue, veiled metaphors, and sometimes-comic overly literal images play at undermining the ego's delusions of rational linguistic dominance. Thus, look at the words in your dream journal. Perhaps hurriedly write out the whole dream narrative the next day (avoid editing or letting your computer spell-check or auto-correct). Then, take some time away from the narrative and return with a fresh set of eyes.

Although often dismissed as mere 'Freudian slips,' considering the potential meaning of these linguistic constructions can help lay bare the tensions dogging us just under the surface of our lives. One particular example still stands out for me from a training exercise I did with a classmate in my Master's program. He had a dream that left him deeply shaken when he awoke from it. In the dream, he is shaving and simultaneously angry at what he perceives as abandonment by a friend. He provides an unusually detailed description of the shaving: long smooth glides up one cheek, careful quick passes above his chin, and then a sudden and inexplicably brutal slash up and across his upper lip that leaves one nostril bleeding profusely. He fixates on the action and its seeming inexplicability. In my glib inexperience, I look at him incredulously, 'You don't see it do you?' He angrily snipes at my taunt and I simply say, 'Cutting your nose to spite your face, much?' In less than five seconds, he flips through a blank stare, a flash of anger, a profound furrow, and finally a deep belly laugh.

You cannot dream of another. I introduce this rejoinder for the benefit of all those romantic partners who have awoken to being pounded with a pillow for having 'cheated' in their partner's dream. We cannot actually dream of another; *we dream of our relationship to them.* Just as we do not 'see' another in the waking world but rather see all of our attributions to them of meaning, reference, and reflection; the dreamworld provides us with the same complexes, but, in this case, unencumbered by the 'objective' presence of the other. The actions of others in our dreams may help us improve or understand our relationships with the person. They can just as easily inform us about those parts of us that become active in relationship to this person or those parts of us that we fear, hope, or otherwise deny are like or resonate with them. This leads us to the next hint.

Everyone and everything in the dream is a part of 'you' — scary parts, stuck parts, hidden parts, hostile parts, parts with whom you want to merge, parts that look like your parents, and parts that look like 'you.' The tricky part is that 'you' as you know you, or at least the 'you' of the dream, defines itself in such as way as to deny these other parts. By taking the perspective that all of these dream-parts are aspects of a larger 'You,' you may gain fruitful imagery for the various tensions you experience in your waking life.

You are having the dream as you describe the dream. Worries that you'll 'forget something,' 'get it wrong,' or 'mess it up' are misplaced. The very act of entering into the description of the dream invites the leviathan that motivated the dream to gently nudge our little conscious rowboat. So, too, our feelings during the retelling, our inability to recall certain words, and our conflicts with someone with whom we share the dream will all be products of this unconscious configuration. Thus, attending to the retelling becomes a whole source of far more direct access to the informing image now present in the room. This is one particular area where a skilled dreamworker can be of immense benefit.

Let go of the dream itself and play! Whether through dance, painting, sculpting, a story, poem, or any other creative act, let some image possess you. In this spirit, even academic investigation of the background of some seemingly mythic image — known as 'amplification' in the classical Jungian community — will prove artistic. Trust that any process growing out of this imagery will lead you to deeper waters and stranger horizons.

These are just the barest of hints of a whole way of living in which we learn to free ourselves from the myopia of literalism and see the massive currents and forces that shape our lives. Unfortunately, an ongoing familiarity with dreams facilitates some people segregating their insights into only their sleeping productions. In part, this conflict plays out in the Jungian community in which some analysts seek to keep psyche's voice firmly grounded in 'individual' and 'internal' landscapes; whereas others, especially the firebrands of Imaginal Psychology, see the waves of psyche on a global scale. Nevertheless, whether we give full voice to it or not, dreamwork transforms our waking lives.

Throughout Jung's writings, he has a gradually developing arc about 'active imagination.' At first, one could believe that he is merely advocating for a technique by which the patient can learn to interrogate or 'work' a particular image. Eventually, however, the very process of encountering these images becomes an attitude toward one's life — an attitude in which we learn to liberate ourselves from entrapping archetypal dyads. In short, what begins as a technique becomes an engagement in the unfolding Individuation of the Self. In the end, we can tell no stories but our own — dream no dreams but those of our unfolding lives. The ability to remain resolutely loyal to this process is what this current work presents as the underlying telos of all life.

In a world in which the ontological obscenity of 'Reality Television' ever expands its tentacular stranglehold, we sense that we are fictional yet have no means of expressing this truth. We yearn for fictions, we live from and through them. We need stories, even ones that are 'true,' to fuel our regeneration, our growth, our loves and passions. By necessity and perhaps by design, we fully fall into our stories, as we must in order, truly, to change. But we lose, in this absorption, the necessary awareness to view our stories *as* stories. And thus, like the idée fixe of an amnesiac, we feel the powerful pull of our dreams and the other fictions of film, literature, biography, and myth — screaming with their message, 'You too are made of these!'

39
A Last Go at the Central Idea
Dream and the Gods

Wake up to the Dream! No-one dreams all the time; but we are all dreamed, all the time. Any particular 'I' is constantly being dreamed. The process of dreaming endlessly produces and represents the fictions upon which we live and has little to do with sleeping. As Chumbley beautifully illustrates, dreaming is the Crossroads. Hecate, Mercury, and Legba are just a few of the gods guarding this axis-point. However, the Crossroads of dreaming are not the mere intersection of life's roads. Dreaming is not simply some utile cognitive process by which we efficiently categorize and store our days' experiences. The Dreaming is the point from which all roads grow.

We can speak neither of the Imaginal nor of the imagination of magic without finally coming to those supernatural entities about whom center our most ancient stories. The gods. Whether in the forms of dread Archangels, the cunning Fae, or breastplate-clad Olympians, neo-pagans continue to struggle with the possibility of an even more radical notion of the gods than the safely sterilized moralisms of middle-school myth curricula will allow. But are we not all struggling with cosmologies that do not yet address our lives as we experience them? Do we not all secretly know that the gods with which we are familiar conceal stranger forces than we allow ourselves to express? Let us briefly deconstruct the convenience of our story-book gods and see if we may not discover the powers that animate and destroy, that drive us—as well as drive us mad.

To begin with, the mythoi of the Northern Europeans, as well as that of your average teenager, understands that the gods must die. The gods are real, to be sure—as real as a sunrise, as childbirth, as an identity, as technology. But the gods are no *more* real than these. Perhaps we might say that the gods are the reality of these constructions. But gods who are not of the lived experiential world condemn us to a life divided against itself. Perhaps one of the best illustrations of this point comes from a surprising source.

I can enjoy nearly all of Lovecraft's stories, with proper perspective, but one particular novella stands out as unusually optimistic and poignant for that brooding Yankee. *The Dream-Quest of Unknown Kadath*, although written in 1927, did not see publication until 1943, six years after Lovecraft's death. In the story, we meet, once again, Lovecraft's Randolph Carter. Once an anxious and cowering man of questionable sanity, the reader now encounters a matured Carter who journeys through a series of dreaming adventures, each more rich with mystic symbolism than the last. Carter seeks a beautiful, shining city that he has only glimpsed in his dreams. Determined to find it, he sets out on a quest through the limitless dreamland to find Kadath, where the gods dwell. Throughout his quest, however, his steps are dogged by the machinations of Nyarlathotep, the faceless god, the Crawling Chaos, the Emissary of the Unspeakable gods dwelling in the black space between the stars. In the story's climax, Carter finally lands on the unimaginably elevated spire of Kadath, only to find it empty. The gods are not here. Carter comes face to face with Nyarlathotep, now in the guise of a pharaoh. This dark trickster explains that the gods have left this place and gone to live in Carter's dream-glimpsed 'sunset city.' He goes on to reveal that this city has always been Carter's own childhood memories of wonder at the numinous world around him. Nyarlathotep explains that Carter must go to the city and force the gods back to dance beneath Nyarlathotep's gaze; but, ever the trickster, when he sends Carter on his way, he gives him passage on a massive bird that heads straight for the center of the universe — a nuclear singularity of insanity. Carter realizes, in a frenzied rush of insight, that this is all a dream and that the city he sought, the city in which now dwell the gods, is his own city. Letting go of the bird, he awakes to a sunset over Boston, and is home.

Though the fear of the voids may lead us to divide up our experiences, the gods rightly live in the streets with us. The only real journey is the one that leads us more fully to exactly where we are, this very moment. All our other realms, spiritual aspirations, and mystic journeys will annihilate us in black madness if we do not tenaciously hold to the reality of *now*.

I cannot sustain a belief that abandons experience. I admire the tenacity of those who can, but my temperament is such that I fail to see the relevance of what is 'back then' or 'yet to come.' To have a mythos, a faith, or a philosophy that guides you through life's pains and trials with a hope of what is yet-to-come or not-quite-here is a powerful thing. But if it pulls you, as it inevitably will, away from the unfolding moment, what was this religion ultimately about? Yes, the gods die, are born again, and die again. Marvelous! But how many gods do more for you than your blender? I mean, think about all that creamy, smoothie-goodness. Gods who cannot account for the blender, gods who do not intersect with 'check-engine' lights, break-ups, mental illness, and credit-card debt are of little use to most of us, other than as a distraction.

Personified, anthropomorphized, and trussed up in anachronisms, our gods too often pull us away from life with the hopes of enriching it. Personification demands relationship and we are fundamentally relational creatures. So, indeed, giving a face to our gods is a fruitful road. But does this practice not also tame that which transcends our easy definitions? Is it not our just due that the Love-craftian Mythos should give us indifferent, unspeakable, and sanity-devouring gods to compensate and complement our sweetly accessible hearth divinities?

Worse yet, though we allow our comic book writers to dabble with the chang-ing relationships of the gods, how often do we see world events as the politics of the gods? Our parlor-friendly, humanistic and figurative gods lack the horror, awe, and numinosity of their forebears. We have little room for gods that yank us screaming into the moment. Usually, we want our gods to pull us away from the intolerability of our lives!

Too often, we only hearken to dream images and 'magical' moments that reso-nate with our fantasy of the gods. We dive into the world of what-we-think-dreams-should-be-like and miss the fact that we often dream of small things, of bloody things, of wiring, and bad hair, and car-trips, and our pets. Are these petty dreams? Should we wait for the dreams where faeries speak and caves glow? These dreams may actually be less important than the one about the light bulb burned out in the closet or when you show up to class naked.

When we wait for 'big dreams,' do we not safely insulate our lives against the real dream that we are having right now? Only when we awaken to this Dream can we come to see the moment in its fullness. Only then can we read our lives aright.

Through identity, thingness, time, and all the other fantastical frontiers of our lives, we confine ourselves to a corner of the dream—through 'a glass darkly,' Paul says. But I have little patience for waiting until after death for his 'face to face.' Let us learn to set aside that mirror, that looking glass, and look, as if for the first time, into this starry abyss that reels around and within us.

Afterword
Is It a Book Yet?

As explained in the Introduction to this second volume, initially, this work was an effort at self-indoctrination — in addition to self-initiation. 'Let's see what happens if I actually believe this stuff and take these ideas to their logical ends.' Becoming so enmeshed and identified with a process can open up opportunities to reassess and remake parts of your life. It can also make you a moody and self-possessed twit. I chose a bracing do-si-do between these two extremes for most of this process.

I offered the second 'Niel Estes' draft of this book as a submission to a relatively prolific publisher. Given the sort of dense esoteric rants he proffered alongside relatively scholarly works, I figured my own underdeveloped, snarky tirade stood a decent chance. After a few months, I received a terse email that stated, 'it isn't quite a book yet.'

After a resentful tantrum in my library in which I counted the number of spelling and grammatical errors in one chapter of the publisher's most recent offering, I was forced to admit that he might have a point. I looked again at my draft and saw, much to my horror, that I was hiding behind hyperbole, symbol, and the worst sort of 'occultization' — the very sins I bemoan in so much of this work. Why wasn't I saying what I meant? Was I ashamed? Afraid? In my smug intellectual acrobatics, I was certainly cagey for sure.

In part, I didn't entirely know *what* I meant to say, and if I did, I didn't yet know *how* to say it. I did not yet fully have the voice and only dimly saw the vocation. I knew I felt a deep and powerful connection between my academic, professional, personal, and magical lives, but I felt that I had to apologize for, dissemble, or equivocate the interconnections. The very act of writing this book in its current form has been an attempt to unmake those divides. The only way to do this, however, was to actually deal with my life, not derivative ideas or concepts, but the stories that represent, and gave rise to, the realizations herein. Only with this lifeblood would the message no longer be an ironic self-indictment.

Rewriting, recasting this work that claims to be about life as we live it, with the testimony of my life as I live it, has yielded a work that I think I can say is now indeed a book.

In Volume One, I said that I meant this book to be of value to everyone. 'The premise of this work,' I said, 'is that *we all yearn for and do magic*. We just don't let ourselves see it.' What we do, how we do it right now, is magic. The imagination of magic is an intuition of, and gateway to, our imaginal reality. Given these perspectives, I hope that, not only through the concepts, stories, and exercises, but through an ongoing commentary with this text, you have been able to feel that yearning for the real anew, and have seen a way to reclaim the magical acts that constitute your life.

When you ask the vast majority of people about their 'spiritual' life, my experience has been that they tend to give one of two types of answers. They respond with either formulaic, doctrinal pabulum, or they offer a series of vague statements that often end with 'I guess I never really thought about it.' Again, in most cases, this response has precious little to do with how these same people lead their lives.

'I'm not religious, I'm spiritual' has become something of a motto in certain circles today. These people put aside dogmatism in favor of—what? A vagueness that seems safer? If anything, I hope that this work has offered another possibility. Perhaps these volumes have even given those retreating from formulaic beliefs a new grounding in the imaginal to move *to*, rather than running *from* the imposition of others' imagery. Even those who cling to rigid literalisms such as spirituality or materialism find themselves haunted by fundamental anxieties. To everyone who has wondered if there is not another way to address this fundamental human longing, I have offered this work.

Our lives are rooted in our stories, our lived beliefs. Not all of them are pretty or pleasant, or even hopeful; but they are ours. Only through claiming the responsibility for our meaning-making can we hope to live purposeful, intentional, deliberate lives. Whether we believe in ancient mysteries, institutional equations, or ephemeral equivocations, these are still *our* beliefs. These are all ways we make this moment. But how do we live with these constructed moments? Do we find guilt, hope, guidance, forgiveness, hate, unity, division? Regardless of what the philosophies, rationales, promises, sacred texts, textbooks, and informative articles of our faiths, beliefs, sciences, and convictions tell us, we are still left with the business of getting on with a life. I hope that this work has provided some aid in that process.

Appendix B

A Grammar of the Voids
Essays, Impressions, Sources, and Glossary of Key Terms

Postmodern philosophy has become increasingly reality-warping and, as such, I am not convinced that overtly, explicitly magical writings are the only or even the best place to learn the technology of experience engineering. Nevertheless, I suspect that, however much of a minority the readers of explicitly occult and esoteric topics are, sincere readers of postmodern philosophy are even fewer. Thus, this collection of personalities and terms contains something of a brief primer of existential and postmodern philosophy, in addition to key figures and concepts from the history of neo-paganism, esotericism, magic, and the occult. I make no claim that it is exhaustive, nor free from controversy.

For this current work, I drew influences from all of the authors below. To the best of my ability, when I borrow an idea directly from an author, I cite the name within the text. I offer this list as a starting point for readers who wish to explore theorists who are often more important and more thorough scholars than most of the 'big names' of occult literature. However, if you plan to cite—whether at a cocktail party or in writing—any of these authors or their ideas, please do them the courtesy of actually attempting to read their works rather than merely scanning a Wikipedia article about them. As this work indicates, the journey of discovering, engaging, and wrestling with an idea is a powerfully personal and potentially transformative path.

In the midst of trying to decipher some esoteric author's cryptic ramblings, I have often wondered if the term 'occult' merely refers to a penchant for 'occulta-tion'; that is, hiding what could otherwise be explained clearly. I suppose that this sort of obscuring can provide would-be initiates with the intellectual fodder to fuel their personal journey; but I worry that it is mostly a poorly constructed substitute for genuine mystery. Frequently, the 'Six Degrees of Francis Bacon' mentioned in Volume One becomes the sole purpose of all this esoteric acumen, as victims of the imagination of magic attempt to cover over their disillusion-ment with impenetrable cross-referencing. Thus, in many of these essays, I have attempted to lay bare as many of the 'secrets' of Western Esotericism as have any relevance to this current work. Such is the case with the numbers that begin this grammar; nonetheless, these are symbolic numbers and fanciful equations, with little to no gemmatria or any other numerological system underpinning them.

Most of these names and terms appear within the text. Others provide enhancements to and clarifications of the book's message or intent. These definitions and annotations are painfully biased and self-serving, but should give the reader enough grounding to pursue these ideas beyond the confines of this current work. Words in SMALL CAPITAL LETTERS indicate definitions or bibliographic references that the reader can find elsewhere within this appendix.

Although I have tried to restrain myself from creating an excess of neologisms, I freely admit to creating unique and SYNCRETIC definitions for pre-existing terms.

0 In the Western Initiatory QABALAH, the numeric label of AIN SOF AUR

00 In the Western Initiatory QABALAH, the numeric label of AIN SOF.

000 In the Western Initiatory QABALAH, the numeric label of AIN.

0=2 ('zero equals two') An equation used within CROWLEY's Thelema. Read from right to left, this formula holds the potential to speak to the transcendence of dyads into nothingness. More typically read from left to right, it describes the avoidance of genuine nothingness through dichotomies. Thus, it is the formula of seeming or appearance, ubiquitous within esoteric systems that are still enthralled by dualistic symbolism. From the checkered floor of the FREEMASONIC Lodge to the derivative gender dyads that plague most magical systems, this formula is utile only if you want to maintain a current stasis or status quo. From this self-sustaining dyadic paradigm, making changes becomes awkward at best. HERMENEUTICALLY speaking, however, becoming aware *of* the dyadic nature of any particular system may prove a gateway to transcending its thrall — that is, hermeneutic awareness of a dyad may be a first step toward some form of METHOD X.

0>N ('zero is greater than any number') For this work, the formula of existence in which nothingness takes precedence over derivative forms and dyads. Consistency is brutally difficult from this perspective. Making alterations, achieving rebirth, and transformation are, however, much easier.

23 A number of chaos. For this text, rather than the personal, individualistic journey represented by CROWLEY's 93, 23 offers a vision of subtle systems, dynamic relationships, and polymorphous transformations. Thus, 23 relates to Kia rather than Thelema. It is most widely presented by Robert Anton Wilson, who credits William S. Burroughs with its discovery.

93 The number of Thelema. CROWLEY bases his famous greeting-formula 'Do what thou wilt shall be the whole of the Law. Love is the Law, Love under Will' on the numerological value of Thelema ('will') and Agape ('love') in Greek both equaling 93. The idea of pursuing one's True Will, assumedly a long and difficult journey of discernment and travail, is central to this number's symbolic power.

111 A number sometimes associated with Kether, the highest sephiroth. Also the enumeration of QTB (QUTUB, 'the point').

222 Since 333 can be seen as a number for a qlipothic level, thus 222 — along with 444 — would assumedly be qlipothic shadow parallels to 555 and 777. However, no publicly available source explains the correspondence. It seems most likely that 444 stands behind 555 and 222 obverse to 777.

333 According to GRANT, the number of Choronzon, and thus, the shadow side — QLIPOTH — of the Rosy Cross's 666. In CHUMBLEY's Sabbatic system, it is the number of Zsin-Niag-Sa, 'The Lunar In-creative Formula of Magick' (*Azoëtia*, 2002, p. 361).

444 In CHUMBLEY's Sabbatic system, the number of Abra-Khu-Zraa, 'Solar Creative/Ex-creative Formula of Magick' (*Azoëtia*, 2002, p. 359). See 333 and 222.

555 The number of the GOLDEN DAWN level of the Western Initiatory Qabalah. It corresponds to the five pointed star: the four elements plus spirit creating a vector toward the ROSY CROSS yet blocked by the VEIL OF THE PEROKETH.

666 The number of the ROSY CROSS level of the Western Initiatory QABALAH. It corresponds to the six pointed star formed by two overlapping triangles, one pointing up and the other down. Some esoteric systems actually portray four triangles, two of them with cross-beams, thus forming symbols for 'raised elements' — no longer base matter, since the Rosy Cross is the symbolic level, protected from the mundane by the VEIL OF THE PEROKETH. However, although initiates may, on this plane, believe themselves to have reached enlightenment, their view of what may lie ahead — the A.˙.A.˙. — is obscured by the abyss of DA'ATH. To a greater extent, this number has been conflated with 'The Great Beast' of the Bible's *Book of Revelation*, a confusion encouraged by CROWLEY's perversity and iconoclasm. However, this level of achievement can become a qlipothic quagmire if the initiate becomes complacently satisfied with the life-wisdom offered by the Rosy Cross and remains ignorant of the Greater Mysteries of the A.˙.A.˙..

777 The number of the A.˙.A.˙. level of the Western Initiatory QABALAH. It corresponds to the seven pointed 'Star of Babalon' — as CROWLEY called it. In the Western Initiatory QABALAH, the seven points of the star correspond to the seven previous sephiroth of the GOLDEN DAWN and ROSY CROSS levels, now visible in a unified system, rather than opposed to each other.

888 A facetious Chaos/Qabalistic number meant as a hyperbolic trump card to all the other symbolic numbers. This number could be used to represent the truth that all qliphoths contain all sephiroth and all sephiroth contain all qliphoths, just as every sephiroth contains a complete Tree of Life. This 888 satire would then emphasize that every qabalistic stance extends in every direction beyond any and all known paths. Peter CARROLL presents such a Tree in his *Apophenion* (2008). 888 links better to KIA than to Thelema. (The number is also the numeric value of 'Jesus Christ' in Greek according to *Godwin's Cabalistic Encyclopedia, 3rd Edition* (2008).)

A.ˑ.A.ˑ. An acronym deliberately conceived to have no single expressible meaning, often thought to mean *Astrum Argenteum* (spellings vary but all mean 'Silver Star'), *Arcanum Arcanorum* ('Secret of Secrets' or 'Mystery of Mysteries'), and other ciphers including 'Angel and Abyss.' It is mostly associated with CROWLEY's reworking of the HERMETIC ORDER OF THE GOLDEN DAWN system into a more solitary magical lineage and order — as expressed in his uncharacteristically restrained poem 'One Star in Sight' (1921); however, the symbolism far exceeds any corporate entity or legally recognized copyright holders. Multiple layers of meaning, which hermeneutically and epistemologically shift depending on the seeker's position, suffuse this term. Stated differently, how one chooses to define the term is representative of one's relationship to what it simultaneously conceals and reveals. In the broadest sense, the A.ˑ.A.ˑ. is one term for the archetype of the True Journey and Order of all Initiates — not merely the Thelemically-minded ones, since the concept predates Crowley. It also can refer to the final triad of the Qabalistic Tree of Life: Kether, Chokhmah, and Binah. In a more specific interpretation, it is the imminent vector underlying the Western Esoteric Current, especially those pursuing the Western Initiatory QABALAH. See SECRET CHIEFS and 777.

Abject A concept from the writings of KRISTEVA. The abject defies, indicts, and undercuts subject and object and frequently evokes a fundamental revulsion. The abject is an ongoing layer of UNDIFFERENTIATION that abides after the construction of various personality structures atop it. The experience of UNSPEAKABLE HORROR is often in the (non)face of the abject. The encounter with the abject may be an important step along a VITRIOLIC journey. A defensive rejection of the ubiquitous mystical path may engender a potentially destructive encounter with the abject.

Abyss The expansive nothingness represented by the empty circle. The term carries a sense of being 'beyond depth'—that is, an indictment of all specificity and limit. In this sense, it is synonymous with some notions of the SUBLIME. Many people try to escape this reality through an inward-focused subjectivism, PSYCHOLOGIZING, or spirituality. A host of encounters may reveal abyss, but more popular ones include community, expansive space, and time. The Western QABALAH's Tree of Life has a rhythm of increasingly expansive abysses beginning with the bridge between Malkuth and Yesod (the path of the World), then the VEIL OF THE PEROKETH, next DA'ATH, and, ultimately AIN SOPH AUR, AIN SOPH, and AIN. See BYSS.

Actor-observer bias A tendency to see your own actions as due to circumstances; however, observers will tend to see these same actions as due to your fundamental character or disposition. Thus, to use an automotive example, when I brake too late and come to a jerking stop, I will tend to blame the driver ahead of me for stopping short. Yet my passenger will tend to see me as a fundamentally careless or distracted driver. Easily blended with, but distinct from, the FUNDAMENTAL ATTRIBUTION ERROR. Both are part of attribution theory.

Adler, Margot (1946-) Journalist, author, and Wiccan, Adler wrote the first comprehensive examination of neo-paganism in America. *Drawing Down the Moon* (1979) was a powerful work of social anthropology, journalism, and personal reflection. It presented a cross-section of the magical, occult, and neo-pagan cultures emerging in 20th century America. Free from unsupported doctrinal assertions, Adler's work slowly opened the door for later scholarly examinations of neo-paganism and the MAGICAL REVIVAL. To the rest of the U.S., Adler is best known for her work on National Public Radio.

Agency The state of asserting meaningful and informed choice within one's life. Although we are always responsible for the events and choices we make in our lives, we cannot assert complete agency over them. The process of claiming increasing agency is integral to the path of authenticity. See FREEDOM AND RESPONSIBILITY.

Agnostic Like ATHEISM, a term defined to the advantage of the speaker. One version is a stance of 'who knows, it could be?' regarding all things divine and spiritual. Another distinct version, championed by Stephen Batchelor in *Buddhism without Beliefs* (1998) speaks to the irrelevancy of any religious or philosophical stance that leaves the limits of the human ways of knowing.

Ain, Ain Sof, and Ain Sof Aur In the QABALAH, the three pre-manifestation voids surrounding the entirety of the Tree of Life. They are, however, typically seen as extending beyond or before the final triad of the Tree (see A.˙.A.˙.).

Although translation of such terms is difficult, Ain, the furthest void can be seen as 'Nothing,' Ain Soph as 'Limitlessness,' and Ain Soph Aur, the closest void, as 'Endless Light.' All previous veils, limits, or abysses on the Tree (the bridge between Malkuth and Yesod, the Veil of the Peroketh, and Da'ath) are mere echoes of these fundamental voids. In the numerology of the Western Initiatic Qabalah, Ain is 000, Ain Sof 00, and Ain Sof Aur 0.

Aizenstat, Steve (1949-) Founding president of *Pacifica Graduate Institute*. Noted for his work with luminaries in the field of Imaginal Psychology, he has also worked extensively with various indigenous groups around the world. He coined the term 'dream-tending' for his approach to dream materials, which he presents most recently in *Dream Tending* (2009).

Alembic The alchemical vessel or flask in which the work of practical alchemy occurs. Portrayals of the alterations of appearance of the vessel and its contents are the central metaphors in much of alchemical literature.

Aletheia One of several Greek words for 'truth,' highlighted by Heidegger. In this case, it is the ditch digger's realization that to uncover one thing you must simultaneously cover over another. This term highlights the profoundly contextual nature of all 'truth' and the limitations imposed by any perspective. See logos.

Allah In addition to the more etymologically standard derivations for this singular God of Islam, Sufis sometimes cite the name as meaning 'Al-lah' — 'the Not.' This definition receives attention in the writings of the Sufi Psychologist Llewellyn Vaughan-Lee. To be clear, referring to Allah as 'the Beloved' is far more common in Sufism.

Alphabet of Desire A system of sigils embodying a cosmology, often also a divinatory system. The Tarot, I Ching, and Runes are prime examples. Spare introduced this term to a wider audience and advanced the technique of creating one's own secret alphabet; however, the practice and its numinous potential clearly extends far into antiquity, and possibly into prehistory with the promethean invention of language itself within any given culture. A grimoire may contain one or more alphabets, whether a collection of talismans, supernatural languages, planetary or zodiacal attributes, gems, elements, spirits, or a host of other vocabularies by which to divide experience. In this text, the true alphabet of desire is exactly that: the language of the various vectors of being, desires, defenses, and identities through which No-one flows. The intersections of these vectors form the fabric of the True Grimoire.

Alterity Otherness, the defining relational orientation that gives rise to the localization of experience ('self') and is simultaneously an indictment thereof. True alterity is inscrutable, as is the other pole of the encounter, identity. The rhythm of alterity hermeneutically defines the mystical journey wherein seekers face new ciphers of otherness challenging their construction of self. In this text, that dance is symbolized by the rhythm of the various BYSSES and ABYSSES one encounters.

Analytic Psychology Term created by JUNG to contrast his approach to psyche with that of FREUD's 'psychoanalysis.'

Angst EXISTENTIAL dread. Literally 'anxiety,' this term has come to mean the ache of inauthenticity, as well as a call to reassess how one lives.

Anima/Animus The contrasexual shadow. In Jung's original sense, a man had an anima and a woman an animus. This systematization characterized the anima as an irrational, sensual, and seductive side to a man's personality and the animus as a rational, stern, and restrictive aspect of a woman's psyche. In an effort to overcome this sexism, theorists have struggled to develop new language to account for a phenomenon that is still quite valid, simply in a more fluid fashion than Jung originally allowed. The contrasexual shadow holds those aspects of one's gender and sexual orientation that one's ego will not allow. As an indicting force against identity, when resisted the anima or animus can be a destructive power. Typically, we project our countrasexual shadows onto our friendships and sexual relationships. Coming to terms with the anima or animus can be a central vector in one's initiatic work, as seen in DANTE's transforming and transformative relationship to Beatrice in the *Divine Comedy*.

Anti-theism An ironic stance that simultaneously acknowledges, at a minimum, the power of the idea of an active God, and opposes it. See also ATHEISM.

Apophasis Mystical path of eliminating imagery. This term may apply to eradicating intermediary language obscuring moment-to-moment experience as well as purging limiting images of the divine or sublime. Although often theoretically contrasted to the imagery of CATAPHASIS, both of these terms may ultimately lead to the same realizations if pursued tenaciously. Many would view forms of Buddhism, especially Zen, as fundamentally apophatic; on the other hand, much of Tibetan Buddhism blurs the apophatic/cataphatic distinction by using imagery to move one to the stance of nothingness. A fanciful etymology might link this term to the enemy of the Egyptian sun god Ra, the snake Apep, known as Apophis in Greek. The motto of aphophatic mysticism may well be *NETI, NETI*. See also MU.

Apophenia Finding meaningful symbolism and connections where none seemingly exist. This term assumes that things unto themselves can actually be, at other times, meaningful and symbolic; and thus ignores the fundamental meaning-making task of existence. In clinical psychology, the pathological version of this stance is the delusion of IDEAS OF REFERENCE. This term, in a more positive sense, figures prominently in CARROLL's work *The Apophenion: A Chaos Magic Paradigm* (2008).

Apotheosis Originally, this term applied to the ascension of a saint into heaven. In a mythopoetic or postmodern sense, it can take on the meaning of a relentless pursuit of values, imagery, or goals that eventually renders the original idea irreplicable and subsumes the practitioner and practice into a greater whole. It is a rarefaction, ATTENUATION, distillation — an alchemical process in which the practitioner dissolves in the quest. After this transformation, any return to the previous context or practice would be empty. On a larger scale, an artist, practitioner, or IMAGONAUT may render a form empty for others as well, should the apotheosis be radical and large-scale enough. In this text, paralleling the compass atop the central FREEMASONIC symbol, the Λ represents this relentless upward ascent. MEMES and IMAGES may also apotheosize, such as the first atomic blast serving as an apotheosis of the solar phallus.

Archetype Widely misunderstood concept advanced by Jung. Archetypes are the structure of experience itself. Archetypes are neither abstractions, nor inherently more 'spiritual' than other ideas. Archetypes are always lived, relational, dyadic, and embody a complete continuum from 'flesh' to 'spirit.' Jung used the metaphor of the visible light spectrum (i.e., red, orange, yellow, green, blue, indigo, violet) and its edges (i.e., infrared and ultraviolet) to express this continuum from the warm infrared of embodiment, through the green of lived relationships, to the uncanny luminosity of ultraviolet spirituality. Thus, the mother/child (there is no 'mother archetype' on its own) archetypal pattern could potentially extend from the motherly embrace, through the caring conversation, to the spiritual Mother Mary. From a Jungian perspective, archetypes are the dry riverbeds into which the specific experiences of our lives pour, creating our complexes. Although experiences of the numinous may give one insight into archetypal structures, one does not truly experience the archetype itself, since archetypes are the structure of experience itself. A somewhat pessimistic interpretation of the archetypes could cast them as greedy ARCHONS seeking to co-opt, subvert, define, and possess the individual (and reality itself) through the process of INDIVIDUATION. From a Jungian perspective, only the SELF is unique within the archetypes in its non-entrapping individuation. Thus, in a GNOSTIC struggle, one seeks liberation from these forces in order to become present to truths that extend beyond the immediate context as archetypally defined. A fresh gloss on the term might call this Neo-Gnostic An-archism.

Archetypal Psychology See IMAGINAL PSYCHOLOGY.

Archons 'Kings' of this world, as 'this world' is most commonly taken up. A term from some forms of GNOSTICISM, the archons are seen as jailers keeping the sparks of the alien God trapped in gross material(istic) illusion. The archons serve the DEMIURGE. The process of transforming the relationship to the archons until they are revealed as archangels is slow and fraught with tears. This classic Gnostic cosmology too easily slips into some form of dualism; however, given that those achieving archon-transcending Gnosis did not immediately ascend into some non-visible spiritual ('pneumatic') realm, one may assume that archontic reality may have been more of a fallen mode of being, rather than some other 'realm.' In this spirit, Hans JONAS presents an intriguing synthesis of EXISTENTIALISM with Gnosticism.

'As above, so below' Central doctrine of the EMERALD TABLET OF HERMETICISM.

Atavism Genetic, ancestral, or racial memory.

Atheism A term used far too broadly and glibly to achieve any clarity of definition. In a technical sense, the word can merely imply a disbelief in a theistic god — an active, changeable divine force that one can propitiate. This disbelieving stance is, more precisely, NON-THEISM. In this sense, one can be an atheist and hold religious, spiritual, mystical, or a host of other views about God, gods, etc.. Too often, critics lob the label 'atheist' to mean a broadly defined ANTI-THEISM, a rabid disdain for any sort of divinity as well as those adherents to religion in any form. In all likelihood, 'atheism' only maintains its marginal terminological utility in the West.

Atlantis A mythic GOLDEN-AGE continent where enlightened beings once ruled in harmony with God and Nature. The origins of the story can be traced at least to Plato. In the spiritualist and New-Age revival of the story, Atlantis has become the origin for all spiritual traditions and, thus, the PERENNIAL PHILOSOPHY. Whether through the song by Donovan or the revelations of various channelers since the Victorian era, believers cast Atlantis as the connecting hub between the pyramids of Egypt and Meso-America. It is also seen as the origin of the gods, especially HERMES TRISMEGISTUS. Stories vary as to Atlantis' demise, but typically some form of hubris or greed corrupts the island and it sinks beneath the ocean. In more expansive cosmologies, Atlantis is only the latest of three great antediluvian continents. See MU and LEMURIA.

Attenuation A tenacious refinement of a concept/image to distill an almost imperceptible (quint)essence. In short, a potentially ridiculous quest of APOTHEOSIS that could remove one entirely from experience, were not the journey toward this unattainable goal so madly rich. Attenuation implies a signal becoming increasingly subtle.

Attribution theory See ACTOR-OBSERVER BIAS and FUNDAMENTAL ATTRIBUTION ERROR.

Autangel A term introduced in this work to convey the inseparability and indistinguishability of an image's content and conveyance. Autonomous, AUTOCHTHONOUS messengers in which the means of conveying the message *is*, in fact, the message. Autangels often carry infectious EPISTEMOLOGIES. These forms usually hide under the content they use to distract and beg the question of their true purpose, which is to modify how, and thus *what*, we perceive. An example would be a Western medical doctor recognizing that the patient has the right to a second opinion, but simply sending the patient to another Western allopathic doctor. No matter what, the underlying means of conveying information has been carried on. Commercials, fields of academic study, politics, sciences, and relationships are common hosts for these entities.

Autochthonous Self-generating or emerging from itself. Without creator or source, de facto, ipso facto, and sui generis. Memes, archetypes, and images are always autochthonous regardless of the intentions of the one who claims to have birthed, created, or conceived them.

Autonomic Nervous System (ANS) The body's self-regulating 'auto-pilot.' The ANS has two theoretical divisions: the sympathetic and parasympathetic nervous systems. The sympathetic side prepares the body for 'fight, flight, or freeze'; the parasympathetic, 'rest and digest.' Interconnected with a wide range of bodily functions, including respiration, heart rate, metabolism, perspiration, perceptual sets, blood flow within the brain, and many others. Meditative techniques tend to begin with establishing some control over the ANS, especially by way of breath control.

Azoëtia Magnum Opus by CHUMBLEY, originally published in 1992 and expanded and re-issued in 2002. This GRIMOIRE conveys the ritual structure and ALPHABET OF DESIRE for the Sabbatic Craft.

Bach, Richard (1936-) American author, most famous for his spiritual books *Jonathon Livingston Seagull* (1970) and *ILLUSIONS: THE ADVENTURES OF A RELUCTANT MESSIAH* (1977) as well as his aviation and ferret-oriented works. Highly influential in the New Age movement more through affection than direct influence. Though semi-autobiographical in nature, his works are all fictional or fictionalized.

Bachelard, Gaston (1884-1962) French philosopher on poetics and the philosophy of science. A major influence on later postmodern philosophers. *Psychoanalysis of Fire* (1938) and the posthumous *Fragments of Poetics of Fire* (1988) are of particular relevance to this current work. Bachelard focuses a tenaciously poetic eye on the nature of imagination.

Baphomet Central figure in the imagination of much of Western Occultism. Historical origins are quite shaky with legends that usually refer back to the accusations against the Templars. Emerging in the 19th century as part of the MAGICAL REVIVAL, Eliphas Levi (1810-1875) created the most memorable image attached to this character with his 'Sabbatic Goat.' Were it to appear in Tibetan Buddhism, this goat-headed, alchemical, hermaphroditic, trans-species, animal, vegetable, mineral, chthonic spirit figure would just be another heady thangka symbolizing integration. But in the West? This figure still carries a powerful satanic resonance, past which most viewers cannot get. This is probably a deliberate foil on the part of generations of occultists who need to simultaneously access their own shadows and deter those who can't. Nevertheless, some groups do use the Baphomet figure as a type of anti-Christian, satanic image. This usage is ironic at best since, in many ways, Baphomet is just as easily a Christ figure. As a SELF-symbol (see ARCHETYPES and INDIVIDUATION) this pseudo-historical pagan divinity represents the potential power of the MORNINGSTAR current for integration and individuation of the Self.

Baudrillard, Jean (1929-2007) Post-structural philosopher who introduced the concept of 'hyperreality' in which we no longer connect to raw experience but only to a haze of referential signifiers. Arguably more referenced than understood, his best known work is *Simlacra and Simulation* (1981) which draws a marvelous metaphor from the BORGES (and possibly Casares) story 'On Exactitude in Science' (1946) in which a map becomes so large as to be on the same scale as the territory, eventually replacing the 'original.'

Black Brother A dated accusatory term lobbed by late Victorian self-righteous moralists within the magical world to indict the practices of those with the audacity to refuse such rigid morality. Sometimes meant to imply that a previously promising Mage has failed to cross the Qabalistic abyss of DA'ATH or has fallen into the QLIPOTHS. Again, this slur usually implies that the accuser believes himself superior to the 'lost' brother or sister. Such fallen practitioners were sometimes associated with the 'Black Lodge' or the LEFT-HAND PATH. Clearly, in today's moderately more diverse esoteric community, the nomenclature is troubling and troublesome at best. Nevertheless, individuals claiming to be mages are, more-often-than-not, deluded. Of those who practice some form of magic, regardless of their self-label, a certain portion refuses to surrender to the gravity of the greater process at work and desperately clings to some ego state. A substitute term has not yet been developed, within the imagination of magic, to accurately speak to this developmental resistance leading to deluded, pathological entrapment.

Blavatsky, Helena Petrovna (b. Helena von Hahn 1831-1891) Spiritualist, prophet, and likely skilled con artist, Blavatsky gathered together disparate elements of spiritualist, orientalist, and classical ideas into a piquant goulash that would eventually become the New Age movement. Her first major work, *Isis Unveiled* (1877), is a massive effort to reform the errors of Western science and religion. The founder of Theosophy, she, along with Dion Fortune, are the most visible advocates for the Right-Hand Path.

Bodhidharma (c. 5th/6th centuries) The first of the 'Six Patriarchs' of Chan (Zen) Buddhism. Various legends abound regarding him, including the likely apocryphal but popular notion that he founded Kung Fu at the Shaolin Temple. Legends explain that he, like Gautama Buddha, was a prince in India who turned to a life of monasticism. He traveled to China and found that the practice of Buddhism was needlessly esoteric and misguided. He retreated to a mountain cave to meditate and achieved the realizations necessary to transmit what would become the Zen Current—a return to the wordless enlightenment of the Buddha's 'Flower Sutra.'

Borges, Jorge Luis (1899-1986) Unrivaled Argentine author, poet, essayist, and imagonaut. Uncategorizable, his short story 'The Library of Babel' (1941) is representative of his genius. He plays with concepts of perception, reality, infinity, categorization, epistemology, and a host of other ideas. Authors such as Eco owe a huge debt to him.

Butcher, Jim (1971-) Prolific American author of the urban fantasy *Dresden Files* series. His Wizard Private Investigator Harry Dresden, first appearing in *Storm Front* (2000), has become an iconic figure in the contemporary imagination of magic. Most notable for successfully weaving together elements of noir, chivalric fantasy, and action/adventure into a mixture that does credit to the label 'pulpy.'

Byss The intimate nothingness represented by the point. The Qur'an reminds the faithful that Allah (the Not) is closer than your jugular vein. In the process of opening to the voids, this closeness can become a discomforting sense of smothering meaninglessness and angst-ridden bleakness. Byss undermines any personal sense of meaning, significance, and identity through petty pathos (the pathetic), Münch-heroics (mundane hubris), and many other ego-deflating realities. The literary sense of bathos (as opposed to bythos) captures one of the indictments brought by byss. When one grounds a cosmology in the denial of the fundamental banality of life, byss will prove to be suicide- or delusion-inducing. Many people attempt to escape this force through finding external significance or an abiding personality structure. See Qutub and 111.

Byss and Abyss The mystical realization of absolute nothingness undermining all divisions. Sigilized by the point *and* the circle. The space contained within the circle up to the point represents existence and the field of our fictions. The point and circle are the frontiers to the voids. See QUTUB.

Bythos and Sige Greek for 'Depth' and 'Silence.' In some systems of Gnosticism, the first two expressible names of the INEFFABLE.

Campbell, Joseph (1904-1987) American mythologist and author of numerous books on the topic, including *The Hero with a Thousand Faces* (1949) and *The Masks of God* (1959-1968). He perhaps came to the widest public attention through a series of televised interviews with Bill Moyers. Highly influential in the humanities for several generations, his ideas eventually became part of the JUNGIAN current.

A Canticle for Leibowitz 1960 post-apocalyptic novel by Walter M. MILLER, JR. The book tells the story of a Roman Catholic monastery in the American Southwest after a nuclear holocaust. The monks preserve scientific knowledge over the millennia it takes civilization to rebuild itself. The work begins with a poem 'The Centuries' which plays a role in this current text.

Caputo, John (1940-) American philosopher and theologian. As most fully presented in *The Weakness of God: A Theology of the Event* (2006), he is the originator of 'weak theology.' This perspective deconstructs the 'strong theology' in which God chooses to hold back his potential to alter the world, for instance choosing to let his son Jesus die. Instead, weak theology finds God in the cries of the oppressed, abused, and victimized. Heavily influenced by Derrida, Caputo's works are dense, poetic, and cryptic.

Carroll, Lewis Pseudonym for English author, photographer, and mathematician, Charles Lutwidge Dodgson (1832-1898), author of *Alice's Adventures in Wonderland* (1865) and *Through the Looking Glass, and What Alice Found There* (1871). CROWLEY was quite fond of these works and crafted his narrative schematic of the Qabalistic Initiatory Tree, *The Wakeworld* (found in *Knox Om Pax*, 1907), to follow their style.

Carroll, Peter J. (1953-) Seminal British chaos Mage with a maths fetish. Strong themes of the ubiquity of magic run throughout his regrettably sparse literary output. *Liber Null and Psychonaut* (1987, originally 1978 and 1982 respectively) is likely his most influential work.

Cataphasis The pursuit of the divine through mediatory imagery. Most of the Western Esoteric tradition is cataphatic in its use of instructive, transformational, and syncretic icons, emblemata, and tracing boards. Often opposed to APOPHASIS.

Change and Finitude In this text, one of the eight VOIDS. In an odd sense 'death' does not exist since we do not experience it, per se. Thus, the existential emphasis on death, to which these terms refer, points more to our undeniably finite nature as well as the metaphorical omnipresence of death. All things change and pass away and, thus, any sense of permanence is an imposed limiting fiction designed to defend us against this void.

Chaos In this text, one of the eight VOIDS. Any form of a discrete causality denies the multiple factors responsible for any 'event.' Moreover, any particular 'event' is a product of an imaginally informed perspective that ignores all the other occurrences, singling out one set of changes as 'salient.' Therefore, 'chaos' refers to the acausal network of interrelationships that yield various convergences from which we may assert the fiction of a particular event.

Chaos Magic (Meta-)Magical current growing out of a diversity of sources including Austin Osman SPARE, Kenneth GRANT, Robert Anton Wilson, the LOVECRAFT Cthulhu Mythos, and any other belief system that 'works,' regardless of origin or provenance. The IOT is currently the largest Chaos Magical order, but many others have effervesced since the introduction of the ideas in the late 1970's. A 'do-it-yourself' approach to magic, the Chaos current is, appropriately, ill-defined, which leads to just as many interpretations of what, exactly, it *is* as there are ways to apply it. Any magical, philosophical, religious, or belief system can be subsumed into a Chaos Magic paradigm if approached with a meta-magical eye on the 'results.' Thus, Chaos Magic is likely the most postmodern of approaches to ritual and magic. Peter CARROLL and Ray Sherwin are frequently cited as the central figures in the early elaboration of these ideas. Phil HINE produced important works in the 1990's, expanding on the central perspectives. The works of both Grant MORRISON and Alan MOORE contain extensive references to this perspective. See also GNOSIS, SIGIL, and KIA.

Chemognosis The use of an array of ingested substances for magical and or ritual purposes. The term is popular in certain magical counter-cultures, especially those associated with CHAOS MAGIC and neo-Shamanism. Ethnobotany devotes a substantial portion of its work to the study of these practices throughout the ages and across world cultures. Advocates frequently refer to their various psychoactive sacraments as 'entheogens' — 'making god in us.'

Christian Science Movement founded in 1866 by Mary Baker EDDY. The fundamentals of the religion can be summed up in the equations flesh=error=death and God=Truth=Life. In the central text *Science and Health with Key to the Scriptures* (1875) Eddy presents not so much a vision of materiality as bad, but as delusion—a mistaken, entrapping, and pathological belief. Her writings are markedly anti-spiritualist, in the strict Victorian sense of the term. Although sharing many ideas with the New Thought Movement, Christian Science is a distinct current. Sometimes confused with L. Ron Hubbard's Scientology, the two movements have nearly nothing in common.

Chumbley, Andrew (1967-2004) British occultist, esotericist, researcher, artist, and author. Although associated with his scholarly and magical works on the Cunning Tradition and his foundation of the *Cultus Sabbati*, Chumbley's associations with the Typhonian O.T.O. and the IOT would seem equally important to his publicly semi-available masterwork *The Azoëtia* (1992/2002). Rumors of a follow-up volume *The Draconian Grimoire: The Dragon-Book of Essex* abound, but its distribution appears to be entirely private to date. Themes from SUFISM inform his works, especially *Qutub: The Point* (1995).

Code-switching In linguistics, the often-unwitting transition to another language, accent, dialect, or vocabulary selection. Examples include slipping into slang, changing languages to match unconscious cues from a potential audience, and the habit of many news anchors of incongruously over-pronouncing Hispanic names.

Community Supported Agriculture (CSA) A more direct relationship between the production and consumption of foodstuffs. This system often takes the shape of a group of people paying a membership fee that supports a farm or group of farmers who then prepare a variety of fruits and vegetables, and sometimes dairy and meat products, typically in weekly batches.

Complex See ARCHETYPE.

Confirmation bias A strong tendency found across a wide range of demographics to interpret, exclusively attend to, or recall information in such a way that it supports an initial suspicion, hypothesis, or prejudice.

Constructivism A blanket term extending into philosophy, learning theory, psychology, and other social sciences. The central concept largely denies 'truth' or other transcontextual structures that would predispose humans to perceive or know in any particular way. Thus, our EPISTEMOLOGIES, rather than in some sort of competition to 'get things the most right,' are actually *producing* knowledge and may be seen as competing for self-reproduction. A MEME-based approach would be consonant with constructivism.

Corbin, Henry (1903-1978) French scholar of Islamic mysticism, responsible for introducing the idea of the IMAGINAL to a Western audience. His term *mundus imaginalis* is a translation of the Arabic *alam al mithal*. He also presents the idea of the IMAGINATRIX. Essential reading for any serious scholar of Islamic mysticism or the imaginal, his major work, *The History of Islamic Philosophy* (1964/1993), lays out many of the ideas he pursues in his later works.

Corbett, Lionel (1943-) Depth psychology educator and psychiatrist. Author of *Religious Function of the Psyche* (1996) and *Psyche and the Sacred: Spirituality Beyond Religion* (2006).

Crooked Path A term used by CHUMBLEY to describe the process of development within the Sabbatic Craft. The reader could surmise that he intended it as an alternative to the term 'LEFT-HAND PATH,' as he presents a unique hybridization of Witchcraft, CHAOS MAGIC, and the Typhonian traditions.

Crowley, Aleister (1875-1947) Fundamentally, the reader of Western esotericism is posed with a burning question: do I *still* need to read this man's often-awful writing? That the question remains speaks to his continuing prominence, yet Crowley is the case-in-point for why self-publishing can be a sign of an author who shouldn't be published. Most of what he wrote is colonial, Edwardian, self-indulgent, sexist rubbish. More often than not, The Great Beast is proven 'right' because somewhere else in his writings he makes up a cryptic justification based on his own mis-interpretation of a cobbled together sense of some other mythos he has mistranslated. However, in the midst of this steaming mountain of esoteric scat, one does occasionally find the purest alchemical gold. Unfortunately, he has been so widely read that other authors have perpetuated not only elements of his genius, but, more often, evidence of his mountainous misunderstandings and misrepresentations. This problem is only compounded by the number of occult traditions founded by, written by, informed by, or borrowing from Crowley—all of this merely engorging the sense of his Münch-importance. Sadly, no author has yet—and probably could never—present a *full* and fair assessment of this man's entire output. This is due in part to the size and breadth of his output and, in part, to the possibility that the keys to some of his works may be hidden within secret documents accessible only to those initiates recognized by those enforcing the copyrights to his works. What is, in all likelihood, the most important part of Crowley's life is not his prodigious production itself, but that he dared to experiment earnestly and tenaciously with the imaginal and (usually) faithfully record his results. Nevertheless, when observing such a range of works, a devotee can hearken to the minutest details of one quarter of Crowley's total works and still be missing the entire point of Crowley's life. Although he often wrote in fevered spiritual hyperbole, he also frequently disparaged the appropriateness of any metaphor to describe the fundamental reality of experience. In addition, he often wrote works with multiple levels of meaning, with the deeper level ironically mocking the shallower levels. Most devoted readers seem to enjoy the existence of this humor but miss the onus of self-scrutiny. Crowley's life was an effort to live his beliefs and although it smacks of an ad hominem attack, the reader might do well to observe how he aged and died to determine the quality of his life philosophy. The main group that follows his teachings call themselves Thelemites — followers of 'Thelema,' the refinement and discernment of 'True Will.' The O.'.T.'.O.'. is the main body of thelemic practitioners. The incorporated body calling itself the A.'.A.'. currently integrates with the OTO at its highest levels. Crowley is also responsible for informing the foundation of GARDNER's Wicca.

Cu Chulainn (kooHOOlin) Protagonist of many parts of the Ulster Cycle. His refusal of the love offered him by the MORRÍGAN leads to dire consequences.

Cultus Sabbati See Andrew CHUMBLEY.

Current 93 British experimental artistic collective founded by David TIBET in 1982. With Tibet alone as well as a series of impressive collaborations, the group has produced neo-folk, industrial, spoken word, and atmospheric musical creations, as well as visual and performance art pieces often integrating esoteric, spiritual, and religious themes in ephemeral and tragic juxtapositions. Most relevant to this current work is the 2000 collaboration of Current 93 and Thomas LIGOTTI, *I Have a Special Plan for This World.*

Da'ath Hebrew for 'knowledge,' it is actually the limit of knowability. It is the abyss that separates the ROSY CROSS level from the A.'.A.'. in the Western Initiatory QABALAH. In the initiatic schematic, the seeker must let go of their various identities to cross into the A.'.A.'. and avoid the monstrous Choronzon who dwells in Da'ath.

Dante Alighieri (1265-1321) The Florentine Poet, author of *The Divine Comedy,* the three parts of which, *Inferno, Purgatory,* and *Paradise,* describe a mystical journey of self-scrutiny, purification, and numinous unity and insight. This current work parallels these three levels with both the three levels of the Western Initiatory QABALAH and three levels of Mystery.

Dawkins, Richard (1941-) British evolutionary biologist, author, and commentator. His *The Selfish Gene* (1976) is a stunning achievement and introduces to a wider audience the idea of a MEME. His rabid atheism is, perhaps, necessary in an era of such fanatical literalism and fundamentalism. However, Dawkins seems entirely blind to the other possibilities of esotericism, mysticism, and religious imagery. Thus it has fallen to other writers to pursue memetics as a field.

Dee, John (1527-c. 1608) English polymath and advisor to Queen Elizabeth I. In addition to his many other contributions, Dee is best remembered in the

imagination of magic for his elaborate rituals involving divination and the channeling, through his one-time friend Edward Kelley, of various supernatural entities. The Watchtower Ritual, expanded upon by the HERMETIC ORDER OF THE
GOLDEN DAWN tradition, is perhaps the most lasting legacy of these workings.
Although the specifics and precautions Dee took in these efforts are imitated to
this day, few hearken to the lessons of his strained relationship with his fellow
aethyr-exploring colleague.

Deism Belief in a Watchmaker God who sets the universe in motion but does
not intervene. This philosophy can also raise Rationality to a Divine Principle
beyond action and is thus often a watered down Neo-Platonism. Popular in
the Age of Enlightenment, this belief pervades much of FREEMASONRY and was
thus, reportedly, widespread within America's Founding Fathers.

Deleuze, Giles (1925-1995) and **Guatari, Felix** (1930-1992) French postmodern, Marxist authors. If only for their two volumes of *Schizophrenia and Society:
Anti-Oedipus* (1972) and *A Thousand Plateaus* (1980), these authors would have
guaranteed their place in postmodern philosophy. They radically recast the very
ideas of identity, culture, society, labor, production, and a host of other heretofore unexamined 'givens' of Western life. Their works present an incredible
extension of Marxist philosophy. Very challenging to read, the intrepid explorer
of their works should have several readers' guides at hand.

Demiurge The Gnostic image of the deluded and deluding false divinity. Gnostics viewed most worship and religion to be of this aborted creation. The demiurge is close to the image of the ego—indispensable but far from absolute.
Many divine names, such as IAO, used in various ritual magic practices, actually
refer to the demiurge. Some APOPHATICALLY minded Gnostics might even say
that *any* name for the divine is ultimately demiurgic. Coming to understand the
existential mechanics and means by which identity works is a major initiatory
accomplishment wherein one transcends the thrall of the demiurge and claims
the power of this agency beyond the politics of identity. In some Gnostic theo-
cosmologies, the Demiurge had fallen archangelic henchmen: the ARCHONS.

DeMolay Masonic youth organization for young men, typically the sons of
Masons. Founded in 1919 by Frank S. Land (1890-1959). See FREEMASONRY.

Derrida, Jacques (1930-2004) Along with Foucault, the most prominent postmodern philosopher. Derrida's work centered on language and the paradoxes
of 'signification.' His form of deconstruction noted the inconsistencies in the
simplest acts of meaning and, thus, rather than hoping to salvage some shred
of representation, Derrida coined the term 'différance' to indicate the potential
interstitial space of free play that contrasting meanings can introduce. *Of Gram-*

matology (1976) is perhaps his most widely read work. His writing is, however, often criticized for being deliberate obscurantism. Caputo raises Derrida to the status of Saint and sees an underlying secret mysticism in Derrida's works.

Dialectical monism The philosophical or theological concept that, although reality is a unified whole, this unity expresses itself through dualities. Depending on approach, these dualities may progress toward transcendence (thus yielding new dyads) or may abide in the realm of 'seeming.' The path of transcending can be seen in the philosophies of JUNG and the ideas popularly known as the HEGELIAN DIALECTIC.

Dialectical nihilism This current work offers dialectical nihilism as a ground against which DIALECTICAL MONISM is an inauthentic mode of being. Rather than constantly transcending any given dyad into some new dualistic configuration, an open relationship to the VOIDS can—albeit usually temporarily—eliminate the various thing-sets that yield further entrapping dyadic fictions. Dialectical nihilism represents transcendence to nothingness. The term is synonymous with this current work's 'mystical nihilism.'

Différance See DERRIDA.

Dream tending Term coined by STEPHEN AIZENSTAT to speak to a cultivating relationship toward dream material.

Dreamwork In this text, a term coined to differentiate a growing relationship toward the imaginal as opposed to 'dream interpretation' in which dream material is a mere analog for some waking material issue. Ultimately a set of attitudes that bring one into a more fruitful relationship with the imaginal.

Dresden, Harry See Jim BUTCHER.

Eco, Umberto (1932-) Italian philosopher and author. Eco first came to wider public awareness with his Medieval mystery *The Name of the Rose* (1980/1983). Eight years later, he brought his same love of language and possibility to *FOUCAULT'S PENDULUM* (1988/1989).

Eco-Kashrut A perspective growing out of RECONSTRUCTIONIST JUDAISM in which the spirit behind Kosher dietary strictures translates into contemporary ethical questions about animal cruelty, sustainability, and health.

Ecopsychology Term coined by Theodore Roszak in *The Voice of the Earth* (1992) to refer to the integration of ecology and psychology. This field is particularly concerned with the alienation of humans from their environment, but especially from nature. Ecopsychologists tend to view human diseases as manifestations of unsustainable lifestyles. Ecopsychological perspectives frequently intersect with those of IMAGINAL PSYCHOLOGY.

Eddy, Mary Baker (1821-1910) Founder of CHRISTIAN SCIENCE. Having suffered ill health for most of her life, the middle-aged Eddy came to view the Bible in a new light—one in which coming into accord with the Divine Principle that is Truth, Healing, and Redemption frees one from death, falsehood, illness, and sin. Her most full statement of this ideology can be found in *Science and Health with Key to the Scriptures* (1875).

Egregore A de facto construct, a collection of MEMES created through intentional, unintentional, and compensatory effects of group interactions, workings, or conflicts. Within occult circles, the term refers to such a pattern that achieves sentience. As used by Eliphas Levi, 'egregore' originally referred to the 'Grigori' or 'Watchers'—semi-fallen angels found in the Old Testament and Apocrypha. Always (at least) dyadic, an egregore is based on archetypal patterns—as such, an egregore is always an IMAGE and thus, as with all life, is experienced through imagination. The form is contextual and often takes possession of various relationships and identities within the group, as well as those with whom group members have contact. In this sense, the egregore attempts to INDIVIDU-ATE—constitute the reality of the system in question. Corporate culture, group hysteria, family dynamics, mass cultural traumas, nations, cults, and groupthink are just a few examples. See AUTANGEL.

Eldritch Linked to a sense of the alien, ALTERITY, the uncanny, and the ABJECT. Some etymologies present a connection to 'elven.' 'Eldritch horror' is another term used to describe the works of LOVECRAFT and his unspeakable compatriots.

Ellis, Warren (1968-) English graphic novelist perhaps best known for his *Transmetropolitan* series (1997-2002). Themes of freedom, transhumanism, and the often tumultuous process of divided worlds coming to unity dominate his work. For the ideas found in this current work, Ellis' *Planetary* (1999-2009) is arguably the most germane. The characters of this work, all exceptional individuals in their own right calling themselves 'archeologists of the impossible,' fight to keep the unusual and extraordinary viable in a world too-easily dominated by tyrannical super 'heroes.' The motto alone is worth the price of purchase: 'It's a strange world. Let's keep it that way.'

Empty nihilism Any stance that leads to the assertion of things having inherent meaning, rather than positioning the ultimate responsibility for meaning-making as fundamental to the human condition.

Emerald Tablet The *Tabula Smaragdina*, a short, dense, and cryptic text purportedly authored by HERMES TRISMEGISTUS. The earliest source may date to 500 CE. Highly regarded by alchemists, Rosicrucians, and central to much of Western Esotericism. The central doctrine is 'As above, so below.'

Enantiodromia Originally used to describe the corrective tragic fall near the end of Greek drama, it is a compensatory force fueled by the degree of the extremity. This effect, demonstrated in the tragic fall of a hubris-laden hero, stands on the entrapping nature of all dyads. JUNG uses this term to describe the painful effects of DIALECTICAL MONISM when denied.

Ensigilization (also 'sigilization') The process of creating a sigil, or the product of crystallizing a magical process into a sigil. Most ensigilizations are unwitting and carry profound unconscious gravity.

Epistemology The study of *how* we know what we know. 'Where a door leads depends on what key you use to open it.' One can also speak of one particular epistemology (or *episteme* as FOUCAULT calls it). In this case, it refers to the way of knowing inherent to a particular IMAGE. Epistemology, as a philosophical science, stands before and beyond all other particular ways of knowing.

Eschaton The end of days, and the end of the world-as-known. Certain esoteric circles set 'immanentizing the eschaton' as their goal; that is, to make real that which they see as the after-life state of humans or the effect of the end of the world 'as we know it.' Within the Western QABALAH, this may be seen as the opening of the 32nd path that divides Malkuth from Yesod—the breaking down of the World of 'seeming' and the unifying with the rest of the tree. Predictions of new GOLDEN AGES, ages of Aquarius, and other utopian visions are of a similar ilk. Largely, these visions ignore the world as it is and fail to see that the eschaton is this very moment. See REALIZED ESCHATOLOGY.

Evans, Dave (1962-) Mentee of Ronald HUTTON and author of several scholarly works on the 20th century history of magic, including *The History of British Magick After Crowley* (2007).

Existentialism The study of the absolute givens of life, concerned more with the experience and description of being than with some sort of metaphysical explanation thereof. From this perspective, 'being' is always contextual—'being-in-the-world' or *Dasein*, in German. Existentialism demands a whole sheet reassessment of life itself and how we each make meaning. The transition from the inauthentic mode of being, in which we rely on others to provide supportive meanings, to the authentic, in which we are each completely accountable for our lives, is always painful and never a permanent shift. Although often characterized as brooding, solitary, beret-wearing, cigarette-smoking misanthropes, this cliché belies the underlying liberation that the pursuit of existentialism can effect. ANGST is indeed a call when we are in the midst of inauthentic fallenness, but the authentic emotion of existence is, according to many existentialists, joy—or, in this text, wonder.

Faceless God See NYARLATHOTEP.

Feynman, Richard (1918-1988) American physicist and Nobel laureate, noted for his efforts to make various aspects of physics more accessible to a wider audience. He stated that he had a form of SYNESTHESIA in which he saw the letters in equations in distinct colors.

Fiction The form of all assertions, perceptions, identities, and stances. All types of 'truth', 'belief', and 'fact' are, inherently, fictional. Certain fictions coordinate with each other to create a story-line of mutual verification; but no stance, information, or perception can be said to be less or more fictive. All are inventions. Contextually, certain fictions may speak more to one organizing IMAGE or the other and thus one can speak of a contextual truth, but never a transcendent one — unless it is a structural truth in which case it may tend to be true across (or under) contexts. Fictions may be more or less limiting depending on what degree to which they veil or reveal the VOIDS.

Finitude In this text, one of the eight voids, paired with Change. See CHANGE AND FINITUDE.

Fortean Referring to the works of Charles Fort (1874-1932), an American author and researcher of bizarre and unexplained phenomena. The term 'Fortean' has come to refer to all phenomena that belligerently refuse all current scientific explanation.

Foucault, Michel (1926-1984) Incalculably important historian, postmodern philosopher, and cultural anthropologist. He introduced the idea of POWER/ KNOWLEDGE and brought EPISTEMOLOGY to the forefront of philosophical discussion. His treatment of the history of the idea of 'MADNESS' in *Madness and Civilization* (1961) is often misunderstood but contains many of the major arcs he would pursue later in equally ground-breaking studies such as *The Birth of the Clinic* (1963/1973) and *Discipline and Punish* (1975/1977). Although his writing itself is fluid and rich in illustrative historical examples, by the end of a paragraph or chapter, readers typically struggle with the subtle implications Foucault intends through the contrast of various narratives.

Foucault's Pendulum 1988 novel by Umberto ECO. In it, three publishers of a vanity press decide to combine the inane conspiracy theories and pseudo-history proposed by their various authors. Eventually, they find themselves overcome by a growing sense of APOPHENIA. The climax of the book contains a poignant illumination of the ultimate meaning of the QABALAH. The 'Foucault' in the title refers to the French physicist, Léon Foucault's (1819-1868) demonstration of the earth's rotation through a pendulum that, in actuality, maintains the same course, although it appears to slowly describe a circle over the course of a day.

Frater Achad Magical name of Charles Stansfeld Jones (1886-1950). Thelemite, member of Crowley's A.˙.A.˙. and O.˙.T.˙.O.˙., Theosophist, and confidante to Crowley. In addition to his many writings on a wide range of esoteric and occult topics, Achad's illustration of a fractal snowflake of multiple superimposed QABALISTIC Trees of Life has had a lasting impact.

Freedom and Responsibility In this text, one of the eight VOIDS. Although threats, programming, social expectations, and habit may seem to curtail our freedom, we are, ultimately, free to make any choice, if only in our minds. Moreover, we are always choosing, though typically unwittingly. We are, thus, also responsible for the outcomes of these choices, even when we did not intend, or want, these consequences. Responsibility also extends to a fundamental existential call to be *responsive to* our lived world *as it is*. Genuine freedom of choice, to whatever extent we can exercise it, only comes through calibrating our choices to a comprehensive assessment of experience.

Freemasonry Initiatory fraternal organization, first becoming public in 1717, with its previous origins hotly debated. Subsequent syncretism between folk traditions, orientalist fantasies, SPIRITUALISM, and Masonry are too common to count. It is not overstating the case to say that one can, currently, trace the mark of Freemasonry in nearly the entirety of the Western Esoteric Tradition. At its heart, Freemasonry was designed to provide a classic Rite of Passage for young men. The Blue Lodge (the fundamental three degrees) forms the heart of the Masonic system with the hyperbolic 'higher degrees' merely amplifying themes from the foundation. Its visible success for 250 years owed to it filling the gap created by increasing urbanization, industrialization, and the collapse of traditional community rituals. Its current decay, with average member ages ranging in the 70's, is due to a refusal to address contemporary issues as well as 20th century purges of even a hint of 'occultism,' especially in American practice. Members of occult initiatory organizations, especially the OTO, are currently making efforts to move into the well-funded and meeting-space-rich structure of Masonry. Conspiracy theories aside, Freemasons have taken on leadership roles throughout the world. Three major revolutions — The American, French, and Bolivar's — made use of the Masonic ideals and its culture of secrecy. Perhaps the most misunderstood aspect of Masonry is its love of myth, allegory, and fiction thinly veiled as secret history. Taking the bait regarding these fantastical stories as 'non-fiction' is the road to madness. INEFFABILITY is a central and reiterated secret of the Brotherhood. Frequently, Masonry's various revealed secret names for The Grand Architect of the Universe are merely fingers pointing at an ineffable moon. See ROBINSON for a levelheaded treatment of Masonry's history. See also DEISM.

Freud, Sigmund (1856-1939) Phenomenally misunderstood pioneer of the psyche. Accusations of Freud's sex obsessions are sustained only by those unaware of the social context of Freud's writings, including the pervasively abusive and perverse practices of medical doctors before and during (and after) Freud's life. Moreover, any drug addictions Freud may have suffered pale in comparison to his suffering with cancer of the palate. Freud gave his school of thought (he would say 'discoveries') the label of 'psychoanalysis.' Freud's contributions were not only novel but his observations, though often scant, reflect phenomena with which researchers still struggle today. That is to say, although Freud often came to interpretations that seem outdated today, he was among the first to actually observe previously unnoticed and unimagined possibilities. Far too many people's rejection of Freud is based in an ignorance of his actual work and its context, as well as a glaringly obvious discomfort with the implications of his theories. Given the parallel history of the Magical Revival and Freud's revelations, much of the imagination of magic's obsession with 'sex magic' seems more than coincidental.

Fundamental attribution error Easily blended with, but technically different than, the ACTOR-OBSERVER BIAS. In this case, we look to the failures of others and tend to blame them on their character while ignoring mitigating circumstances. This cognitive bias is the other half of attribution theory.

Gaiman, Neil (1960-) English author of novels, short fiction, and graphic novels. A master of Imaginal Realism, his fame is widespread and his fans are deeply devoted. Although often placed in the science fiction and fantasy genres, Gaiman's work typically speaks to the intersection of the initial banality of the everyday world with the unexpected wonder and horror of an otherworld. Gaiman's stories are profoundly developmental and often amplify a rite of passage for a character faced with a crisis or a need to grow. Often with tongue firmly in cheek, Gaiman draws freely from the world's mythologies, fairy and folk tales. Author of a wide range of fiction, including the *Sandman* series, *The Books of Magic* (1990-1991), *Neverwhere* (1996), *Stardust* (1999), *American Gods* (2001), and *Coraline* (2002).

Gardner, Gerald (1884-1964) Late in his life, CROWLEY mentored Gardner and encouraged the establishment of Wicca, Gardner's cooption of the imagery of the Witch for an earth-based neo-pagan initiatory religion and magical current.

General Semantics Originated by KORZYBSKI, a system of philosophy designed to liberate the practitioner from assumptions embedded in habitual thought patterns, especially those thoughts grounded in the belief in the adequate representativeness of concepts that are more realistically a product of the simultaneous convenience and oversimplifications of language. General semanticists seek to unravel the confusion resulting from equating terms that stand in differing levels of abstraction. See HAYAKAWA.

Giegerich, Wolfgang (1942-) Jungian analyst and author, most famous for his sometimes-contentious efforts to remind readers of their shadows, especially those related to violence, death, and technology. He has also leveled substantive critiques against psychotherapy and analysis.

Glossographia As used in this work, a written form of glossolalia, this practice differs from 'automatic writing' (psychography) in that it does not strive to use a coherent, conscious symbol system.

Gnosis In CHAOS MAGIC, a directed ecstasy, a momentary suspension or elimination of identity and other confining fictions allowing an in- or outflow of more primary forces. Often channeled toward a sigil as a means of empowering, charging, or casting. In GNOSTICISM, the term refers to a special type of divine knowledge in which one experiences an awakening to true divine reality and cosmology. Early experiences with this form of Gnosis tend to yield a disoriented and devastated individual, awoken from a sleep of which they were unaware, to the horrific imprisoning freak show nature of this world. Some systems of ancient Gnosticism would seem to have had multiple levels of awakening.

Gnosticism A disparate collection of philosophical and religious systems dominant just before, and during, the establishment of Christianity. Although once thought to be a single movement, the term seems to cover a range of ideas ranging from the extremely esoteric to ecstasy-focused, nearly-Pentecostalist practices. Many Gnostics considered themselves Christians, but those currents that would eventually become the first orthodoxies in Christianity rejected and eventually pursued genocidal policies against these now-'heretics.' Many forms of Gnosticism had a far more central role for the Divine Feminine, often in the form of the Sophia — Divine Wisdom and Compassion. Through a broader range of Old and New Testament texts, Gnosticism also had radical cosmologies that portrayed the DEMIURGE as the creator of the world as we know it. The True God was, thus, alien to this world. The struggle of the Divine Sparks, entrapped in materialist delusion, to return/awaken becomes the central archetypal journey in many Gnostic texts. Although few direct accounts of Gnosticism were available until the mid-20th century, its imagery has attracted many writers, theorists, and alternative religious leaders. The MAGICAL REVIVAL, especially as related to ritual or high magic, drew heavily from their imagery. Many New Age philosophies can be characterized as neo-Gnostic. Since the discovery of the Nag Hamadi Library in 1946 and its gradual translation, a broader view of

Gnosticism has emerged, leading to a wider acceptance of the ideas. Although CROWLEY introduced a 'Gnostic Mass' and an *Ecclesia Gnostica Catholica*, his use of the term is idiosyncratic to Thelema.

Goetia The practice of invocatory and evocatory sorcery, especially related to the Grimoire known as *The Lesser Key of Solomon* or *Lemegeton* (17th century, C.E.). Although a rather extensive system of magic, the most referenced part of the work is its pack of 72 demons. Sorcerers of today tend to refer to, and, occasionally, perform the demonic evocations as a type of Shadow Work. Jungian analysis is, admittedly, more expensive, but a somewhat less smelly and more relevant (and pro-social) means of achieving similar results.

Golden Age Any mythic time for which sentimentalists pine as being 'the good old days.'

Golden Dawn (level of the Western Initiatory Qabalah) The first four sephiroth of the Western Initiatory QABALAH's Tree of Life: Malkuth, Yesod, Hod, and Netzach. The name refers to the solar splendor of Tiphareth—the 5th sephira from the bottom—remaining always just beyond the horizon of the VEIL OF THE PEROKETH which divides the Golden Dawn from the ROSY CROSS level. In this text, this first level is the 'secrets' level of mysteries in which one must discover the basic cosmology of the overall journey, but will ultimately be left with only puzzles to decipher. This level is also associated with DANTE's descent into the *Inferno* and thus the alchemical motto V.˙.I.˙.T.˙.R.˙.I.˙.O.˙.L.˙.. The numeric value associated with the Golden Dawn level is 555—the five pointed star, which adds the vector of spirit to the four points of the elements seen in the first sephira, Malkuth.

Grant, Kenneth (1924-2011) British occultist, former secretary to CROWLEY, and innovator of the former's tradition. He is responsible for drawing greater attention to his friend A. O. SPARE's innovative works. Inheritor of the leadership of the O.T.O. in England for a time, his eventually distinct organization was commonly known as the Typhonian O.T.O., during Grant's lifetime, due to his explorations of the Setian current. His explorations into applied occultism, rather than pedantic pretension and repetition compulsion, earned him the derision of many. Nevertheless, Grant seemed keenly aware of the fundamentally fictional nature of all of the Great Work and stands out as a father of the CHAOS MAGIC current. His works are all, to date, limited editions and difficult and expensive to come by.

Grimoire A book of magic usually attributed to more ancient sources than the work's author. In its most powerful form, it is not just a book about magic, but a magical book—that is, an icon to which a seeker relates as a fetish. The

Book of Shadows, both created and copied, is an ongoing form of the Grimoire legacy. This type of work often presents deities, demons, talismans, and spells, and may contain its own inherent cosmology. In this current grimoire, The True Grimoire is our life itself written in the language of our ALPHABET OF DESIRE.

Guanyin 觀音 (sometimes 'Kuan Yin') Chinese Goddess of Compassion. The name is a shortening of Guanshi'yin, 'Observing the Cries of the World.' In Buddhist tradition, she is widely thought to have evolved from the Indian bodhisattva Avalokitesvara. However, Taoists hold her as an Immortal with different stories of origination.

Gurdjieff, G. I. (1866?-1949) Widely traveled Russian mystic who integrated elements from many esoteric traditions to form an evolving system of enlightenment. In a neo-GNOSTIC fashion, Gurdjieff views nearly everyone as asleep and sees ordinary life as inherently opposed to awakening. He was among the first to use the enneagram as a core symbol.

Hagakure (Japanese for 'hidden leaves') Japanese guide for samurais drawn from the sayings of YAMAMOTO TSUNETOMO but compiled by Tsuremoto Tashiro during their conversations between 1709 and 1716. A strange and bittersweet collection, it extols the bushido code and bemoans its decay. It provides inspiration and interspersed quotes for Jim Jarmusch's film *Ghost Dog: The Way of the Samurai* (1999).

Haber, Fritz (1868-1934) German Jewish chemist and Nobel Laureate, responsible for the technology that would eventually yield artificial fertilizer, thus averting global famine at the dawn of the 20th century. This same technology also enabled the birth of modern chemical warfare, an application Haber proudly oversaw during World War I. Haber did not live to see the use of the resultant Zyklon B in the genocide of the Shoah.

Halal Islamic dietary and foodway strictures.

Hayakawa, S. I. (1906-1992) General semanticist, psychologist, academic, and political leader. His most important work, *Language in Thought and Action* (1949) set the groundwork for many later innovations such as NLP and E-Prime. However, the radical implications of Hayakawa's work, rooted in KORZYBSKI'S GENERAL SEMANTICS, is rarely realized by proponents of newer techniques.

Hegelian dialectic Thesis + antithesis = synthesis. A formula popularly attributed to Hegel, although present in several other philosophers of the same era. See DIALECTICAL MONISM.

Heidegger, Martin (1889-1976) German existential phenomenologist. His *Being and Time* (1927) is a radical effort to recapture the question of the meaning of being, a question Heidegger believes is lost beneath 2000 years of premature, foreclosing answers. A student of HUSSERL, he took the nascent ideas of PHENOMENOLOGY and made them the grounding science beneath an examination of the human condition — EXISTENTIALISM. Although not postmodern in any real sense of the term, his ideas form the ground from which philosophers such as DERRIDA and FOUCAULT grew. Heidegger's philosophy is a type of apotheosis of Western philosophy as can be evidenced by the Zen resonances many see in his writings, including, late in life, Heidegger himself. As a prominent academic leader in Germany, Heidegger joined the Nazi party in 1933 and remained with it until the end of the War. Though romanced by some of the rhetoric initially, Heidegger contends that he remained a Nazi in name only once he saw the brutality of the movement by the mid-30's.

Heraclitus (535-475 BCE) Pre-Socratic Greek philosopher most notable for placing change as the central constant of the universe, 'You cannot step twice into the same river.'

Herbert, Frank (1920-1986) American author of science fiction, best known for his epic *Dune* saga (1965-1985). His writing often focuses on internal dialogs and unfolding levels of subtleties.

Hermeneutics The study of interpretation. 'What you see depends on where you stand.' Founded on the idea of shifting perspectives, this current text presents hermeneutics as inferior to EPISTEMOLOGY since hermeneutics almost always assumes the primacy of the object being interpreted. This current text also proposes a hermeneutic means of interpreting the Western Initiatory QABALAH.

Hermes Trismegistus 'Three-times Great Hermes.' Central figure of HERMETICISM, in Hellenistic Egypt, a combination of Hermes and Thoth.

Hermetic Order of the Golden Dawn (HOGD) Post-Masonic magical order existing in its first form from 1887-1901. Utilizing the initiatory structure of various Freemasonic sources, this order sought to practice the invocation and evocation of spirits — 'theurgy' — in an initiatic structure. This format concretized the Western Initiatory QABALAH into the form now widely used. A wide range of groups claim direct descent from HOGD, but the organization itself was fracturing into dissipation by 1899. CROWLEY had his first major occult experiences and controversies while in their ranks. Among their numbers are claimed to have been Maude Gonne, Bram Stoker, Algernon Blackwood, Arthur Machen, A. E. Waite, William Butler Yeats, and many others who went on to establish threads of 20th century esotericism, occultism, and the imagination of magic.

Hermeticism Originally, a loose collection of esoteric beliefs rooted in neo-Platonism, GNOSTICISM, and the hybridization of late Greek and Egyptian thought. This canon gained cohesion around the figure of HERMES TRISMAGIS-TUS and the doctrines contained in texts such as the EMERALD TABLET. Eventually, their revitalization during the Renaissance integrated with alchemical and Rosicrucian thought and became the grounds for much of Western Esotericism and the MAGICAL REVIVAL.

Hillman, James (1926-) The founder of Archetypal Psychology as a means of criticizing and innovating the practice of more classical approaches to Jung's analytic psychology, as well as psychotherapy in general. From Hillman, readers gain the radical notion that images are not so much what is seen, but how we see. This shift to a PHENOMENOLOGICAL and EPISTEMOLOGICAL perspective enables Archetypal (IMAGINAL) PSYCHOLOGY to outpace nearly every other form of psychology and to remain more radical, according to this text, than most forms of magic. Hillman's major works include *Re-Visioning Psychology* (1975), *The Dream and The Underworld* (1979), *We've Had a Hundred Years of Psychotherapy—And the World's Getting Worse* (with Michael Ventura) (1993), and his summary of the movement, *Archetypal Psychology* (2004).

Hine, Phil (1960-) Prolific and readable author of relatively canonical texts of CHAOS MAGIC, such as *Prime Chaos* (1993), *Condensed Chaos (*1995), and *The Pseudonomicon* (1996). Marked by a facile sense of humor and a healthy grounding in results, his writings remain influential well beyond the bounds of self-declared Chaotes.

Holy Guardian Angel (HGA) A metaphor drawn from *The Book of the Sacred Magic of Abremelin The Mage* (1458). This imagery was overlaid with Western Esoteric QABALISTIC schematics and became a HERMENEUTIC revelation based on the aspirant's perspective on the middle pillar of the initiatory Tree of Life. In a sense, the HGA is the relational aspect of one's vector toward the Voids. For most, this relationship is obscured by UNSPEAKABLE terror, proscriptive beliefs, or deadening rationality. The awakening to the reality of the HGA is, for some esotericists, the fundamental goal of spiritual work. Within the Western Esoteric Qabalah, so-called 'knowledge and conversation' with the HGA represents the achievement of the first major arc of the Great Work. If pursued further, the HGA will appear to abandon the journeyer since a later step involves the stripping away of the very identity that was in relationship to this other aspect. This esoteric paradigm would seem to stand on a unilinear metaphor of a singular journey for most seekers. A more KIA-based paradigm might allow for relationships to a host of entities at various phases of the Great Work and Play. Other traditions from around the world have spirit guides, tutelary spirits, daemons, genii, familiars, and many other relationships that lead (and/or distract) the practitioner along the Way.

Howard, Michael (d.o.b. unknown, still alive at publication) Author, researcher, and editor on neo-paganism, Witchcraft, and the occult. Due to his interest in 'TRADITIONAL WITCHCRAFT' — non-Wiccan legacies — he is associated with the Sabbatic Current as found in his *Book of Fallen Angles* (2004) and, with Nigel Jackson, *The Pillars of Tubal Cain* (2000).

Huineng (638-713) Daijin Huineng 大鑒惠能, Sixth patriarch of Chan (ZEN) BUDDHISM. The summation of his life and thoughts can be found in *The Platform Sutra*, a central text of Zen Buddhism.

Huson, Paul (1942-) Screenwriter and researcher of occult topics, Huson wrote a primer on TRADITIONAL WITCHCRAFT, *Mastering Witchcraft* (1970). In 2004, he released an authoritative presentation of the origins of the Tarot, *Mystical Origins of the Tarot*. In it, he links the 'trumps' of the deck to the *triumphi* ('triumphs'), mobile morality play 'floats' of medieval Italy.

Husserl, Edmund (1859-1938) Mathematician, philosopher, founder of PHENOMENOLOGY, and mentor to HEIDEGGER.

Hutton, Ronald (1953-) The man neo-pagans, magicians, and esotericists *should* be reading to get their history and not the series of oft-repeated nonsense from popular New Age publishers. Hutton's *The Triumph of the Moon: A History of Modern Pagan Witchcraft* (1999) is the first and best scholarly work on the topic to date. Other, more social anthropological works, such as ADLER's *Drawing Down the Moon* raise important questions that Hutton decisively answers. Hutton explains, with excellent resources, how the pseudo-feminist myth of Wicca's ancient origins began and was perpetuated, and finally lays to rest any whisper of provenance in MURRAY's works. Hutton's work has given rise to new scholarship on the topic, including the works of DAVE EVANS.

Hyatt, Christopher (b. Alan Ronald Miller 1943-2008) Publisher, occultist, clinical psychologist, academic, friend to Israel REGARDIE, author, and sometime-Thelemite. A towering figure who attempted to update the metaphors and methods of occultism beyond the limitation of Western culture and tradition. In many ways more of a chaos mage than a ritual magician, he brought long-needed physiological and psychological grounding to practices previously accepted merely on authority. Most of his major insights are contained in the various incarnations of his *Undoing Yourself/Energized Meditation* (1993).

Hypersigil A large-scale ensigilization. An intentional hypersigil may be a work of art, but many hypersigils are corporate logos, signatures, or other EGREGORIC ensigilizations. The term was popularized by Grant MORRISON.

IAO In Thelema, the formula of Isis, Apophis, Osiris, a symbol of death and rebirth as well as a HEGELIAN DIALECTIC. Historically, a barbarous name from Gnosticism linked to the DEMIURGE.

Ideas of Reference (IOR) Psychotic delusions in which seemingly meaningless things take on deep significance not apparent to anyone else. Similar to APOPHENIA

Illusions: The Adventures of a Reluctant Messiah 1977 brief novel by RICHARD BACH. In it, our barnstorming narrator meets another pilot in the plains of the Midwest. He discovers that this man is an enlightened individual, a 'Messiah' even. The book contains this Master's tutelage to the narrator.

Image Not so much what one sees but a prepackaged locus of *how* one sees. Self-perceptions, identities, pasts, futures, configurations of ALTERITY, senses of embodiment, and a host of other qualities are inherent to images. All images are MEMEtic in nature and flow within ARCHETYPAL patterns.

Imaginal The entirety of what exists—experience—bounded only by the voids. Materialism, spirituality, rationality, identity, cosmology and a host of other ideas/images/fictions all exist within the imaginal. Imagination occurs within the Imaginal.

Imaginal Psychology Also known as archetypal psychology, this field began as an attempt to reconsider the assumptions of psychology in general and the practice of JUNG's ANALYTIC PSYCHOLOGY in particular. Since then it has broadened its influence to architecture, gender, politics, ECOPSYCHOLOGY, as well as all the areas traditionally addressed by psychology. Imaginal psychology tends to emphasize the polycentric nature of the personality and casts a suspicious eye at any monological perspective, especially the reification of Jung's SELF into a thing-like 'center' to psyche. Thus, Imaginal Psychologists are more apt to speak of a sense of 'soulfulness' rather than any literalistic 'soul.' In many ways, this perspective returns to Jung's writings with fresh eyes, setting aside the sacred doctrines of the first generations of adherents to Jung's Analytic Psychology. An imaginal perspective sees IMAGES as primary and our various perceptions, ideas, and attitudes as products of these informing epistemologies. Key figures include James HILLMAN, Henry CORBIN, Thomas Moore, Rafael Lopez-Pedraza, Marion Woodman, and Wolgang GIEGERICH among others. This current work is a synthesis of Imaginal and EXISTENTIAL perspectives using the language of the IMAGINATION OF MAGIC.

Imagination of magic The ostensible subject or at least interrogatee of this work. Since we cannot speak of 'MAGIC' in the same way we would discuss 'iguanas,' it must be a different order of phenomenon. Moreover, to limit the definition of 'magic' to only those practices by self-avowed 'magicians' would seem, again, to relegate it back to an iguana-like level. If magic can be seen as an expression of psyche, a vector of being, and an act of the imagination, then the view radically changes. Now, the investigator must consider all those ideas about magic, whether contained in film, literature, heresies, dreams, or the many forms of 'ritual magic' and neo-paganisms that apply to this genre of imagery. Therefore, rather than addressing magic as a thing, we must see it as a form of imagination — a form of imagination rooted in some of our earliest perceptions as children and remaining with us throughout even the most rationally-constricted lives. In this work, through an examination of the imagination of magic, we come to a view of magic as not only an indigenous language of the Imaginal, but as the very physics of the IMAGINAL.

Imaginatrix Term coined by Henry CORBIN to refer to the organ of the imagination. That which dreams the 'I' in which we each locate experience.

Imagonaut A willful neologism asserted in this work as an alternative to CARROLL's 'psychonaut,' merely to emphasize the primacy of imagination. The imagonaut journeys through the imaginal realms, exchanging identities, paradigms, cultures, beliefs, futures, pasts, genders, and many other supposedly permanent attributes. See NO-ONE.

Imagopathy A disorder of the imagination first coined by this author in his doctoral research on the criminal profiling of serial killers. Serial killers, like many brand-loyal consumers, show three distinct deficits of imagination: rigid fantasies, failures of empathy, and rampant projections. Many psychopaths are imagopaths, but most imagopaths are not psychopaths.

Immediacy In this text, one of the eight VOIDS. This term refers to the necessarily qualitatively distinct actions of remembering a past or predicting a future as projections from a constantly unfolding now.

Individuation The process of all images, EGREGORES, MEMES, and ARCHETYPES attempting to manifest, define, and dominate reality. Within some forms of Jungian Psychology only one form of individuation is not fundamentally ARCHONtic: the individuation of the Unfolding Path of the SELF. In many cases, this particular form of individuation is what authors intend when they use the term 'individuation' alone. From a KIA-based meta-system, one might speak more of the unfolding of kia, rather than the Self. For most people, the first arc of development is about the individuation of the ego and its function as the reality principle. We then spend most of the rest of our lives trying to transcend this achievement.

Ineffable An idea, a state, or an experience is not ineffable because it has some term for it that we have forgotten, cannot utter, have not learned, or have not yet conceived; but rather because the full reality of it is beyond or before the very capacity to conceptualize and thus speak. Much as the full reality of a Qabalistic idea of G-d is to be found in the *entirety* of the Tree and the Voids, the Name (Hebrew: *ha Shem*) of this G-d is ineffable not because it has been forgotten, per se, but because we have forgotten that the entire name of G-d is, within that cosmology, the entirety of existence. Elaborate vows that threaten an oath breaker with evisceration, devouring demons, stabs through the heart, or having one's tongue removed reveal a deeper secret of ineffable doctrines. That is, the full revelation of the ineffable truth is found in the entirety of life within the frontier of mortality. In this work, ineffability is the highest Mystery of Mysteries in which the initiate is open to the VOIDS. A denial or rejection of these voids leads to UNSPEAKABLE horror instead of the wonder in the face of the ineffable.

Integration See SELF.

Intentional living In a sense, everyone engages in intentional living, since whatever intentions we have, lead to, or are part of, are products *of* our current way of living. However, this term more typically applies to ways of living in which one deliberates on the impact of all aspects of how one lives and aims to bring them into accord with one's ethics or goals. In most cases the objective is a sustainable lifestyle that supports one's values and attempts to reduce participation in any counterproductive patterns. Intentional communities in which people band together to support shared ethics and goals are one example of this practice. As such, many religious communities have engaged in this practice since time immemorial. Most of this work's exercises are efforts toward gaining clarity regarding one's lifestyle toward the ends of a more intentional lifestyle.

Introjection In psychodynamics, an internalization — 'taking in' — of some emotion, idea, behavior, or experience in such a way that it becomes part of oneself. Since a child is born UNDIFFERENTIATED, the first several years are an ongoing and intensive process of introjections as the infant and toddler establish something like a demarcation between self and other. The process continues throughout life. See PROJECTION and REINTROJECTION.

Initiate One who has undergone a significant enough transformative experience to begin to utilize the powers of imagination to alter their life course. Having awoken to some degree of the fundamental reality of the IMAGINAL, this individual can no longer return to a previous way of living although, to any outside observer, they may seem to be living the exact same life they lived previously.

I.·.N.·.R.·.I.·. Esoteric motto with multiple layers of meanings. Supposedly the placard hung above the crucified Jesus' head by the Romans to indicate that he was Jesus of Nazareth, King of the Jews, few mottos have so many alternate and fanciful meanings, including levels of reality, the Divine Name, and the four elements. In this text, the motto carries its alchemical meaning of *Ignis Natura Renovatur Integra*; that is, 'through fire nature is reborn, whole.' This is the motto of the remarkable chaparral — plant seeds that depend on the heat of wildfires to open them. With its association with crucifixion and sacrifice, INRI is sometimes linked to the ROSY CROSS level of the Western Esoteric QABALAH. With its transformative fire, it is also well placed on DANTE's Purgatory level, in which he must step through a curtain of fire to transform lust into Love and thus enter into the reborn Nature of the Garden of Eden.

IOT *Illuminates of Thanateros.* CHAOS MAGICAL (dis)Order founded in the late 1970's. A reaction to the increasing irrelevancy of Western Esotericism, the group draws influences from A. O. SPARE, H. P. LOVECRAFT, psychedelia, and any other available set of images. It is a DIY approach to magic — or perhaps, more accurately, an approach which acknowledges that all magic is DIY and thus lays claim to universal fictionality. A strong current of observable results underpins this group's approaches, as seen in its frequent use of the term 'results-based' magic.

Irving, John (1942-) New England novelist, author of *The World According to Garp* (1978), *The Cider House Rules* (1985), and *A PRAYER FOR OWEN MEANY* (1989). Noted for his often quirky, humorous, and poignant stories, Irving's works maintain a decidedly humanistic optimism in the midst of often difficult circumstances.

I-tal Rastafarian diet and foodway varying in application. The word derives from 'vital' combined with the 'I-and-I' construction by which Rastafarians recognize the continuity of all living creatures in Jah. The main goal is to enhance 'livity' — vitality and connection to nature — and to these ends many Rastafarians avoid artificial additives. Some practitioners are strict vegans, many avoid certain suspect foods much as in Kosher practice. Ital is a personal commitment and continues to develop as Rastafarianism faces the challenges of the new millennium.

Jackson, Nigel (1963-) British-born artist, author, and esotericist.

Jonas, Hans (1903-1993) Existentialist, ethicist, environmentalist, and interpreter of Gnosticism. Jonas was the sort of tough-minded and grounded philosopher existentialism should help to create. His *The Gnostic Religion: The message of the Alien God and the beginnings of Christianity* (1958) is an indispensable classic. Although his work's assumptions about historical Gnosticism have since been revised by the translations of collections of ancient texts such as the Nag Hammadi Library, his creative synthesis of Gnostic mythology and Existentialism is brilliant. His later works have profound implications for bio-ethics and environmentalism.

Jones, Charles Stansfeld See FRATER ACHAD.

Jung, C. G. (1875-1961) To date, no one has yet written the critical comparative biography paralleling the lives of CROWLEY and Jung. Born the same year, they were inspired by strikingly similar source material and created globally influential visions of a sort of neo-Gnosticism. Notably, both men also used themselves as the central subjects for their experiments in esoteric transformation. (And, not coincidentally, both were eventually supported by the wealth of others.) Jung's influence, however, is exponentially broader and more significant than Crowley's often over-blown reputation. However, like his contemporary, Jung's writing can be a crossword puzzle of obscure references. *Memories, Dreams, Reflections* (1963), his autobiography, is the best place to start to understand the scope of his ideas. Sadly, New Age writers and lecturers bandy about terms, such as ARCHETYPAL, with little or no understanding of Jung's intent. Thus, once readers approach any particular essay, text, or lecture, they would do well to remember that Jung probably innovates or disagrees with that particular stance in another work. The 2009 publication of Jung's *Red Book* represents a watershed event in Imaginal Psychology, as the reader is able to see how Jung created and refined his own GRIMOIRE to represent and fuel his development.

Kadath In Lovecraft's *The Dream-Quest of Unknown Kadath* (1927/1943), the central spire of the Dream Lands where the protagonist meets NYARLATHOTEP. See QUF.

Kairos Ancient Greek term for the time of opportunity, a time that breaks through the quantifiable inevitability of chronological time. Kairos is personified as a fleet youth with long forelocks who must be seized if the moment is not to pass. CAPUTO links the idea to the Event of Christianity in *The Weakness of God* (2006).

Kali A powerful and primordial Hindu Goddess of time, fundamental energy, and the cycles of destruction and regeneration.

Kia Concept for a fundamental unit of (non)being first introduced by Austin

Osman SPARE. CARROLL presents it as the truth behind concepts such as 'spirit' or 'soul.' Kia offers an alternative to the defensive 'real inner me' of an individual, personal soul. Rather than a linear personal growth vector, Kia would seem to prosper with possibility, imagination, and diversity (see DERRIDA). In many ways, this concept is closer to the sense of psyche and 'soulfulness' advocated by IMAGINAL PSYCHOLOGISTS. In this work, it is equivalent to 'NO-ONE.' (Author's note: I would have been happy to continue to use the term 'kia', but the South Korean carmaker has made the term difficult to use with a straight face.)

Kierkegaard, Søren (1813-1855) Danish philosopher, proto-psychologist, and theologian. With a focus on the struggles of individual experience and a rejection of the abstract in favor of human reality, many scholars view Kierkegaard as an early EXISTENTIALIST.

Klien, Fritz (1932-2006) Psychiatrist and sex researcher, famous for his *Klein Sexual Orientation Grid* that responded to the limitations of the Kinsey Scale, offering many more dimensions with which to define affection, gender, intimacy, and sexual orientation. His work informs many parts of this current text, but especially 'Application 4: Love, Intimacy, Sex,' in Volume One.

Kohut, Heinz (1913-1981) Psychoanalyst most associated with his creation of Self Psychology, a school of thought that integrates and complements Object-relations. Kohut's sense of 'working through' — rather than the baffling self-destruction of Freud's 'repetition compulsion' — seeks to explain the puzzling acts of traumatized individuals who seemingly seek out unhealthy relationships or put themselves at unwarranted risk. Kohut believes the impulse is fundamentally based in the urge to resolve the incomplete business represented by the trauma.

Korzybski, Alfred (1879-1950) Creator of GENERAL SEMANTICS. Famous for his remark that, 'The map is not the territory; the word is not the thing defined' (a concept BAUDRILLARD might contextualize by stating we have only maps left). His major work, *Science and Sanity* (1933), remains rich with fascinating notions for training one's thinking to avoid the confusion of various classes of abstraction.

Kristeva, Julia (1941-) Bulgarian-French philosopher, feminist, psychoanalyst, and novelist. Her most important contribution may be her concept of the abject introduced in *Powers of Horror, An Essay on Abjection* (1982), but she has amazing and radical notions on a host of other topics.

Lacan, Jacques (1901-1981) French psychoanalyst and philosopher. One of the first thinkers to claim the radical potential of FREUD's writing and revise the role of language in constituting both the conscious and the unconscious. As such, he can be seen as predicting and informing postmodern philosophy, while giving it grounding in concrete psychological moments. One of his earliest contributions was an analysis of the MIRROR PHASE. His development of ideas of ALTERITY still resonates with innovative sizzle. His ideas of 'the imaginary,' 'the symbolic,' and 'the real' represent a well-developed system approaching the same themes as this current work.

Lao-tse (somewhere between the 6th and 4th century BCE if he was, in fact, a single actual person) The story goes that, tired of the noise and complications of an urban life, this wearied bureaucrat slowly rode a water buffalo toward the West of China to retire. At a last gate, a guard asked this clearly wise elder to reveal what he had learned in his years. The result was the central work of Taoism, the *Tao te Ching* (6th century BCE). The briefest sentence from this work can induce enlightenment if the reader allows it to open into him or her.

Left-Hand Path (LHP) This work takes a rather dismissive tone relative to the imagination of the Right-Hand Path/Left-Hand Path dichotomy. In spite of how cool and dark the term may seem, LHP would appear today to be mostly an aesthetic consideration by occultists who rebel against the solar phallic or White Light assumptions of other mages. In all, it is a meaningless distinction based on false assumptions, bad faith, and leveled mostly as an accusation by later Victorian and Edwardian esotericists to describe the bogeymen of the Black Lodge. Although often seen to have its origins in the *vamachara* or *vamamarga* of Tantric practice, this distinction is ineffective for its application in Western practice in which asceticism and meditation are painfully rare. Any hopes of bringing back the Gnostic sense of the Sophia and her Left-Hand Path appear impractical — new terminology may be necessary to reclaim this potential. Some contemporary practitioners claim this label with pride but each practitioner, and each collective of practitioners defines the term in ways idiosyncratic to their perspective. In many cases the behaviors, expressed ethoi, or goals of individuals adopting the label of Right or Left-Hand Path may be indistinguishable. See RIGHT-HAND PATH.

Lemuria In several New Age cosmologies, a GOLDEN AGE, antediluvian continent coming between MU and ATLANTIS. Originally proposed by a zoologist Philip Sclater (1829-1913) to explain lemur (thus the name) fossils outside of Madagascar, BLAVATSKY first introduced it into the imagination of magic.

Ligotti, Thomas (1953-) American author of Weird and Horror fiction. In many ways, the inheritor of H. P. LOVECRAFT's legacy of UNSPEAKABLE Horror — except Ligotti is a better writer with more sophisticated psychology and philosophy girding his works. Themes of emptiness, the abyss, madness, and black, black, black nothingness abound in his fiction. Also a scholar of the genre, he has written some distinction-bending essays and prose poems. His work *I Have a Special Plan for This World* (2000) stands as a singularly perfect piece of NIHILISM. S. T. Joshi presents a scholarly treatment of Ligotti in the context of other authors in *The Modern Weird Tale* (2001).

Lived world The phenomenal world, the world of experience. A term from PHENOMENOLOGY, it can be contrasted to a derivative 'world' of things—a supposition built, according to this text, on informing IMAGES and their FICTIONS.

Logos Greek term for logic that implies a situational logic or truth. By abandoning the fantasy of transcendental Logic, one may come to understand the logos of a particular situation or image, thus gaining access to the imaginal.

Lovecraft, H. P. (1890-1937) New England author who gathered together a few threads of existing speculative fiction and horror to create the genre of the Weird tale and the Cthulhu Mythos. His obsession with creeping madness and UNSPEAKABLE horror place him as a central prophet of NIHILISM. Yet, as with Nietzsche, Lovecraft was not exactly praising the Great Devouring Abyss; rather, he is reporting, perhaps, what *is*, rather than what he would have be. Look to his dream worlds writings for a moderately more optimistic side of his personality. Although much of his writing for the pulp magazines of his day is rightly forgotten, his prodigious output also contains ample examples of brilliance. Figures within the Chaos tradition have taken up his mythos as a means of undoing the authority of historicity, provenance, and established religion, thus asserting the ubiquity of fiction. The prime example of the power of this approach is the now-reality of his MACGUFFIN, the NECRONOMICON.

Lukyanenko, Sergei (1961-) Russian Science Fiction and Fantasy author, most noted outside of Russia for his *Night Watch* tetralogy (1998-2006). Due to his background in psychology, Lukyanenko's works are rife with ethical dilemmas demanding psychological insight and transformation on the part of the protagonists. His vision of the 'Twilight' or 'Gloom' presents a fascinating commentary about spiritual hierarchies, especially since, by the end of the NightWatch books, the ultimate shape of the various levels reveals a mystical secret.

Lynch, David (1946-) American filmmaker as well as practitioner and advocate of transcendental meditation. Although the *Twin Peaks* (1990-1991) television series and film may have established his reputation to the widest possible audience, his many mind-bending films are brilliant, heartrending, and often-terrifying glimpses into the mad parts of all of us. To a greater extent his films can be categorized as psychological realism.

MacGuffin Term first widely used by Alfred Hitchcock to describe a plot element, sought after item, or motivating quest that drives the story toward its climax. In this text, it is any driving force for life that helps us avoid encounters with the VOIDS (but simultaneously leads us all the more toward them). See NECRO-NOMICON.

Madness In this text, one of the eight VOIDS. Closely linked with the existential idea of the absurd, madness reminds us that no explanation, rationality, system of logic, or reason can exceed or transcend this unfolding moment. Explanations are fictions, products of the images that typically constitute the moment. Behind the vertiginous maw of the inadequacy of our various logics, a funda-mental human quality offers its liberation in the form of this void's indictment of all binding fictions. As in FOUCAULT's use of the term, madness here does not equate to mental illness although it has a complex relationship to it.

Magic For this work, the physics of the imaginal. All acts are magical acts because, for those creatures who are 'experience,' all acts are grounded in the imaginal. Magic is the means by which any other technology, science, or philosophy oper-ates. Most of the technologies that lay claim to the intentional application of magic rarely describe their efforts as such; conversely, most practitioners who claim to perform magic are rarely doing so with any efficacy. The now popular (re)addition of the 'k' — 'magick' — was an effort by CROWLEY to distinguish will-working from stage 'magic' and other pedestrian uses of a term that he sought to define, instead, scientifically. Layered with multiple implications, Crowley also intended the 'k' to indicate an association to the 'kteis' or vagina. From a chaos perspective, the k might as easily stand for 'kaos', 'KIA', or the Erisian 'kallisti' ('for the fairest') — the inscription on the golden apple thrown into an Olympian feast, from which the subsequent strife amongst compet-ing goddesses led to the Trojan War. This work dropped the 'k' in order to expand the sense of magic to embrace more poetic, daily, and fantastical senses of the term. Were this work to add the 'k' back on, it would need to stand for 'KAIROS' — the 'moment' — or 'khora' — an interval or space before becoming.

Magical Revival A somewhat amorphous term, it refers historically to a Romantic movement beginning in the late 18th century in response to the Industrial Revolution. In it, scholars, artists, Freemasons, and many other groups found themselves looking to the past — usually imagined or inter-preted through mauve colored glasses — for an alternative to the urbaniza-tion of the world around them. The Revival intersected strongly with the invention of various nations in Europe in the mid-19th century, seeking foundation myths. Often a rustic sentimentality drove the dreamers to create sylvan groves, forests primeval, and ancestors more in touch with the cycles of nature. (Never mind the fact that the world population was rapidly making such a relationship near impossible.) Eventually occult ORIENTALISM, fueled by questionable translations and even more questionable interpretations, led to strange syncretic creations. This coincided with the emergence of SPIRITUALISM, laying the groundwork for the New Age movement. Several works of seemingly exhaustive scholarship fueled a fantasy that Europe's ancestors shared a relatively homogenous, often matriarchal pagan religion. The two major advocates of this pseudo-history were James George Frazer (1954-1941) and Margaret Murray (1863-1963). Only with HUTTON's *Triumph of the Moon* (1999) has a complete and thorough accounting of the Revival fully dismissed these previously canonical perspectives. World War II was a culmination of the Cults of Nationalism coming into apocalyptic conflict. In the years following, the Revival became far more of a counter-cultural movement and by the 1970's a second 'Occult Revival' emerged spawning the dizzying array of neo-pagan, Wiccan, Witchcraft, folk magical, Satanic, and esoteric groups abounding today. For further scholarship, see Dave EVANS and Margot ADLER.

Magical thinking A derogatory term, drawn from developmental and clinical psychology, for dysfunctional cognitions including all the forms of superstition, delusion, shoddy reasoning, and blind faith in which what a person thinks, says, or does has a seemingly supernatural or 'psychic' effect on his or her environment. What psychology isolates as examples of 'magical thinking,' this text presents as cases not of 'overactive' but rather *underdeveloped* imaginations.

Mala Necklace of prayer or meditation beads originating in ancient India. The beads are used to track repetitions of mantras or prayers. Typical malas in Hindu and Buddhist practice have 108 beads, however other quantities are common, although the number is always highly symbolic. The mala is likely the progenitor of most other prayer beads including the Islamic misbaha and the Christian rosary.

May, Rollo (1909-1994) Although sometimes not as linguistically radical as his subject demanded, May was the most approachable and readable of the writers on EXISTENTIALISM in its hey-day in the mid-20th century. His introduction to *Existence* (1956) was one of the first comprehensive statements in English of the basic tenets of Existential Psychotherapy.

Meaninglessness In this text, one of the eight VOIDS. An encounter with this void reminds us that life itself has no transcendent goal, finish line, or instruction manual, and that the world itself has no inherent purpose or significance. We are those beings that have our own existence in question and are thus those that make meaning. This meaning-making function rips our ontology out of derivative thing–filled worlds and into the IMAGINAL.

Messiaen, Olivier (1908-1992) French composer. A SYNESTHETE, he saw particular colors associated with certain chords.

Method X An inherent, unique means of extrication from an image's monomania and archontic individuation. A Method X may emerge with each image, but no method is a transcendent Method X applicable to all images.

Meme Term coined by Richard DAWKINS in his *The Selfish Gene* (1976). A meme is a self-replicating pattern of behavior, perception, and/or thought paralleling the patterns of genes. In this text, it is linked to IMAGES and AUTANGELS.

Miéville, China (1972-) English author of fantasy and science fiction literature, as well as critical and political academic works. Miéville lays claim to 'weird fiction' to label his novels and short stories that embody themes of alterity, multiculturalism, revolution, man/machine, and other Marxist-informed perspectives.

Miller, Jr., Walter M. (1923-1996) American science fiction author of many short stories and *A CANTICLE FOR LEIBOWITZ* (1960).

Mirror Phase Psychological developmental stage occurring anywhere between six and 18 months in which children come to (somewhat mistakenly) recognize their reflection as their self. In the language of LACAN, the child creates a small other within that redefines experience through the lens of this model. Although an indispensable development (i.e., the formation of the ego), this INTROJECTION is ultimately an inaccurate mediation of experience.

Modernity the period of history beginning with the Renaissance and continuing until the present. Although, popularly, 'modern' may mean 'contemporary' or 'high-tech,' historiographically, this term refers to the urbanization, decline of agrarianism, focus on rationality, progress, and materialism that find their origins in the humanism of the Renaissance. This era has also seen the rise of the bourgeoisie, the advance of European colonialism, and the fracturing of philosophy into the manifold sciences. In many ways, the force of modernity came into full flower with the Industrial Revolution of the late 18th century. Just as the Renaissance did not instantly take root across the globe, neither has modernity faded into a POSTMODERN era. However, as industrialization moves into parts of Asia, this once-vanguard development of modernity has morphed to the point that some might speak of modernity ending. See PERIMODERN and POSTMODERN.

Moore, Alan (1953-) British author and mage mostly known for his work in graphic novels. His works are often postmodern bricolages drawing from every conceivable genre of literature, art, music, advertising, occult practice, conspiracy theory, and politics. An imagonaut of encyclopedic erudition, he is often too clever for his own good. His masterful *Promethea* series (1999-2005) does a far better job of explaining the Western Esoteric Tradition than any author to date—a welcome replacement for Manley P. Hall's (1901-1990) *The Secret Teachings of All Ages* (1928).

Morningstar An ambivalent term applied to both Christ and Lucifer, and as such, according to this text, containing an important secret. The term also applies to the planet Venus whose symbol, in some Western esotericism, is the pentagram. One important Luciferian legend asserts that Emerald Tablet of Hermeticism was, in fact, the crown jewel of the Lightbringer, Lucifer, knocked from his crown in his defeat by the Archangel Michael. Luciferian currents, somewhat distinct from Satanic ones, in the imagination of magic are often well-guarded for fear of public persecution. However, Traditional Witchcraft has come to have a rather sophisticated promethean mythology which places Lucifer back within the Divine Pantheon.

Morrígan Celtic Goddess, known by various names, including 'Phantom Queen.' She is the 'Washer at the Ford' who portends death. She is an ancient Goddess of Death, Battle, Magic, and Sex. In this text, a Western analog of Kali and the Vajrayogini. See Cu Chulainn.

Morrison, Grant (1960-) Scottish essayist and author of numerous graphic novels. Known for taking other standard superheroes and adding elements of meta-fiction and counter-culture to the storylines. Amongst his most famous works is the masterpiece *The Invisibles* (1994-2000) which portrays the struggles of a cell of anarchist chaos mages fighting the influx of life-sapping archons into our dimension. Morrison considers the work an ensigilization of a Chaos current.

Mu Japanese word roughly meaning 'without' or 'none.' It is the only proper response to a query for which any answer so profoundly begs the question as to be unable to satisfactorily extricate itself from the assumptions contained in the query. Basically equivalent to 'Wu' in Chinese.

Also, a mythic continent, first proposed by Augustus Le Plongeon (1825-1908) and, later, James Churchward (1851-1936), presented by spiritualists and channelers of the New Age as the oldest civilization on earth. In their systematizations, it preceded Lemuria and Atlantis.

Murray, Margaret (1863-1963) Egyptologist and anthropologist most associated with her theory of a pre-Christian Witch-cult in Europe, against which the various Witch-trials were pitted but failed, thus leading to its re-emergence in the MAGICAL REVIVAL. This theory has been systematically deconstructed by several scholars, especially Ronald HUTTON.

Mystical Nihilism Central informing stance for this current work and contrasted to EMPTY NIHILISM. The term asserts that a return to an open relationship with the voids ought not to prove entirely annihilating, but potentially authentic and rejuvenative. See DIALECTICAL NIHILISM, NIHILISM, and APOPHATIC.

Nabokov, Vladimir (1899-1977) Russian-American Novelist, best known for his extended metaphor on life in post-World War II America, *Lolita* (1955). A synesthete, he had strong associations between certain numbers, letters, words, and colors. These elements show up in his writing, as well as some of his characters.

Narrative Therapy A movement anchored in the pioneering works of Michael White (1948-2008) and David Epston (1944-). Their seminal work, *Narrative Means to Therapeutic Ends* (1990), extends ideas from postmodern philosophers such as FOUCAULT, offering the psychotherapist tools by which to help the client deconstruct the limiting singular narratives that constitute their pathology. The resultant multiple narratives, and more flexible sense of identity, provides the client with more opportunities for adaptability and future extrications from entrapping narratives.

Necronomicon The oft-reported neo-koan about this Grimoire of Grimoires is that if it didn't exist as a historical reality before, it does now. The Necronomicon, one of the greatest literary MACGUFFINS of all time, became an incredible archetypal cipher for the image of the GRIMOIRE. LOVECRAFT's introduction of the term in 1922 spurred countless later authors, directors, game designers, and occult junkies to spread its legends through further dark fictions. Lovecraft asserts that this madness-inducing tome's author is Abdul AlHazred (one of HPL's pseudonyms) 'the Mad Arab', and that its original name was *Al Azif*—the demonic, nocturnal buzzing of insects. Perhaps, unwittingly, the author and title present other perversely playful potential meanings for the A.·.A.·.—in its Qlipothic form? The Necronomicon has become a powerful MEME, based on archetypal potentialities, that has become a potent EGREGORE for many groups, literary genres, and individuals. This current work could be considered another iteration of the Necronomicon, dealing, as it does, with the inscrutable boundaries of life, the VOIDS.

Neti, neti Hindu mantra and term for 'not this, not this' or 'neither this nor that.' See also MU.

Neuro-Linguistic Programming (NLP) A term introduced by Richard Bandler (1950-) and John Grinder (1940-). The theory includes elements of Family Systems and Gestalt psychotherapy as well as hypnosis. The practice rests on an assumption-free assessment of what thoughts, language, and embodiments tend to go along with what behaviors and effects. The term is now widely used to mean any manipulation, engineering, or alteration of language that intends a largely unconscious effect on the subject. To a greater extend, NLP liberated hypnosis from the backwards counting, watch-waggling confines of the consulting room. The term is, however, overly used by a cadre of ethically questionable individuals who might benefit from a bit more time studying the rest of psychology.

Nietzsche, Friedrich (1844-1900) Does anyone actually read him, or do we just misquote him? Far too often, he is turned into a sort of jackbooted punk with a bushy mustache. Few caricatures could be farther from the truth. Terrified by the misdirection the West had taken with reason, power, and religion, Nietzsche prophetically warned of an impending EMPTY NIHILISM from which no one would escape. In his ongoing critique of the abysmal state of Western philosophy and culture, he challenges his readers to question what power is, and to liberate themselves altogether from the master/slave dichotomy that pervades religion, politics, and life itself. Although credited as an important influence, CROWLEY likely misunderstood much of Nietzsche.

Nihilism No single definition can suffice to describe the many (anti)philosophies claiming this title. In general, it is lobbed as a form of derision—as it was by NIETZSCHE who saw Western rationalism leading inexorably to an EMPTY NIHILISM born of a fundamentally flawed theory of meaning. However, as East Asian and sub-continent philosophies have been better represented in the West, ideas of emptiness, nothingness, APOPHASIS, and other key mystical concepts have come to challenge a purely derisive sense of the term. This current work's sense is of a MYSTICAL NIHILISM, which speaks to a fundamental conviction that not only can one not seek out meaning in an external sense of a thing-like world, but that any meaning one can find—through discovering existential structural truths, for instance—still sits upon and gains significance from an ultimate NOTHINGNESS. Only through an increasingly less-mediated relationship to the VOIDS does one make any headway in extricating oneself from the nightmare of ARCHONtic domination and certainty.

Non-theism A philosophy free from the belief in an active God as an agent who modifies events in the world. This stance can, however, allow for other images of God or gods, such as DEISM, principles of enlightenment, the INEFFABLE, etc. Many forms of Buddhism could be considered non-theistic. 'Non-theism' is only useful in contrast to ATHEISM if the speaker intends to salvage some sort of religious, ritual, transpersonal, or philosophical ground of meaning. See AGNOSTICISM and ANTI-THEISM.

No-one A term introduced in this text to indicate the centerless field of psyche, KIA. The inter-related field of vectors of desire and experience out of which emerges the ego structure. The IMAGINATRIX is the central organ of no-one.

'Nothing is true, everything is permissible' Magical motto strongly linked to the CHAOS MAGICAL tradition. The term is popularly attributed to Hassan i-Sabbah, the richly storied founder of the 'assassins.' Although sources as far back as the 14th and 15th centuries—in particular, the Egyptian historian Al Maqriti (1364-1442)—link the saying to some leader of this Islamic secret brotherhood, the persistence of the myth in the imagination of magic is now far more important than its origins. NIETZSCHE quotes it, having likely read it in the work *Die Assassinen* (1818) by the ORIENTALIST Joseph von Hammer-Purgstall (1774-1856). Thus, by the mid-20th century, it had become a password in secret societies seeking to hearken to the heretical, deadly, and 'orientalist' resonances of this now-mythic order. The Chaos Magical order of the IOT adopted it as a motto and, today, gamers the world around know the phrase from the *Assassin's Creed* series of videogames. Regardless of provenance, the fact that this phrase has multiple layers and potentials for meaning is frequently lost in a haze of antinomian fantasies. (Thanks go to Steve Snair for his fine legwork in tracking down the provenance of this phrase.)

Nothingness In this text, one of the eight VOIDS. This void undermines and erodes the various things, thing-sets, as well as fundamentalisms and literalisms that distract us from the essentially imaginal nature of all experience. The term, in part, means 'not-thing-ness.' It is the truth behind things that renders any 'thing' uncanny with the slightest scrutiny.

Nyarlathotep (From LOVECRAFT's Chthulu Mythos) The Crawling Chaos, Soul and Messenger of the Other Gods. First introduced by Lovecraft in a 1920 prose poem of the same name, inspired by a vivid and disturbing dream. In *The Dream-Quest of Unknown Kadath* (1927/1943) he holds sway over the gods of this world on the immeasurable Spire of KADATH. The following invocation, created by this current author, gives a sense of the roles in which Lovecraft cast this figure:

An Invocation of Nyarlathotep

I am Nyarlathotep, the Crawling Chaos, Soul and Messenger of the Other Gods. I do not lie. I do not deceive.

My depths are Void.

I am Legate and Ambassador of the Demon Sultan, Azathoth.

I am all, when Others are not.

When you seek, the blackness of my eyes is all that you will find.

Be wary in your thirst for knowledge lest you should learn my truth;

Yet to avoid me is to inexorably approach my court.

I am Absolute Frontier.

I am the Black Man of the Sabbath.

I am Perfect Midnight.

Nameless and Faceless, I am the Haunter of the Dark.

Propitiate me not,

Worship me not.

From my emptiness, the gods of earth, in their caprice and machinations,
 are subject to me—

While idiot throngs dance to the bone flute's skirl.

I speak with the bloodied tongue and

I am the last voice you will hear before annihilation.

I am Nyarlathotep, the Crawling Chaos, Soul and Messenger of the Other Gods.

Object-relations Post-Freudian school of psycho-dynamics focused on the tone of early childhood experiences constituting the structure of the personality. Object-relations has gained wide cachet within the world of depth psychology due to its strong research record, intensive training of analysts, and modification of Freud's less-supportable tenets.

Orff, Carl (1895-1982) German composer and innovator of music education. Orff is best known for his *Carmina Burana* (1937), a powerful piece intended to be performed by a large community-based group of instrumentalists, choristers, soloists, as well as dancers and visual artists. Orff saw music as a fundamental human vector and thus created an innovative system of child music education in addition to his efforts at engaging the larger society in performance.

Orientalism Fantasies of the East, both Middle and Far. Originally a term for the study of these territories, Edward Saïd (1935-2003) in his *Orientalism* (1978), levels it as criticism of the wide range of fantasies Westerners created about this perpetually 'exotic' frontier of their knowledge. Due to its almost complete absence from the academy, the study of the occult and Western Esotericim has been, and too-often remains, rife with these unexamined imaginings.

Panentheism The belief that God pervades all of the universe but is bigger than it. This perspective has wide variance and is a label applied externally to try to distinguish various disparate perspectives into generalized categories.

Pantheism The belief that the entirety of the world or the universe is synonymous with God.

Pathologizing A term with two distinct meanings. The most common meaning in the world of psychology and psychiatry is an accusation against the tendency of diagnosticians to find something wrong, and often *very* wrong, with everyone. In this sense, one can speak of certain instruments (psychology tests) as pathologizing since the subject cannot somehow 'pass' the test and come out looking normal and healthy. Rather, these measures tend to leave everyone looking at least moderately 'sick.'

The second meaning came as a reaction against humanistic psychology's tendency to view everyone as healthy and disregard diagnosis. HILLMAN popularized 'pathologizing' to mean a native expression of the psyche. Thus, Hillman asks mental health practitioners, and humans in general, to hearken to the voice of their pain and suffering as a call from an individually and culturally repressed source.

Pathology In ANALYTIC and IMAGINAL PSYCHOLOGY, the language (logos) of pain (pathos), a native expression of psyche. Although all suffering sits within psyche, one can also speak of psychopathology — the language of the pain of the soul — to refer to more specifically 'mental' suffering. However, this distinction relies on questionable mind/body differentiation.

Perennial Philosophy A notion — present in a wide range of philosophies, metaphysics, religions, and occult beliefs — that the fundamental Truth or Secret of Life, The Universe, and Everything Else has been present, to varying degrees, throughout history. Thus, adherents can look to various minds over the past 2000, 6000, 10,000, 200,000 or 2 million years to gain validation of their current beliefs. ATAVISM, the akashic records, archetypes, and other perspectives may be used to explain this phenomena. In this text, the existential givens and thus the VOIDS are inherent to the human condition. Therefore, every philosophy or religion will have to encounter them, either through defensive distraction and denial, or acknowledgement.

Perimodern A term, coined in this work, referring to those traditions running in parallel to the MODERN — post-Renaissance — era. These traditions may have their origins before the emergence of modernity and, later, industrialization, but were changed in reaction to the urbanization, reduction of agrarianism, division of 'philosophy' into the sciences, and the continued progress of the bourgeois that modernity brought with it. A group may be considered perimodern to the extent that its philosophy differs from the rational, materialistic, individualistic, or progress-obsessed agenda of the 'dominant' modern culture. Thus, alchemy, folk traditions, luddites, a host of 'heresies', syncretic amalgams such as Vodoun, Candomblé, and Santería, as well as the Cunning Tradition of the British Isles describe a surprisingly large periphery of alternatives to the mainstream that has controlled the use of language and accounts of history. Although many esoteric traditions can be described as perimodern, such as TRADITIONAL WITCHCRAFT, many others capitulated to modernity's agendas and merely supported the dominant paradigm, albeit dressed in ritual robes. Though a hotbed for the creation of perimodern traditions, FREEMASONRY cannot be considered perimodern since its goals are insufferably modern.

Phantasy In psychoanalysis, and especially OBJECT-RELATIONS, unconscious fantasies.

Phenomenology A critique of any approach to the human condition that harbors natural scientific assumptions. By bracketing these assumptions in what HUSSERL called an 'epoché,' the field examines *how* the subject describes experience (phenomena). This process bears a strong resemblance to aspects of Buddhist meditation techniques. As a Western philosophical development, this early 20th century movement soon allied with Existentialism, especially in the writings of HEIDEGGER.

Philo of Alexandria (20BCE-50CE) Hellenistic Jew famous for his Biblical exegesis that later contributed to early Christianity.

Pike, Albert (1809-1891) Confederate and Freemason. Most widely known for his *Morals and Dogmas of the Ancient and Accepted Scottish Rite Freemasonry* (1871). His ideas became highly influential in those esoteric circles surrounding Freemasonry in the late 19th and early 20th centuries. Many of his works contain elements of Promethean Luciferianism. Although historical scrutiny indicates Pike did not found the Klu Klux Klan, it would be hard to cast the man as a proponent of multiculturalism.

Postmodern a term used to describe both: 1) a historical period with its roots in the industrialization of the Victorian period, but coming into its own at the beginning of the post-World War II era; and 2) a loose collection of philosophies addressing this condition. Attempting to define the postmodern condition, or its philosophy, is an almost impossible task since words themselves are at stake in both cases. The philosophy grows out of Marxist, existential, feminist, phenomenological, and psychoanalytic foundations. Age-old questions such as 'how do I know what is real?' and 'to what extent is individual identity a social construct?' find new relevance in an era of multiculturalism, media super-saturation, and virtual lives. Harbingers of the decay of modernity can be seen in the collapse of colonialism, corporations overshadowing nations, the re-emergence of pre-modern empires such as China to global dominance, and the progressive decay of nation-states into smaller regional ethnic states (i.e., 'Balkanization'). Postmodern philosophy can embrace a wide-range of philosophies that speak to the postmodern condition, but most make use of the technique of deconstruction. This practice takes the component parts of a long-held understanding and turns these pieces against each other in order to yield a new perspective, usually one that opens more possibilities, but deteriorates the prospect of a universal understanding. See DERRIDA and FOUCAULT.

Power/Knowledge Concept introduced by FOUCAULT to emphasize the inextricability of the two ideas. Those in power may define what is knowable — that is, shape an epistemology; but, so too does a system of knowledge define what power *is*. In these self-referential loops, aspects of experience may all but disappear if they become epistemologically inaccessible.

Practical Magic 1998 contemporary fantasy film directed by Griffin Dunne (1955-) based on the 1996 novel by Alice Hoffman (1952-). It portrays the lives of the Owens sisters, witches who bear a centuries-old curse of finding that any true love they experience leads to the death of the beloved.

Pranayama The control of breath and life-force from yogic practice. In its simplest sense, it is a form of breath-work that complements the asanas (yoga postures) and opens the way for more advanced yoga. More complex forms of pranayama involve esoteric teachings usually transmitted from guru to student. Great care should be taken in the practice, and it should involve a seasoned expert as mentor.

Pratchett, Terry (1948-) British author of comic fantasy novels. Best known for his Discworld (1983-) series beginning with *The Colour of Magic* (1983) and *The Light Fantastic* (1986). In the Discworld, an eighth magical colour exists — 'ocatarine.'

A Prayer for Owen Meany 1989 novel by John IRVING. The story describes the titular character and his best friend growing up in a New England town. Owen has a powerful sense of calling that gradually takes shape over two decades, integrating seemingly impossibly disparate elements of his narrative. Strong messianic themes, along with fundamental religious questions punctuate the often comic novel.

Projection The unconscious denial of aspects of one's self or experience that are then attributed to some outside source, often another person. See PROJECTIVE IDENTIFICATION.

Projective identification A psychoanalytic term for the successful, unconscious infection of person B by person A's projections. That is, B begins to unwittingly act and feel in accord with A's projections. Obvious examples are easily explainable without recourse to the unconscious, such as when a person is so worried that he is hated that he drives others away with his incessant 'checking-in' on their relationship, thus confirming his suspicions. However, more complex examples must resort to subtler explanations such as when a traumatized individual can, without mentioning their history of victimization, engender historically-resonant hostility in another.

Prophecy Epistemological advocacy. A clear-sighted statement of what has become hidden in plain sight in a culture. A call for social transformation based on a new way of seeing, often demanding an elimination of hypocrisy, and, as such, the destruction of the current POWER/KNOWLEDGE structure. From the perspective in this current text, the association of prophesy with the psychic power of prescience is a misunderstanding. Any predictions of future events that grow from prophesy are typically due to a fuller sense of current events and their logical consequences. Most of the figurative and often apocalyptic language applied by prophets is not so much predictive as descriptive.

Psi Phenomena Parapsychology examining supernatural events, abilities, and perceptions. A tradition with deep roots in the history of psychology with luminaries such as William James and Carl JUNG bringing sober level-headedness to its ranks.

Psychoanalysis See FREUD.

Psychologizing Offering explanations of experiences that reduce them to 'mere' manifestations of mental processes. Ultimately, a form of EMPTY NIHILISM.

Qabalah, Western Initiatory Also known as the HERMETIC Qabalah and intertwined with the Christian Qabalah. Spelled variously cabalah, kabbalah, etc. Strongly linked to the creative and initiatory schematic Tree of Life, this system must be distinguished from the Jewish Kabbalah. Although overlap exists, and the Western practice profits from any influx from the Hebrew, they are distinct currents opposed in some key ways. The Western Qabalah dates to Moorish Spain (711-1492) where Christian, Muslim, Jewish, and Hermetic scholars intersected. By the emergence of Roscrucianism in the early 17th century, the Western Qabalah was already producing fascinating SYNCRETIC ideas. It was not, however, until the HERMETIC ORDER OF THE GOLDEN DAWN that this system came to its fullest articulation.

Qi Gong (氣功, also 'ch'i kung') 'Qi Cultivation.' A broad range of Chinese exercises that may involve breath, often slow movements, and the stimulation of various points on the body. Although Qi Gong may be a part of various martial arts practices, it has no direct martial applications unto itself, unlike the practice of Tai Chi Chuan. Most of the controversy surrounding these practices concedes the benefits of the practice but debates the idea of Qi. Blaming these misunderstandings on 'mistranslation' would be convenient, but many Chinese practitioners address Qi with similar New Age concepts as those used by Westerners. Since Qi (氣) has such a wide range of possible meanings and associations, the Western reader would do well to become familiar with these potentials. One sense of the term can indicate the 'way of things working.' Qi Gong practice is intimately related to TAOISM, as well as other Asian philosophies and religions.

Qlipoth 'Husks' or 'broken shells'. Often presented as some sort of shadow tree behind the Sephirothic Tree. The Qlipothic tree would, in that system, have levels of 444, 333, and 222 rather than the 555 (GOLDEN DAWN), 666 (ROSY CROSS), and 777 ('A.˙.A.˙.') of the Sephirothic levels. In this text, the Qlipoths are the reality of any conception of the Sephiroth, in that any expressible idea of the shape of reality is inherently a failed, or at least different-than, image. In the Qabalah of Isaac Luria (1534-1572) the upper three sephiroth could bear the divine inflow; however, the next lower six sephiroth were broken by the supernal light and became 'figures' or 'faces.' That one should search through the Qabalistic Tree and somehow imagine the schematic, as presented, to be perfected is a questionable practice at best. Furthermore, relegating the Qlipoths to some sort of preliminary shadow-work to be overcome before proceeding to the Sephiroths, would seem to ignore the importance of the concept. Kenneth GRANT, in his innovation of the Western Initiatory Qabalah, introduced the paths of the Qlipoth as the TUNNELS OF SET.

Quf, Mount In Sufism, a mountain that is simultaneously the central axis/hub of this world as well as its furthest boundary rim of mountains. Strikingly similar to the spire at the center of H. P. LOVECRAFT's KADATH on which dwells NYAR-LATHOTEP overseeing the gods of this world. Quf's simultaneously central and ringing locations also resonates powerfully with the point and the circle of BYSS AND ABYSS, as well as DANTE's final vision of the Cosmic Rose in the *Divine Comedy*. See QUTUB and 111.

Quotidian Day-to-day, mundane, everyday.

Qutub Arabic term meaning 'point' or 'axis.' It indicates a saint, prophet, messenger, or spiritual leader who anchors an era. The term is widely used in Sufism. Since many Sufi traditions ground their cosmology in the imaginal, the Qutub may be seen as a gateway, usher, wedge, or prophet who belies the division between worlds. CHUMBLEY uses these ideas to great effect in his *Qutub: The Point* (1995/2009). See 111.

Ram Dass (b. Richard Alpert 1931-) American psychiatrist turned New Age guru. His most famous work, *Be Here Now* (1971) integrates psychedelic, transpersonal, yogic, and mystical themes into a blaze of atemporality. Likely one of the more influential humans of the 20th century, he is unquestionably central to the New Age movement.

Realized eschatology In theology, the stance that creation and the end of the world are all *now*. Some versions, perhaps best labeled 'esoteric realized eschatology,' agree with this definition, but point out that most people do not achieve this perspective. Thus one must undergo initiation in order to become aware of the immediacy of these dynamics. From the perspective of this imagery, the end of the world is creation played backwards.

Reconstructionist Judaism A progressive movement growing originally out of Conservative Judaism. Founded by Rabbi Mordecai Kaplan (1881-1983), the movement embraces a diversity of expressions of Judaism but holds to Kaplan's tenet that 'the past has a vote, but not a veto.' The movement seeks to re-invigorate the practice of Judaism through an engaged ethics of life, tradition, and a relationship to the Divine. Female Rabbis, the bat-mitzvah, and ECO-KASHRUT are expressions of such considerations.

Red Pine (b. Bill Porter 1943-) Author, commentator, and translator of Buddhist and Taoist texts, especially those focusing on Chan Buddhism—the Chinese movement that would become Zen Buddhism in Japan. Influential in American Zen Buddhism.

Regardie, Israel (b. Francis Israel Regudy 1897-1985) One-time secretary to Crowley and apologist for the HERMETIC ORDER OF THE GOLDEN DAWN. A chiropractor and psychotherapist, Regardie's well-regarded legacy is one of the less ambiguous of the 20th century's major figures in occultism.

Reincarnation Any of a wide range of beliefs in the movement of the soul from one body to another after death. In its most common sense, the term refers to metempsychosis, the transmigration of a distinct individual soul from one body to the next after death. This is far from the only definition. Variations exist: do animal souls reincarnate?; can human, plant, and animal souls develop or devolve into one another?; does the soul remain with an individual throughout incarnations?; are there multiple souls, some of which may continue on, others not?; is it unavoidable?; and many other questions. A vague sense of reincarnation has entered the wider public imagination, as evidenced by the number of people, both religious and otherwise, who endorse the belief.

Reintrojection Reintegration of projected material. An often difficult but developmentally necessary process. See INTROJECTION and PROJECTION.

Responsibility In this text, one of the eight VOIDS, paired with FREEDOM. See FREEDOM AND RESPONSIBILITY.

Rhizome In botany, a creeping stem that can give rise to new roots or shoots. DELEUZE AND GUATRI refer to rhizominc thinking, in which an idea is pursued to a new position, which may yield an entirely new cartography-of-understanding of its newly relativized position of origin.

Right-Hand Path (RHP) Increasingly irrelevant term that is contrasted to the LEFT-HAND PATH (LHP). In its purest form, one might imagine a sex-free, ascetic approach to esotericism in which the individual perfection and transformation of self into Light is the only goal. Nonetheless, this description refers to a scant few in Western Esotericism, regardless of labels. Thus, the term, although possibly rooted in some reference to Tantra, is oblique and obfuscatory. The ill-conceived fantasy of the RHP is that one could somehow perform magical acts, let alone simply exist, without impacting other individuals adversely. Both the terms RHP and LHP would seem to lack a certain agrarian veracity.

Robinson, John J. (1925-1993) Author of important references on FREEMASONRY that link their rituals to the Knights Templar, in imagination if not history. Although speculative in nature, the works provide level-headed assessments of the current state of Freemasonry and dispel many uninformed conspiracy theories. His most direct work is likely *Born in Blood* (1989) — readable and fair.

Rosarium Philosophorum A 16th century series of alchemical woodcuts and commentaries. JUNG used the images, somewhat re-ordered to match his needs, to describe the therapeutic processes of transference and countertransference in his *Psychology of the Transference* (1946; *Collected Works* Vol. 16).

Rosy Cross The second level of the Western Initiatory QABALAH, preceded by the VEIL OF THE PEROKETH, and bounded above by DA'ATH, containing Tiphareth, Geburah, and Chesed. Linked to the alchemical motto I.'.N.'.R.'.I.'. and the number 666. In this text, this level corresponds to the Wisdom and life insight level of mysteries, as well as DANTE's Purgatory. Sacrifice, self-overcoming, and rich symbolism are some of the positive attributes associated with this level, just as ego-inflation, spirituality unencumbered by relevancy, and crypticism/occultation are a few of its potential shadows.

Sabbatic Craft See CHUMBLEY.

Scientism Literalist, materialist, and fundamentalist belief in the ultimate validity of applying the scientific method to any and all problems. Monomaniacal adherence to this un-nuanced, un-contextualized zealotry passes for 'education' in much of the Western world.

Secret Chiefs A fanciful term coined in the Victorian Period to refer to the ascended masters that led various secret societies. At times this term could merely refer to living, incarnate individuals who led various traditions in relative anonymity or secrecy. Other interpretations involve figures, living or dead, from a host of cultures who exercised influence from their transcendent states—possibly having achieved the A.˙.A.˙.. Still more arcane interpretations place these Masters as hyperdimensional, extraterrestrial, or entirely spiritual forces that exercise the spiritual gravity behind various esoteric orders' initiatory courses. One might safely say that the EGREGORES of various traditions are their true Secret Chiefs. For some writers, these forces/leaders were synonymous with the Great White Brotherhood (a painfully dated and easily racist term) which was contrasted to the BLACK BROTHERS who exercised their influence from their Black Lodge. The term has a powerful hermeneutic meaning within the snakes and ladders of the Western Initiatory QABALAH.

Self Jungian term for the ongoing journey of integration—overcoming the entrapping dyadic configurations of various ARCHETYPES. In many cases, the term INDIVIDUATION refers to an engagement with this process; a more exacting use would be the 'individuation of the Self.'

Shadow Term from JUNG for those aspects of the personality that a person denies, represses, or does not acknowledge. Shadow contents are typically perceived as negative, but can easily be positive aspects of oneself that one cannot accept. Nevertheless, the fermentation within the Shadow tends to make the contents perverse, dark, and contrarian as they strain for integration.

Sigil An imaginal construct carrying constellations of intent, perception, and identity. A magical crystal-seed designed to create novel fractals, memes, and maps—and possibly new cartographies. Often charged with some form of GNOSIS. See ENSIGILIZATION.

Silver Star See A.˙.A.˙..

Skafte, Dianne (1944-) Depth psychologist focused on history, psychological assessment, and, in particular, 'oracular consciousness.' Author of *Listening to the Oracle: The Ancient Art of Finding Guidance in the Signs and Symbols around Us* (1997), revised and now available as *When Oracles Speak* (2000).

Solipsism A form of EMPTY NIHILISM in which 'everything is whatever I make it.' This arch-subjectivism ignores the fact that more fundamental images underpin the very identity that claims to create the world it beholds.

Spare, Austin Osman (1886-1956) Grandfather of the chaos tradition through his introduction of ENSIGILIZTION, ALPHABET OF DESIRE, and novel means of effecting reality. His was a first important effort to overtly fictionalize magic and liberate it from the pedantry of the previous generations. An associate of CROWLEY and an important mentor to GRANT.

Spiral Dance See STARHAWK.

Spiritualism Victorian belief system centered on contact with spirits of various sorts, especially those of the dead. Mediums and channelers formed the core of this movement—most of whom were either self-deluded fakes of various levels of intuition or skilled charlatans. Incalculably influential, spiritualism was, however, oddly overlooked by historians of religion and the occult due, perhaps, to its ubiquity well into the 20th century, as well as the conflation of the term, more recently, with the generic SPIRITUALITY. Reducing the movement to the table-tappings investigated by the likes of Houdini and Sir Arthur Conan Doyle misses its wide-spread influence. Nevertheless, concepts such as lost continents like ATLANTIS, REINCARNATION as the transmigration of a disembodied 'soul' and other New Age chestnuts owe much to this movement.

Spirituality A term becoming increasingly misleading but tenaciously clutched by masses afraid of letting go of the spirit/matter fiction. Under this aegis, Western bookshop owners pile countless religions and philosophies together, many of which may not have any concept of a 'spirit' as such. In the field of psychology, terms such as 'transpersonal' and, now, 'contemplative' are being advanced as alternatives. The term 'wisdom traditions' is also used to avoid the ambiguities of 'spirituality.'

Splendor Solis 16th century series of elaborate alchemical images depicting death and rebirth, as well as a sequence of seven ALEMBICS.

Starhawk (b. Miriam Simos 1951-) Author, ecofeminist, and central figure to post-hippie neo-paganism. Best known for *The Spiral Dance: The Rebirth of the Ancient Religion of the Goddess* (1979).

Stone Soup A widespread folk tale in which the pleas of hungry visitors to a village are initially rejected until the visitors begin making a 'Stone Soup' to which each of the passing curious villagers contribute a bit of their own meager ingredients, eventually creating an overflowing pot that feeds the whole village. Arguably a lesson on communalism.

Stoppard, Tom (1937-) Prolific playwright and script doctor, best known for his *Rosencrantz and Guildenstern are Dead* (1966). His works are always multi-layered, existential, and often overly clever. As noted in this current work, one visual trope found in many of his works is the flight of pages across the stage or screen.

Structural truth Existential truths realized through an unflinching observation of the nature of experience. These truths include the VOIDS and the flow of experience.

Sublime Although frequently linked to 'beauty,' the sublime refers more to an encounter with the undeniable power of the moment. Even horrific events can be sublime in their undeniable reality. Often linked with the indifferent power of nature.

Sufi Narrowly, this term identifies a range of esoteric traditions in the Islamic world. Broadly, it refers to the everyday enlightened travelers who do not need to wed themselves to elaborate traditions or trappings. They are lovers of the INEFFABLE and omnipresent ALLAH — to whom they refer as 'the Beloved' as can be beautifully found in the works of Rumi, a patron saint of their wanderings. Many Sufis make use of ecstatic states as part of their practice. See also QUTUB and QUF.

Syncretism A cross-fertilization of disparate traditions yielding a unique creation. Although the effects of colonialism often effect such hybrids — such as some forms of Vodun, Santeria, and Condomble — other, less obvious cases also exist. For example, The Cunning Tradition seems to have emerged from a combination of British Isles folk traditions, and FREEMASONRY. The Western QABALAH itself is a syncretic combination of Jewish Esotericism with Western European traditions. And, the intersection of ancient Greek and Egyptian traditions, into early HERMETICISM, is quite likely responsible for the foundation of the majority of Western Inner Traditions. In the often-preposterous search for 'authenticity' and 'provenance' within the world of occultists, a more fruitful pursuit might be a devotion to the creation of such lively hybrids. Such combinations seem far more clearly to be the way of things since time immemorial, rather than any unblemished preservation of a single initiatory line.

Synesthesia Cross-sensory experience such as hearing color or seeing sound. In its milder forms, it can enhance creativity and open new interconnections and non-linear possibilities. In its more severe and diagnosable forms it can be a cruel disability in which a person may not be able to read, add, or otherwise cognitively function due to rigid associations between certain experiences and their cross-sensory analogs. It is likely that children are born as natural synesthetes in their UNDIFFERENTIATED state. As such, they must 'learn' the various senses and, thus, unlearn their creative birthright.

Systems thinking A perspective in which everything that has ever happened has led to this exact moment in its entirety. Sometimes glibly expressed as, 'remember, the brightest minds in the world have brought us to exactly where we are today.' Systems thinking attempts to not be swayed by labels or intentions, and soberly addresses all the various factors coming together within a given system. In systems thinking, practitioners often find it necessary to shift the definition of the system in question in order to account for the factors contributing to the outcomes. 'Systems analysis' is a particular application of these perspectives and is not necessarily synonymous. Typically, a systems analysis will describe a limited number of feedback loops and narrow the field of observable outcomes. Systems thinking is linked, in this current work, to the VOID of CHAOS.

Tabula Smaragdina See EMERALD TABLET.

Taoism Ancient Chinese philosophy wedding the contemplation and participation in the Tao (道, 'the way'). Two distinct branches exist within Taoism, philosophical and religious. The philosophical current moves easily from LAO-TSE's *Tao Te-Ching* to Zen Buddhism, whereas the religious practice aligns more closely to shamanism, Taoist alchemy, and various healing practices. The branches are not necessarily mutually exclusive, but distinct poles.

Telos (plural: teloi) A lived prediction of the future, based in the current moment. This can be as simple as the adumbration that some object, were we to look behind it, would continue to be, more-or-less, that same object. In the bigger picture, we are constantly living with unacknowledged predictions, desires, hopes, and the like. These units of intentionality often create the moment, far more than our immediate circumstances.

Thelema See CROWLEY

Tibet, David (b. David Michael Bunting 1960-) See CURRENT 93.

Tick, the Comic-book hero created by Ben Edlund (1968-). Seen in his series of comics (1988-1993), animated television show (1994-1996), and a live-action treatment (2001). The Tick involves spoof, satire, and a nigh-invincible dose of the absurd.

Traditional Witchcraft A term used to signify those currents of Witchcraft that trace their origins neither to nor through Gerald GARDNER nor Alex Sanders. Some forms of Traditional Witchcraft trace their origins to the syncretic

Cunning Tradition. CHUMBLEY'S *Cultus Sabbati* calls to such provenance. See Michael HOWARD and Paul HUSON.

Tree of Life See QABALAH.

True Grimoire See GRIMOIRE.

Tunnels of Set The paths connecting the QLIPOTHS as introduced by GRANT.

Ubu Central character in three plays by Alfred Jarry (1873-1907). The plays provide social commentary on a range of human foibles in the form of proto-surrealism and an early form of absurdism. In this current text, Ubu is graphically linked to the void of MADNESS.

Undifferentiation In this text, one of the eight voids. It reminds us that our identities and various ALTERITIES stand upon informing images that shift and dissolve depending on context. That is, 'self' and 'other' are two poles within a field of intersecting meaning vectors.

Unspeakable The shadow of the INEFFABLE. When the mysteries of the ineffable are denied, they frequently fester into the ELDRITCH horror of the unspeakable. Largely, the ABJECT expresses this repulsed relationship to the ineffable.

Vajrayogini A central figure in the meditative practice of Vajrayana Buddhism, she is a Buddha of liberation. Though portrayed in many ways, among the most common is a red-skinned young woman, nude, dancing with a brain bowl raised in one hand, spilling its contents into her fanged mouth. Linked, in this text, to the MORRÍGAN.

Via negativa The path of undoing. A contemplative tradition in which practitioners undo or eliminate imageries' idolatrous thrall upon them. See APOPHATIC.

Veil of the Peroketh In the Western Initiatory QABALAH, a divide between the GOLDEN DAWN and ROSY CROSS levels.

V.ˑˑI.ˑˑT.ˑˑR.ˑˑI.ˑˑO.ˑˑL.ˑˑ Alchemical and FREEMASONIC acronym for *Visita Interiora Terrae Rectificando Invenies Occultum Lapidem.* 'One must journey to the center of the earth to rectify the hidden stone.' Vitriol was the alchemical term for sulfuric acid—a cleansing agent used to burn away impurities. As such, it is associated with the nigredo phase of the alchemical process. In this text, vitriol represents the path of this world, a system of descent into the emptiness of things. Like the square at the base of FREEMASONRY's central symbol, the V is the right angle of this world's plane. Vitriol that becomes encumbered with entropy becomes the worst sort of violating, wallowing in filth, leading only to diseased dissipation. Early Romanticism and 20th century romantic mysticism often followed the vitriolic path. This text presents vitriol as the appropriate motto for the GOLDEN DAWN phase of the Western Esoteric QABALAH.

Voids In this text, these are eight underlying indictments of the supposed-unchangeablity of key fictions in life such as identity, materiality, and linear temporality. The voids are limits of knowing and being. Since they have no substance, and relate only to relational vectors of being, their enumeration is somewhat arbitrary, zero being a better count than any. However, in this text, there are eight: IMMEDIACY, UNDIFFERENTIATION, MADNESS, CHAOS, NOTH-INGNESS, MEANINGLESSNESS, FREEDOM AND RESPONSIBILITY, and CHANGE AND FINITUDE.

Watkins, Mary (1950-) IMAGINAL psychologist, educator, and author of *Waking Dreams* (1976) and *Invisible Guests: The Development of Imaginal Dialogs* (1986/2000). She created the idea of 'dream necklacing' as a means of loosening dream material from its initial sequence and assumed causal connections.

Whitehead, Alfred North (1861-1947) British mathematician turned philoso-pher. Perhaps somewhat lost in the haze of the later 20th century's philosophical morass, Whitehead makes a last effort to repair Western philosophy and theol-ogy, rather than allow it to consume itself in an orgy of EMPTY NIHILISM. His 'process philosophy,' as most fully presented in *Process and Reality: An Essay in Cosmology* (1929), challenges the reader to imagine a reality in motion, unfold-ing, and in which the individual plays an integral role. Although his stance on 'meaning' may have an antiquated ring for many postmodernists, his presenta-tion of process can be reconciled to ideas about MEMES and ARCHETYPES in crea-tive ways. Many of his stances proved important in the formation of the next generation of thinkers.

Wiccan Sabbat The eight seasonal revels celebrated by neo-pagans, growing out of the synthesis of various European pre- and peri-Christian festivals.

Witch's Sabbath The various imaginings of heresiologists, artists, novelists, histo-rians, occultists, and club goers to portray the orgiastic revels of mythic 'witches.'

Yamamoto Tsunetomo (1659-1719) Samurai and originator of the sayings compiled by Tsuramoto Tashiro in *HAGAKURE*.

Zen Buddhism A tradition of meditation and ritual centered on the realization of enlightenment. The founding story is of the BODHIDHARMA traveling to China to innovate the practice of Buddhism. His legacy became known as 'Chan,' a Chinese form of the Hindi 'dhyana'—'meditation.' When the term made its way to Japan, it became 'Zen.' The Bodhidarma was the first of the 'Six Patriarchs' of Zen, the sixth was HUINENG. However, Zen Buddhism traces its origins to Gautama Buddha's 'Flower Sutra' in which, rather than speaking an elaborate intellectual or metaphorical sermon, the Buddha simply held up a flower. Of the gathered disciples, only one smiled in response and his legacy carried on through the Bodhidharma to the rest of the Six Patriarchs. The practice spread throughout East Asia but did not make it to the West until the 20th century where it is slowly establishing its own traditions. In China, Zen clearly integrated elements of philosophical TAOISM. Zen has many forms even within the same country; nevertheless, its central message is one of an immediate realization of the True Nature of reality, which is the True Nature of each person, liberating one from the entrapping illusions of what passes for reality for most people.

Zenny A playful term meant to convey an esthetic of seeming Zen sparseness and pseudo-profundity free of any real engagement with the tenets or practices of ZEN BUDDHISM.

Index